HOLMAN
Old Testament Commentary

HOLMAN *Old Testament* Commentary

Ezra, Nehemiah, Esther

GENERAL EDITOR

Max Anders

AUTHORS

Knute Larson and Kathy Dahlen

HOLMAN
REFERENCE

Nashville, Tennessee

Holman Old Testament Commentary
© 2005 Broadman & Holman Publishers
Nashville, Tennessee
All rights reserved

Bible versions used in this book:

The King James Version

10-digit ISBN 0-8054-9469-3
13-digit ISBN 978-0-8054-9469-3

Dewey Decimal Classification:
Subject Heading: BIBLE. O.T. EZRA, NEHEMIAH, ESTHER

Ezra, Nehemiah, Esther / Knute Larson and Kathy E. Dahlen

p.   cm. — (Holman Old Testament commentary)
Includes bibliographical references. (p.).
ISBN
  1. Bible. Ezra—Commentaries.   I. Title.   II. Series.

—dc21

3 4 5 6   09 08 07 06
L

Contents

Contents

Editorial Preface

Today's church hungers for Bible teaching, and Bible teachers hunger for resources to guide them in teaching God's Word. The Holman Old Testament Commentary provides the church with the food to feed the spiritually hungry in an easily digestible format. The result: new spiritual vitality that the church can readily use.

Bible teaching should result in new interest in the Scriptures, expanded Bible knowledge, discovery of specific scriptural principles, relevant applications, and exciting living. The unique format of the Holman Old Testament Commentary includes sections to achieve these results for every Old Testament book.

Opening quotations stimulate thinking and lead to an introductory illustration and discussion that draw individuals and study groups into the Word of God. Verse-by-verse commentary interprets the passage with the aim of equipping them to understand and live God's Word in a contemporary setting. A conclusion draws together the themes identified in the passage under discussion and suggests application for it. A "Life Application" section provides additional illustrative material. "Deeper Discoveries" gives the reader a closer look at some of the words, phrases, and background material that illuminate the passage. "Issues for Discussion" is a tool to enhance learning within the group. Finally, a closing prayer is suggested. Bible teachers and pastors will find the teaching outline helpful as they develop lessons and sermons.

It is the editors' prayer that this new resource for local church Bible teaching will enrich the ministry of group, as well as individual, Bible study and that it will lead God's people truly to be people of the Book, living out what God calls us to be.

Acknowledgments

Special gratitude to Kathy Dahlen, who not only carried her agreed-upon part of the project but also helped so much on mine. She is not only a fine writer but also a faithful, fastidious student of the Word of God. I am grateful.

And I lovingly dedicate this endeavor with deep appreciation to fifties-on-up people of The Chapel in Akron and Green and other seniors of other churches who will use this commentary. They are like the builders in Nehemiah who have given so much of themselves to the church. They still pray and teach and love and encourage. In spite of change in the church, some of which they don't like, they remain strong and faithful. Sometimes the younger members of the church do not recognize what these older people did to give such vision and grace to the church, but these seniors know why they did it—for Jesus their Christ and Lord.

Perhaps they came to the church like Esther, "for such a time as this." They care about God's Word, as Ezra did.

Knute Larson

For my children, Lara and Erik:

You have been my teachers and fellow adventurers in life's journey. Being a parent has given me a richer understanding of God's deep, enduring love; it has awakened me to his faithfulness, humor, and brilliance; it has assured me of his passion for our growth and maturity. I love you both.

Mom (Kathy Dahlen)

Holman Old Testament Commentary Contributors

Vol. 1, Genesis
ISBN 0-8054-9461-8
Kenneth O. Gangel and
Stephen J. Bramer

Vol. 2, Exodus, Leviticus, Numbers
ISBN 0-8054-9462-6
Glen Martin

Vol. 3, Deuteronomy
ISBN 0-8054-9463-4
Doug McIntosh

Vol. 4, Joshua
ISBN 0-8054-9464-2
Kenneth O. Gangel

Vol. 5, Judges, Ruth
ISBN 0-8054-9465-0
W. Gary Phillips

Vol. 6, 1 & 2 Samuel
ISBN 0-8054-9466-9
Stephen Andrews

Vol. 7, 1 & 2 Kings
ISBN 0-8054-9467-7
Gary Inrig

Vol. 8, 1 & 2 Chronicles
ISBN 0-8054-9468-5
Winfried Corduan

Vol. 9, Ezra, Nehemiah, Esther
ISBN 0-8054-9469-3
Knute Larson and Kathy Dahlen

Vol. 10, Job
ISBN 0-8054-9470-7
Steven J. Lawson

Vol. 11, Psalms 1–75
ISBN 0-8054-9471-5
Steven J. Lawson

Vol. 12, Psalms 76–150
ISBN 0-8054-9481-2
Steven J. Lawson

Vol. 13, Proverbs
ISBN 0-8054-9472-3
Max Anders

Vol. 14, Ecclesiastes, Song of Songs
ISBN 0-8054-9482-0
David George Moore and Daniel L. Akin

Vol. 15, Isaiah
ISBN 0-8054-9473-1
Trent C. Butler

Vol. 16, Jeremiah, Lamentations
ISBN 0-8054-9474-X
Fred M. Wood and Ross McLaren

Vol. 17, Ezekiel
ISBN 0-8054-9475-8
Mark F. Rooker

Vol. 18, Daniel
ISBN 0-8054-9476-6
Kenneth O. Gangel

**Vol. 19, Hosea, Joel, Amos,
Obadiah, Jonah, Micah**
ISBN 0-8054-9477-4
Trent C. Butler

**Vol. 20, Nahum, Habakkuk,
Zephaniah, Haggai, Zechariah, Malachi**
ISBN 0-8054-9478-2
Stephen R. Miller

Holman New Testament Commentary Contributors

Vol. 1, Matthew
ISBN 0-8054-0201-2
Stuart K. Weber

Vol. 2, Mark
ISBN 0-8054-0202-0
Rodney L. Cooper

Vol. 3, Luke
ISBN 0-8054-0203-9
Trent C. Butler

Vol. 4, John
ISBN 0-8054-0204-7
Kenneth O. Gangel

Vol. 5, Acts
ISBN 0-8054-0205-5
Kenneth O. Gangel

Vol. 6, Romans
ISBN 0-8054-0206-3
Kenneth Boa and William Kruidenier

Vol. 7, 1 & 2 Corinthians
ISBN 0-8054-0207-1
Richard L. Pratt Jr.

**Vol. 8, Galatians, Ephesians,
Philippians, Colossians**
ISBN 0-8054-0208-X
Max Anders

**Vol. 9, 1 & 2 Thessalonians,
1 & 2 Timothy, Titus, Philemon**
ISBN 0-8054-0209-8
Knute Larson

Vol. 10, Hebrews, James
ISBN 0-8054-0211-X
Thomas D. Lea

Vol. 11, 1 & 2 Peter, 1, 2, 3 John, Jude
ISBN 0-8054-0210-1
David Walls and Max Anders

Vol. 12, Revelation
ISBN 0-8054-0212-8
Kendell H. Easley

Holman Old Testament Commentary

Twenty volumes designed for Bible study and teaching to enrich the local church and God's people.

Series Editor	Max Anders
Managing Editor	Steve Bond
Project Editor	Dean Richardson
Product Development Manager	Ricky D. King
Marketing Manager	Stephanie Huffman
Executive Editor	David Shepherd
Page Composition	TF Designs, Greenbrier, TN

Introduction to

Ezra

AUTHORSHIP

- The chronicler: Most scholars believe the Book of Ezra was written and compiled by a chronicler, quite possibly the same person who wrote 1 and 2 Chronicles.
- Government documents: The Book of Ezra contains insertions of Aramaic text—memos and correspondence from Persian officials relating to events occurring in and around Jerusalem at that time.
- Ezra: Portions of the book appear to come from the personal journal of Ezra himself, a Jewish priest and possibly a Persian high official.

READERS

- Postexilic Jews.

DATE

- Written between 440 and 400 B.C., probably a few decades after the return of exiles under Ezra and the purifying of the community. It is uncertain if the Book of Ezra or the Book of Nehemiah was written first.
- Covers events from 538 B.C. to approximately 438 B.C. during the reigns of the Persian kings Cyrus the Great, Darius I, Xerxes I, and Artaxerxes I.
- Certain events are contemporary with the prophets Haggai, Zechariah, and Malachi.

we will touch on later

CHARACTERISTICS

- Originally, the books of Ezra and Nehemiah were a single book in the Jewish Scriptures.
- Ezra was not written in strict chronological order, nor does it include all events related to that time. Instead, the compiler used

records and information that served his purpose of reestablishing Davidic and Deuteronomic authority.

- The book traces the historical events of the return of exiles from Babylon to Jerusalem to rebuild the temple, the opposition encountered, and the lapse of the Jews into religious compromise. It also describes the completion and dedication of the temple and, under Ezra, the purifying of the people.
- The writer emphasizes the need for individual and communal purity for God's people. These are the true recipients of God's blessing.
- The book highlights the mysterious cooperation between the sovereign will and power of God, and the initiative and choices of people.

Ezra 1

Between God and Man

I. INTRODUCTION
A View from Above

II. COMMENTARY
A verse-by-verse explanation of the chapter.

III. CONCLUSION
The Chief End of Man

An overview of the principles and applications from the chapter.

IV. LIFE APPLICATION
Lessons from Preschool

Melding the chapter to life.

V. PRAYER
Tying the chapter to life with God.

VI. DEEPER DISCOVERIES
Historical, geographical, and grammatical enrichment of the commentary.

VII. TEACHING OUTLINE
Suggested step-by-step group study of the chapter.

VIII. ISSUES FOR DISCUSSION
Zeroing the chapter in on daily life.

Quote

*E*verything that is incomprehensible does not,

however, cease to exist.

B l a i s e   P a s c a l

Use this quote. The people scattered, the temple in ruins. Impossible But is it really ??

Ezra 1

IN A NUTSHELL

*T*he time of Babylonian captivity for the Jews was at an end, just as the prophet Jeremiah had predicted. It was time for the exiles to return to Jerusalem and rebuild the temple. In the first chapter of Ezra, we see the divine and mysterious workings between the sovereignty of God and the will and purposes of people—a pagan king and a community of faith working together to accomplish what God purposes.

Between God and Man

I. INTRODUCTION

A View from Above

"*L*ook at this!"

It was something of a warning; in a split moment my daughter had thrust a paper within an inch of my nose. Suddenly the universe was filled with a scrawled version of our family, all neckless, longlegged, and crookedly smiling ear to ear. Perhaps, like the primitive tribes and medieval monks before her, symbolism far outweighed realism. Portraying a happy family took precedence over identifying these round-eyed, three-fingered figures from out of a crowd.

And yet, as we viewed her portraits, I had the distinct impression that to her, the resemblance was remarkable. After all, the hairstyle was perfect, the orbs at the end of my wobbly legs matched the color of my shoes, and four figures of various sizes filled the page—just like our family. Perhaps from her vantage point, nearer ground level, heads did appear to sit on bodies, arms to sprout from chins, and legs to extend toward some distant point.

From the viewpoint of ordinary human beings, life appears governed by power and wealth, by international relationships built on confusing alliances of greed and self-interest, and by policies that come and go without enduring purpose. It probably seemed so to those who lived around the Mediterranean Sea and throughout Palestine after Nebuchadnezzar's Babylonian Empire crumbled under the strength of Persia's King Cyrus. One empire rose only to fall to another, ruthless men conquered and subdued smaller nations, and decrees were issued and withdrawn according to political advantage.

But in the opening verses of the Book of Ezra, we are given a different perspective. We are taken from ground level, with its distortions and limited vision, and given a view from above. At this clarifying distance we see that life on earth is not directed by the whim of rulers or the might of armies but by the determination of God.

Viewpoint makes all the difference in the world.

II. COMMENTARY

Between God and Man

MAIN IDEA: *God's all-encompassing sovereignty and humanity's capacity for choice exist together. God—absolute and unrivalled in his actions and authority; man—free and responsible.*

A God Is Sovereign (1:1–4)

SUPPORTING IDEA: *God often reveals his overarching plans and design in history. His purposes will be accomplished. It remains for individuals and communities to cooperate in his great enterprise. The choice is ours.*

[handwritten: God chose His people, they however, do not hold up their end, but His will will be done.]

1. Prophecy fulfilled (1:1)

1:1. Ezra opens by echoing the concluding words of 2 Chronicles. Such a device brought continuity and underscored the importance of these opening verses.

Immediately we are placed in historical context. This was not myth but current events: **In the first year of Cyrus king of Persia**. In truth Cyrus had reigned over Persia for some time, but it was his first year as king over the Babylonians and their collapsed empire (see "Deeper Discoveries"). This was the first year in which Persian rule came to bear on the Jews and other subject peoples; for most of them it was welcome relief. *[handwritten: Mention size of kingdom]*

Cyrus, however, was mere introduction. The true king is God who establishes his glory and redeems his people through his Word (delivered by prophets) and power (demonstrated in the heart of a pagan). Cyrus, his kingdom, and his role in releasing the Jews from Babylonian captivity, were predicted even before he was born (Isa. 44:28). "I will raise up Cyrus in my righteousness: I will make all his ways straight. He will rebuild my city and set my exiles free" (Isa. 45:13). Cyrus's conquests and administrative policies originated not only in Persian statesmanship but also in God's will. Interestingly, Isaiah's prophetic words are not mentioned by the chronicler. Instead, he explained the actions of Cyrus as fulfilling **the word of the LORD spoken by Jeremiah**.

The chronicler (Ezra) wanted his readers to understand the exile was over. It was time to return to Palestine, to reestablish the community of faith. He supported this idea, already alluded to in 2 Chronicles 36:21, by referring to Jeremiah's prophecies: "When seventy years are completed for Babylon, *I will come to you and fulfill my gracious promise to bring you back to this place*" (Jer. 29:10, emphasis added; see also Jer. 25:11–14). It was time to go home, and God **moved the heart of Cyrus king of Persia** to bring it about.

[handwritten left margin: Hiram and others. I don't have the means. Just as God used Hiram to built and others. We cannot say He used Cyrus to restore. He used]

Cyrus sent a proclamation throughout the empire orally and then put it **in writing** for official documentation. Most likely a herald went from place to place and read the announcement.

2. Proclamation of a king (1:2–4)

1:2–4. Cyrus began his proclamation by stating: **This is what Cyrus king of Persia says**. It was the official language of political authority.

At first glance the opening statement of Cyrus's decree seems to indicate an unusual reverence for Israel's God. He acknowledged that the Lord, **the God of heaven, has given me all the kingdoms of the earth**. Cyrus's position, however, was very similar to the pluralistic outlook popular in our own culture. He was willing and ready to credit any and all gods for his successes as well as to seek their blessing for his rule.

By appealing to every nation's deity, Cyrus offended few people while gaining the support of many. His kingdom retained strength not through suppression but through support of each people's beliefs. In this way the various populations remained content, their cultural identities preserved, as they were incorporated into the greater empire.

With this political motivation in mind, Cyrus claimed God had appointed **him to build a temple for him at Jerusalem in Judah**. Ironically, God had appointed Cyrus to do that very thing, as both Isaiah and Jeremiah foretold. Whether or not Cyrus truly understood the predictive nature of his assignment is debatable. Quite likely he claimed the divine appointment in order to secure the support of the Jews. But with many Jews serving in high-ranking positions throughout the empire, it is possible Cyrus knew of the prophetic texts. Even so, he probably did not consider the Lord of any greater importance or power than other gods.

In fact, by referring to God as **the God of Israel, the God who is in Jerusalem**, it seems the king considered the one true God to be a local, tribal god of the Jews. Cyrus declared that those who belonged to this God of Israel should **go up to Jerusalem in Judah and build the temple of the LORD**. It seems the choice to return or stay was left up to each person. This was not a forced relocation.

In order to ensure the success of his policy to reinstate local gods and worship, Cyrus's decree compelled non-Jews, **the people of any place where survivors may now be living**, to help those who had returned to Jerusalem. These Gentiles were to contribute **silver and gold . . . goods and livestock . . . and freewill offerings** so the temple in Jerusalem would be rebuilt and worship would be restored there.

B Cooperation (1:5–11)

SUPPORTING IDEA: *God works through people, using a person's natural disposition to accomplish his greater purpose.*

3. The Jews (1:5)

1:5. Responding to Cyrus's proclamation, the Jewish leadership prepared for the mission of rebuilding the temple. But, just like Cyrus, they were people **whose heart God had moved.** In giving credit to God for awakening individual desire and purpose, the writer of Ezra emphasizes the holy nature of the enterprise. The rebuilding of the temple was not a human plan or project. From king to citizen, this was a work of God.

Though the king's decree was circulated and proclaimed throughout the empire, not surprisingly those from the ten northern tribes chose not to return and help. The splitting of the nation into northern and southern kingdoms after Solomon's reign (1 Kgs. 11–12) was a historical fact that continued in present loyalties. Instead, **the family heads of Judah and Benjamin, and the priests and Levites** answered the call. The chronicler notes that only these two tribes were stirred by God; only these tribes represented the true community of faith.

God ruled through Judah and the Davidic throne, centered in Jerusalem. On the road to rebuild the temple were **family heads,** probably extended family including slaves; **priests,** those from the tribe of Levi who traced their family line to Aaron; and **Levites,** members of the tribe whose ancestry could not be linked to Aaron.

4. The Gentiles (1:6)

1:6. As Cyrus decreed, so it happened. In Ezra 1:4 Cyrus outlined precisely how Gentile inhabitants were to assist those returning to Jerusalem. When the time came, the people living throughout the region did, in fact, contribute to the rebuilding project and to the welfare of those returning: **all their neighbors assisted them.** *All,* in this instance, should be understood as representing a respectable number and not an all-inclusive figure.

Reminiscent of the exodus in which the Egyptians gave to the departing Jews gold, silver, and clothing (Exod. 12:35–36), the Gentiles in the neighborhood of Palestine gave what Cyrus demanded: **silver and gold . . . goods and livestock . . . valuable gifts . . . freewill offerings.** As is regularly the case, God provides for his people in ways unexpected.

In putting together a supply list, it is doubtful the Jewish family heads considered asking the Gentile citizenry to help out. But it is in keeping with God's methods and power to use the unregenerate to accomplish holy purposes. It underscores God's sovereignty, it reflects glory upon his supremacy, and it displays his dominion over all people. Though some people are specially regarded as belonging to the community of faith, all individuals live beneath his rule.

5. The king (1:7–8)

1:7–8. Cyrus threw his support behind the project by bringing **out the articles belonging to the temple of the LORD, which Nebuchadnezzar had carried away.** Cyrus was the great restorer. He initiated plans to restore Jews to their homeland, to restore the temple building in Jerusalem, and to restore worship by giving back the sacred articles.

Cyrus had **Mithredath the treasurer** take the Jewish valuables from the royal treasury and **count them out to Sheshbazzar the prince of Judah.** Clearly Mithredath was a Persian official. Sheshbazzar's identity, however, is not so certain. His name was Babylonian, but his title, *prince of Judah,* suggests he was Hebrew. It is possible that, like other deported Jews, he was given a Babylonian name.

It is also possible that he was the son of the captive Judean king, Jehoiachin. Nebuchadnezzar's successors considered Jehoiachin the rightful monarch of Judah (2 Kgs. 25:27–30), and he enjoyed royal favor until his death. Sheshbazzar, if he was Jehoiachin's son, would have been considered the heir apparent, or prince. But this is mostly conjecture, because there is no certainty about the identity of Sheshbazzar.

6. The king's treasure (1:9–11)

1:9–11. The following two verses give an **inventory** of the captured temple articles counted out to Sheshbazzar. Our English translations contain a list of gold dishes and bowls, silver dishes and pans, and other articles. Across from each description a number is given corresponding to how many items of each were counted. The difficulty comes in adding the numbers together. As given, the total number of gold and silver articles comes to 1,499 plus 1,000 **other articles** which may or may not have been precious metals. Either way, the number does not agree with the total given in verse 11 of **5,400 articles of gold and silver.**

Some interpreters suggest translation difficulties, others that the inventory reflects the actual articles from Solomon's temple, whereas the total includes pieces from other places which Nebuchadnezzar looted in Jerusalem and the temple area. At any rate, the figures do demonstrate the vast wealth which resided in Solomon's temple and which was amassed during the height of Israel's glory.

The chapter concludes by declaring that Sheshbazzar brought all the temple treasures **along when the exiles came up from Babylon to Jerusalem.** This chapter has carefully laid the validating groundwork for the temple restoration. God's sovereign power, together with the chosen tribe of Judah, the sacred objects from Solomon's temple, and the divine edict from fulfilled prophecy, combined to prove the legitimacy of the enterprise. This was the true community of faith restoring true worship in God's holy city.

MAIN IDEA REVIEW: *God's all-encompassing sovereignty and humanity's capacity for choice exist together. God—absolute and unrivaled in his actions and authority; man—free and responsible.*

III. CONCLUSION

The Chief End of Man

Pinwheel galaxies, rose-colored nebulae, and spheres of rocks and gas spin beyond our outward gaze, too distant to explore or touch or know. Orbed cells written with code and atoms subdivided to mythic quarks display another cosmos too deep for us to plumb. With intricacy of thought, God declares a universe that expands and contracts to infinitude.

God exists in dimensions we cannot comprehend. He is transcendent yet knowable. He is distinct in three persons, yet he is not divisible. He maintains perfect oneness and perfect community in himself. Eternal, preexisting all things visible and invisible—he is self-sufficient and self-sustaining.

When God brought the Jews out of captivity and directed them to return to Jerusalem, he did so to establish worship. The reestablishment of the community of faith and the rebuilding of the temple represented the proper ordering of life—that people should acknowledge and live within God's majesty, his goodness, and his authority.

He desires the same today because true worship is not a means to an end but an expression of reality. From start to finish, it is all about God.

PRINCIPLES

- God is sovereign and has authority over all creation, visible and invisible.
- The course of history is determined by God.
- Each person is responsible for the choices he or she makes.
- Worship acknowledges the reality of God's authority and wonder.

APPLICATIONS

- It makes sense to follow the wisdom of God rather than rely upon your own limited understanding and knowledge.
- Remind yourself continually of your dependence on God (1 Cor. 4:7).

- Understand worship as expressing the reality of God's sovereignty and goodness; it is not confined to church services, but it encompasses all of life.
- Understanding God's sovereignty, your response should be continual thanksgiving for his grace.

IV. LIFE APPLICATION

Lessons from Preschool

A little boy rushed into his grandmother's house, eager to tell her about everything. He told her about the scrambled eggs at breakfast, the color of the sky, how Dad drove too fast to church (according to Mom), and how the wind blew some papers across the street and into a tree.

"And what did you learn in Sunday school?" the grandmother asked.

His eyes opened wide; his voice became hushed. With the slowness of solemnity, he said, "We learned about God." Then in a rush of excitement and conviction, he blurted, "And we learned that he is very great. And . . . and, do you know what else Grandma?"

"What?"

"I am not *him.*"

Unfortunately, we often take a lifetime to learn this truth—if ever.

It would serve us well to remember that God adorns himself with glory and splendor, honor and majesty. He brings the proud to nothing and crushes the wicked (Job 40:9–14). He knows when we sit or get up; he perceives what others cannot—our thoughts. He is familiar with our habits, personality, and manners. Before a word is formed in our mind, he knows it completely. He determines how long we live (Ps. 139). There is no place that escapes God's presence because he fills heaven and earth (Jer. 23:24).

To live willingly beneath the sovereignty of God is simply to submit to reality. To delight in his supremacy is to live in the wonder of grace. Were it not for his dominion and the free exercise of his nature, we would all be condemned by our sin. His sovereignty allows him to have compassion on whom he chooses and to extend mercy to whom he wants. Were God not free to do as he pleased, we would never experience redemption. Far from encroaching on mankind's freedom, sovereignty allows God to display his goodness, kindness, compassion, and forgiveness. Without it, we would be without hope.

Let us not presume to understand more than we do, to instruct God on what is best for us, to suggest ways to run the universe or our lives, to make recommendations of judgment or mercy, to propose who deserves what. Instead, let us live in perpetual gratitude.

God sets the course of history. He has no rival. He creates and destroys. He judges and redeems . . . and we are not him.

V. PRAYER

Eternal God, when we consider who you are, we can only give echo to what David sang thousands of years ago: "What is man that you are mindful of him, the son of man that you care for him?" Who are we that you should hear us? And more, who are we that you should redeem us? Indeed, there is no explanation except that you are sovereign—full of mercy and compassionate. And so we whisper "thank you" and worship. Amen.

VI. DEEPER DISCOVERIES

A. Cyrus (1:1–2,7–8)

When Cyrus ascended the throne of Persia, he ruled a relatively small kingdom. But he met with quick and amazing victories among neighboring nations, including Media and Lydia. Cyrus continued his victories and, in 539 B.C., added Babylonia to his sprawling realm. According to ancient records (the Cyrus Cylinder), the people throughout the Babylonian cities welcomed Cyrus as a liberator since they had become disenchanted with their own king, Nabonidus. Cyrus claims to have won Babylon without a fight.

Cyrus eventually controlled an extensive empire stretching beyond Persia (modern Iran) into the territories of present-day Israel, Jordan, Syria, Turkey, Iraq, Pakistan, Afghanistan, and Russia. Persia rose from a moderate kingdom to a dominating empire, effectively changing world history.

Cyrus died in battle in 530 B.C. and was followed on the throne by his son, Cambyses. He furthered his father's conquests in Egypt but ruled only eight years. After his death, Darius assumed the throne.

B. Religious Pluralism (1:2)

When Cyrus issued the decree giving the Jews permission to return to Jerusalem so they could rebuild the temple, he claimed, "The LORD, the God of heaven, has given me all the kingdoms of the earth and he has appointed me to build a temple for him at Jerusalem in Judah." Cyrus appeared to be aware of God, his sovereignty, and the Jews' special place in history. But Cyrus was a firm believer in pluralism.

Wherever Cyrus went, he placated all the gods in order to win public favor. When he marched into Babylon, he reestablished the worship of Marduk, whom their King Nabonidus had neglected. Cyrus declared, "At the command of Marduk, Great God of Babylon, I restored the gods taken by Nabonidus. . . . May all the gods whom I have resettled in their former sanctuaries intercede daily on my behalf to Marduk" (the Cyrus Cylinder).

It was Persian policy to restore religious worship, shrines, and temples throughout the empire. Therefore, it was in keeping with his policy of tolerance to allow the Jews to return to Jerusalem. Cyrus viewed it as nothing more than restoring another tribal god to its territory.

Cyrus's outlook infected Jewish thinking. In fact, pluralism was a continual temptation for Israel. Over and over again they included foreign deities in their worship. It was not so much that the Jews discarded the one true God; they simply assimilated other beliefs into their system so that, during Persian rule, the influence of Zoroastrianism could be detected with its highly dualistic view of the universe.

As is often the case, religious pluralism seems kinder, more accepting, less restrictive. It appeals to our desire to fit in; it protects us from being different. While it is certainly right to respect the beliefs and choices others make, it is essential that Christians embrace the exclusive claims of Christ and commit to the revealed truth of Scripture. If we embrace more than what Christianity affirms, we have embraced nothing. Truth is singular and cannot contradict itself. Religious pluralism is irrational because conflicting beliefs cannot all be right.

Jesus claimed to be the only way to the Father, and God the Father demands undivided worship. As the apostle Paul instructed, we must speak the truth with love. Compassion does not necessitate a compromise with truth.

VII. TEACHING OUTLINE

A. INTRODUCTION

1. Lead Story: A View from Above
2. Context: Seventy years had passed since Nebuchadnezzar and his armies pillaged and burned Jerusalem. During that time a great number of Jews were forced into Babylonian exile and lived under the domination of a pagan culture. But those years also witnessed the deterioration of Babylonia, and it eventually fell to the Persians, led by Cyrus the Great. Cyrus initiated reforms marked by religious tolerance.
3. Transition: Though Cyrus ruled an expansive Persian Empire, God still ruled over the affairs of man. In fulfillment of divine prophecy, Cyrus issued a decree allowing Jews to return to Jerusalem and rebuild the temple.

B. COMMENTARY

1. God Is Sovereign (1:1–4)
   a. Prophecy fulfilled (1:1)
   b. Proclamation of a king (1:2–4)
2. Cooperation (1:5–11)
   a. The Jews (1:5)
   b. The Gentiles (1:6)
   c. The king (1:7–8)
   d. The king's treasures (1:9–11)

C. CONCLUSION: THE CHIEF END OF MAN

VIII. ISSUES FOR DISCUSSION

1. Discuss pluralism. Is it a positive force within society? Are there ways in which pluralism can be destructive?
2. Knowing that God is sovereign, what difference does that make in your daily life?
3. If God is in control, why does the world seem so out of control?
4. Brainstorm ideas about ways believers can worship God outside the walls of the church.

Ezra 2

Making the List

I. INTRODUCTION
Under the Spreading Family Tree

II. COMMENTARY
A verse-by-verse explanation of the chapter.

III. CONCLUSION
Family Ties

An overview of the principles and applications from the chapter.

IV. LIFE APPLICATION
Hobbit Habits

Melding the chapter to life.

V. PRAYER
Tying the chapter to life with God.

VI. DEEPER DISCOVERIES
Historical, geographical, and grammatical enrichment of the commentary.

VII. TEACHING OUTLINE
Suggested step-by-step group study of the chapter.

VIII. ISSUES FOR DISCUSSION
Zeroing the chapter in on daily life.

A minority is powerless while it conforms to the majority.

Henry David Thoreau

I N A N U T S H E L L

In order to demonstrate the legitimacy of the exiles in rebuilding the temple in Jerusalem, the writer of Ezra carefully assembled his evidence. The previous chapter established God as the instigator and the nation of Judah as the chosen people. The sacred objects from Solomon's temple brought back to Jerusalem further validated the project. Now the chronicler confirms the holiness of the community.

Making the List

I. INTRODUCTION

Under the Spreading Family Tree

A friend recently described a few findings from some genealogy research he had conducted. He traced his way back through the years and discovered a direct relative who sailed from Ireland to America and fought in the Revolutionary War. But as he followed subsequent generations, he discovered a few members who were less commendable.

One relative he discovered was a man named Daniel. When the powers-that-be decided to run a road through his favorite corner of the world, he and three friends decided to go calling at the home of the roadwork foreman to raise their objections to the road. The four were neither welcomed nor invited in. Daniel took aim through the man's front door and killed him on the spot. Daniel finished out his days in prison.

The second chapter of Ezra presents the reader with a family tree of sorts. It is not a fully developed tree, designating who "begat" whom, but it does provide an accounting of exiles who returned to Palestine and from whom they descended. The compiler of the Book of Ezra was intent on demonstrating that those who returned had legitimate claim to the task of reconstructing the temple. No fringe characters surfaced in this assembly. Those who returned came from acceptable family lines. Those who could not prove their heritage were not allowed full participation in the holy work.

II. COMMENTARY

Making the List

> **MAIN IDEA:** *The writer of Ezra provides a genealogical short form, compiling a list of returned exiles and their ancestry. His purpose was twofold—to reaffirm the legitimacy of the newly settled Jews to rebuild the temple and to establish continuity between the old, preexilic line of David and Solomon, and the newer, postexilic inhabitants as the true and faithful Israel.*

A The Community (2:1–63)

> **SUPPORTING IDEA:** *The chronicler compiles a list from available sources, creating a register that reflects the validity of those who resettled in Palestine. These were not interlopers but true Israelites.*

1. Background (2:1)

2:1. Having described how it came about that Jews returned to Palestine, the chronicler next focused on the exiles themselves: **Now these are the people of the province who came up from the captivity of the exiles.** The people described in the following verses already resided in Palestine. The list was not an account of a particular caravan of Jews recently arrived but of those currently living in the province who had returned because of Persia's more lenient internal policies. These were not expatriates but Jews forced from their homeland by **Nebuchadnezzar king of Babylon**; they had not left willingly but had been **taken captive to Babylon.**

More importantly, however, they returned home, **to Jerusalem and Judah, each to his own town.** Here they settled in with the other inhabitants—non-Jews and Jews who had never departed, those whom the Babylonians had left behind as undesirable. In keeping with the chronicler's purpose of connecting the new Judah with the Davidic kingdom, the towns listed throughout this chapter (with the exception of three) were close to Jerusalem and within the preexilic kingdom borders.

2. The leaders (2:2a)

2:2a. Having identified the exiles in general terms, the chronicler turned to specifics. First, he named the leaders: **Zerubbabel, Jeshua, Nehemiah, Seraiah, Reelaiah, Mordecai, Bilshan, Mispar, Bigvai, Rehum, and Baanah.** Missing from this register, but included in a corresponding list found in Nehemiah 7:7, is the leader Nahamani. If we include Nahamani, we have twelve leaders. These men symbolized the twelve tribes, confirming again the link to the God-ordained kingdom.

Despite the familiarity of several names in the list, such as Nehemiah and Mordecai, most scholars agree that only the first two names, Zerubbabel and Jeshua, can be identified. Where the person's identity can't be established, it is best to remain silent.

Zerubbabel, though given a Babylonian name, was a descendant of David and established his Jewish identity by being referred to as the "son of Shealtiel" (Ezra 3:2). He emerged as the governor of Judah, taking on political authority in the region. Jeshua, known as the "son of Jozadak" (Ezra 3:2), was the grandson of the last official preexilic high priest. In time Jeshua advanced to this same spiritual position within the community.

With a son of David exercising political authority, and a descendant of a high priest assuming religious authority, the messianic expectations of the people were high in and around Jerusalem at that time, especially in context with the prophetic messages delivered by Haggai and Zechariah.

3. The laymen (2:2b–35)

2:2b. This portion of the list includes the men of the people of Israel. This term distinguished these people from the priesthood. Most scholars agree that the list was probably obtained from older, diverse sources. Consequently, the numbers found here do not agree with a parallel list in Nehemiah 7. In addition, the categorizing within the list (switching from family heritage—"descendants of" to town associations—"men of") seems controlled by the material from which the chronicler drew his information.

2:3a. The record begins with those classified by family name: the descendants of . . . It was a grouping common in Israel in which the tribes were subdivided by family groups. These were not individual family units but larger groups comprised of several extended families that could trace themselves back to a particular family head.

2:3b–20. Few specifics are known about the clans listed, though translation of certain names can be made. For instance, Parosh means "flea" and is listed as a clan name again in Ezra 8:3 and 10:25. Shephatiah means "Yahweh has judged." Others of this group returned with Ezra (Ezra 8:8).

In Ezra 2:6, the name Pahath-Moab (through the line of Jeshua and Joab) actually means "governor of Moab." Most likely it refers to those related to a particular governor of that region. Consequently, the distinction is made to those descended from Jeshua ("God saves") and Joab.

2:21–35. At this point the list changes from personal family names to groups designated by towns. The list begins with the men of Bethlehem. Three hundred years before the return of the exiles, Micah prophesied that out of Bethlehem would come "one who will be ruler over Israel, whose origins are from of old, from ancient times" (Mic. 5:2).

Anathoth was located about three miles north of Jerusalem and held the distinction as the birthplace of Jeremiah the prophet. **Netophah, Azmaveth, Ramah and Geba, Micmash,** and **Magbish** were towns scattered five to ten miles outside of Jerusalem. **Kiriath Jearim, Kephirah, and Beeroth** were three towns in the area of Gibeon.

Bethel was an important religious site for Israel but was later taken into the southern kingdom of Judah by King Josiah. The location of **Ai** is uncertain. **Nebo** was possibly on a hill overlooking Jerusalem.

The entry, **the other Elam**, is a precise repeat from Ezra 2:7 where it was listed as a family name. The number associated with each is also exactly the same, raising questions about whether this is a scribal error rather than a new listing.

Harim is a common family name, but there is no evidence of a town by this name. In fact, numerous descendants of Harim are found among the returning priests (Ezra 2:32). **Lod, Hadid and Ono** are a cluster of three towns far from Jerusalem (about twenty-five miles).

Jericho was annexed into Judah by King Josiah. Men from this town helped Nehemiah rebuild Jerusalem's walls. It is uncertain whether **Senaah** represents a town or a family, though records of neither have been found (Clines, pp. 50–53).

4. The priests (2:36–39)

2:36–39. The next group, the priests, accounted for a significant number of returning exiles. Since the main purpose for returning to Jerusalem was to reestablish worship, a large proportion of temple priests accepted the call to return. In addition, a hierarchy within the priesthood was emerging by this time, giving the priests more influence within Jewish society. The powerful role of the priests was just forming during the time of Ezra, but it continued to gain strength until, by the time of Jesus, it had become a formidable institution.

The four families listed in Ezra 2 traced their ancestry to Aaron, who had four sons. Two died without heirs. Aaron's sons, Eleazar and Ithamar, had twenty-four sons (sixteen and eight, respectively). The descendants of these twenty-four men established an order of ministry within the temple (see 1 Chr. 24). From these four families, **Jedaiah, Immer, Pashur,** and **Harim**, the priests of the returning exiles traced their heritage and claim to authority.

When mentioning the descendants of Jedaiah, the writer notes that these descendants included the **family of Jeshua**. It is possible that this footnote was intended to add validity to the current high priest, Jeshua, by establishing his family line with this distinguished family.

5. The Levites (2:40)

2:40. Compared with the sizable group of returning priests (4,289), the number of Levites was few (74): **the descendants of Jeshua and Kadmiel (through the line of Hodaviah).** It is believed that the status of the Levite had come on hard times. As a group, the Levites had never enjoyed the same prestige as the priests. During the exile their position is believed to have declined even more. Consequently, they would probably not have felt the same motivation to return to Judah as the priests did.

Away from the temple during the exile, the Levites may have taken on other occupations and so were absorbed into other groups. It is also possible that since the Levites were not an elite group, as the priests were, relatively few were forced into exile. Perhaps they remained in the Palestine area with those commoners whom the Babylonians considered undesirable.

6. The singers (2:41)

2:41. Historically, temple singers came from three family lines—Asaph, Jeduthun, and Heman. Appointed by King David, these families and their descendants were trained "for the music of the temple of the LORD, with cymbals, lyres and harps, for the ministry at the house of God" (1 Chr. 25:6). In the accounting of Ezra 2, however, only **the descendants of Asaph** are mentioned.

7. The gatekeepers (2:42)

2:42. Originally selected by King David, the gatekeepers were to guard the gates of the tent of meeting and later the temple. The gatekeepers came from among the Levites and were responsible for protecting not only the gates but rooms and treasuries of the temple as well. They were in charge of temple articles used in worship services, the furnishings of the temple, "as well as the flour and wine, and the oil, incense and spices" (1 Chr. 9:29). Those families numbered among the returning exiles were **Shallum, Ater, Talmon, Akkub, Hatita and Shobai.**

8. The temple servants and servants of Solomon (2:43–58)

2:43–54. The temple servants, or slaves, came from people captured during the Israelites' conquest of Palestine. According to Numbers 31:25–47, when the Israelites defeated a town, they divided the spoils among the soldiers and the community. Then, from out of these two larger divisions, a smaller part was given to the high priest as a portion to God, and another to the Levites "who are responsible for the care of the LORD's tabernacle" (Num. 31:30). These shares included animals and people.

Those conquered people selected for service to the Levites were given the lowliest jobs and are believed to be the temple servants. Their names indicate their foreign origins, or, in the case of nicknames, their humble role within the community. **Ziha** is Egyptian, **Rezin** is Aramaic (2:48), and **Besai** may be Babylonian (2:49). **Hasupha** means "quick" (2:43); **Lebanah** means "white" (2:45); **Nekoda** means "spotted" (2:48) (see Clines, p. 57).

2:55–58. Those termed **servants of Solomon** were also temple servants first conscripted by King Solomon as his slave-labor force from among the conquered Canaanites (1 Kgs. 9:20–21). Of the temple servants, **392** left Babylon. In comparison to all those returning to Palestine, relatively few came back from among the lower, more humble ranks.

9. The disenfranchised (2:59–63)

2:59. **The following came up from the towns of Tel Melah, Tel Harsha, Kerub, Addon and Immer.** These were five Babylonian towns from which some exiles returned. The difficulty for these people came in that **they could not show that their families were descended from Israel.** The concern was to demonstrate not only racial purity in the community but also continuity with the Davidic monarchy. Those people whose genealogy was unproved were excluded in some way. What form this exclusion took is unclear.

2:60. The particular families whose ancestry had become muddled or untraceable were **the descendants of Delaiah, Tobiah and Nekoda.** There is no evidence about whether these families ever established their Israelite roots.

2:61. There were also **priests** who could not establish their ancestry—the families of **Hobaiah, Hakkoz and Barzillai.** Hakkoz appears to have eventually provided proof of his priestly lineage because during the time of Nehemiah, a relative from this family was an acting priest who helped rebuild the wall (Neh. 3:4). The fate of the other two is unknown.

Barzillai, however, is identified as **a man who had married a daughter of Barzillai the Gileadite and was called by that name.** Evidently this man, a priest, had taken his wife's family name. It is uncertain why he did this unless it was to gain his wife's inheritance of land. Traditionally, priests had no claim to land—their inheritance was the Lord (Num. 18:20). If land was this man's objective, it may have been seen as a denouncement of his priesthood.

2:62–63. The uncertainty of priestly ancestry was viewed more seriously since impurity among the priests could result in communal impurity. Consequently, though **these searched for their family records,** they were **excluded from the priesthood as unclean.** This ceremonial uncleanness meant they could not function as priests before the Lord.

The governor, most likely Sheshbazzar or Zerubbabel, ordered the priests **not to eat any of the most sacred food until there was a priest ministering with the Urim and Thummim.** The restriction against eating sacred food was a cautionary measure to ensure ceremonial correctness. There was great concern for acting according to law and not exceeding its bounds. Rather than risking the ritual purity of the community, the governor placed these priests on probation until a priest with sufficient authority (the high priest) could decide the matter. The Urim and Thummim represented a system of casting lots by the high priest to determine divine guidance.

B The Totals (2:64–67)

SUPPORTING IDEA: *The chronicler concluded his accounting by referencing all those who accompanied the exiles, including pack animals.*

2:64. **The whole company numbered 42,360.** As with the earlier discrepancy in counting the temple articles (Ezra 1:9–11), the totals given here (42,360) do not agree with the individual numbers provided throughout the genealogy list (29,818)—a difference of 12,542. Some believe the numerical notations included only the men, whereas the "whole company" incorporated women as well. If so, the number of returning women was relatively small. Others suggest a scribal error since the chronicler used outside information which could have become corrupted over time. In fact, we can't be certain why disagreement in the figures exists.

2:65–67. The inclusion of 7,337 **menservants and maidservants** points to the wealth of the returning exiles, as does the addition of **200 men and women singers**. Servants were considered personal property, much like the animals later in the list. The large number of servants suggests a returning population accustomed to a comfortable lifestyle. The men and women singers were personal musicians of the wealthy who provided entertainment. The Babylonians had carted away from Jerusalem the leaders, the highly educated, the most promising among the Israelites. It appears that these people and their families had done well even in a captive nation. This may explain why so few actually returned to Palestine.

Their personal property also included **736 horses, 245 mules, 435 camels and 6,720 donkeys**—pack animals crucial for a long trip. The inclusion of servants and animals in the list demonstrated the status of the exiles, their resources and capabilities.

C Temple Gifts (2:68–69)

SUPPORTING IDEA: *Worship was the objective of the return so, upon arrival, gifts were given toward the temple building fund.*

2:68–69. In discussing the Book of Ezra, one must remember that the text is ancient, the materials used by the compiler are diverse, and the intention of the author supersedes the purely historical. The text reads: **When they arrived at the house of the LORD in Jerusalem, some of the heads of the families gave freewill offerings.** Most scholars agree that the list is a compilation of several groups of exiles over a period of time. Some arrived in Jerusalem, and those who did gave freewill offerings **toward the rebuilding of the house of God**.

Once again there is a discrepancy between the numbers of Ezra and those of the corresponding account in Nehemiah 7. It is possible that the **61,000 drachmas** in Ezra were achieved by combining two different building funds delineated in Nehemiah. The family heads also contributed **5,000 minas of silver**, or about three tons, and **100 priestly garments**. These were linen coats used by the priests.

D Resettlement (2:70)

> **SUPPORTING IDEA:** *The people have returned and reconnected with their ancestral lands and towns. They are home to stay.*

2:70. The author concluded his list much the same as he began it (Ezra 2:1)—by affirming the resettlement of the exiles. He wrote that **the priests, the Levites, the singers, the gatekeepers and the temple servants settled in their own towns**. Certainly a high proportion of those involved in religious duties and responsibilities, along with others, settled in or very near Jerusalem. **The rest of the Israelites settled in their towns** throughout Judah.

> **MAIN IDEA REVIEW:** *The writer of Ezra provides a genealogical short form, compiling a list of returned exiles and their ancestry. His purpose is twofold—to reaffirm the legitimacy of the newly settled Jews to rebuild the temple and to establish continuity between the old, preexilic line of David and Solomon, and the newer, postexilic inhabitants as the true and faithful Israel.*

III. CONCLUSION

Family Ties

Peppered throughout the Old Testament, and three times in Ezra alone (including this chapter), are lists of families and their descendants. Why this Jewish preoccupation with bloodlines?

The concern for heredity grew out of the understanding that God's promises were extended to the heirs of Abraham. More specifically, his blessing rested on the descendants of Jacob. From out of Jacob came the priestly line of Levi and Aaron and the political line of David. These figured most prominently in the national sense of identity and purpose. During the postexilic time in which Ezra was written, the tracing of blood relations helped secure the rights and privileges of the family, nation, and priesthood against interlopers. It helped preserve continuity between past glory and present ambition as well as assure continuance of the national character into the future.

God never intended to establish an elite enclave in the Middle East. He desired to create a holy people who would bless the world. It was not about superiority and privilege but about honor and responsibility; it was not about bloodlines but about God's faithfulness.

God chose Israel to demonstrate his glory through that nation. While the Jews traced their heritage through the bloodlines of generations and centuries to Abraham or David, Christians trace themselves through the blood of the promised one, Jesus Christ. It is through him that the riches of God are distributed generously to those whom God has adopted into his family. In the end, it is still about God's faithfulness.

On the surface, Ezra 2 is merely an ancient listing of people. But the list speaks volumes about the faithfulness of God. What he says happens; what he intends comes to pass. Despite the devastation of war, the threats to identity, and the disruption of captivity, the line continued. God always preserves his people; his promises always hold true.

PRINCIPLES

- Nothing disrupts the purposes of God.
- Outward appearances often mask the workings and power of God.
- God is faithful.
- The path to God has always been through faith, evidenced by obedience to his revelation.

APPLICATIONS

- Base your understanding of God and life not upon what you observe but upon God's revelation in Scripture.
- God's Word is inviolate. Trust God and have full confidence in him.
- God's faithfulness assures you that you are never alone, nor are you ever abandoned. Despite the experiences of hardship or confusion, rest in God's presence and faithfulness.

IV. LIFE APPLICATION

Hobbit Habits

In the classic tale *The Hobbit,* J. R. R. Tolkien assembled a world inhabited by dwarves, elves, giants, goblins, dragons, and, more importantly, hobbits.

The tale centers on Bilbo Baggins, *the* hobbit. He is singular not because he is the only one but because he breaks with hobbit convention. Respectable hobbits, we are told, "never had any adventures or did anything unexpected." Even so, Bilbo embarks on an adventure, a very extraordinary one that consumes almost three hundred pages. Notwithstanding the fantastical creatures and events, the harrowing escapes and daring battles, the most extraordinary aspect to the story is that Bilbo, a hobbit, joins in the quest at all. For, despite often wishing he was at home in his "nice hole by the fire with the kettle just beginning to sing," he can't escape having been chosen by Gandalf, the great wizard. Faithful to his calling, he participates with amazing pluck right to the very conclusion.

In the end, of course, he helps the dwarves reclaim their hoard of gold, silver, and jewels that the terrible dragon Smaug had stolen and kept for a long time. It was not a simple job, and his companions rarely appreciated his efforts. Even so, he did his bit—and that was satisfaction enough.

For most modern readers, the listing of names in Ezra 2 elicits only a quick scan, or a skip and a jump to chapter 3. We know next to nothing about these people. They seem rather ordinary and unexceptional, a dusty group repossessing a dilapidated city in Palestine.

But these people were "hobbits" of an ancient time because they broke with convention. While the majority of Jews remained in Babylon, complacent and content, the list gives evidence of those hearty souls who followed God's call and set their face toward Jerusalem. They probably didn't feel extraordinary in and of themselves, but they did feel the compelling force of God's purpose and their role in that great design. So they broke from the crowd; they ventured out and participated in the adventure God set before them.

We, too, can have a hand in the purposes and events of God's design. It will be enough if we do our bit because in this wide world it is not about us but about the glory of God.

V. PRAYER

King of the universe, ruler over all creation, guardian of our souls, protect us from the subtle tugs of complacency, from the mediocre life that finds contentment in the distractions of society. Open our eyes and fortify our spirits to follow you, even into the ordinary corners of our daily lives. In our weakness help us find our pleasure in you alone. Amen.

VI. DEEPER DISCOVERIES

A. Zerubbabel (2:2)

Zerubbabel, though a Jew, had a Babylonian name. Within his name the term *babel* comes from the ancient city that later gave rise to the empire. Like so many Jews in captivity, he was probably given a Babylonian name to assimilate him into the new society while separating him from his own culture. But Zerubbabel is identified as the son of Shealtiel, and thus the grandson of King Jehoiachin—part of the Davidic line. He is mentioned in the opening of Matthew's Gospel as part of the genealogical line of Jesus Christ.

In the context of Ezra, Zerubbabel provided the leadership necessary for advancing the reconstruction of the temple. Nothing more is known about him.

B. Urim and Thummim (2:63)

The Urim and Thummim date back to Aaron, the first high priest. Exodus 28:30 states, "Also put the Urim and the Thummim in the breastpiece, so they may be over Aaron's heart whenever he enters the presence of the LORD. Thus Aaron will always bear the means of making decisions for the Israelites over his heart before the LORD." Urim is mentioned in the commissioning of Joshua (Num. 27:21), and, during the early monarchy, both are used in discerning truth between Saul and his son Jonathan (1 Sam. 14:41).

Urim and Thummim are thought to have been either stones or sticks kept within the fold of the high priest's garment. These objects were marked in such a way as to give answers to perplexing questions. They were cast as lots, or dice, with *Urim* meaning "curses" and *Thummim*, "perfection." If the symbols were mixed, it was considered "no reply." By postexilic times the system was not used, and it is possible that the stones or sticks did not exist beyond this time.

Many interpreters believe that the reference to Urim and Thummim in Ezra simply implies authority. Consequently, the governor's command that certain priests not eat sacred food "until there was a priest ministering with the Urim and Thummim" could simply mean they were to abstain from these foods until the arrival of a high priest who had the authority to decide on spiritual issues.

VII. TEACHING OUTLINE

A. INTRODUCTION

1. Lead Story: Under the Spreading Family Tree

2. Context: While the majority of Jews remained in Babylon, a few caravans of exiles returned to Palestine to rebuild the temple. These returning Jews were proof of God's faithfulness to his people and his promises.

3. Transition: The heritage of the returning Jews was linked, for the most part, to families of the preexilic kingdom. The listing of the clans was signifcant in establishing their legitimacy for temple reconstruction as well as the reinstitution of temple worship.

B. COMMENTARY

1. The Community (2:1–63)

   a. Background (2:1)

   b. The leaders (2:2a)

   c. The laymen (2:2b–35)

   d. The priests (2:36–39)

   e. The Levites (2:40)

   f. The singers (2:41)

   g. The gatekeepers (2:42)

   h. The temple servants and servants of Solomon (2:43–58)

   i. The disenfranchised (2:59–63)

2. The Totals (2:64–67)

3. Temple Gifts (2:68–69)

4. Resettlement (2:70)

C. CONCLUSION: FAMILY TIES

VIII. ISSUES FOR DISCUSSION

1. Discuss situations where times were difficult or confusing and yet, looking back, God's faithfulness was evident.

2. Name some of God's promises for believers today.

3. Is family heritage important within the community of faith today? Can it be a benefit? Are there times when it can be a hindrance?

4. The casting of lots, the message of prophets, and the writings of the law were used to understand the will of God in ancient times. What are the primary ways in which we discern God's will today?

Ezra 3

A Time to Build

I. INTRODUCTION
Back to Basics

II. COMMENTARY
A verse-by-verse explanation of the chapter.

III. CONCLUSION
Out of Order

An overview of the principles and applications from the chapter.

IV. LIFE APPLICATION
The Business of Fear

Melding the chapter to life.

V. PRAYER
Tying the chapter to life with God.

VI. DEEPER DISCOVERIES
Historical, geographical, and grammatical enrichment of the commentary.

VII. TEACHING OUTLINE
Suggested step-by-step group study of the chapter.

VIII. ISSUES FOR DISCUSSION
Zeroing the chapter in on daily life.

$\mathcal{W}$e all want progress. But progress means getting nearer

to the place where you want to be. . . . If you are on the

wrong road, progress means doing an about-turn and walking

back to the right road; and in that case the man who turns

back soonest is the most progressive man.

C .   S .   L e w i s

I N   A   N U T S H E L L

$\mathcal{S}$ome time after the exiles returned to Palestine, they assembled in Jerusalem to repair the temple altar and begin the prescribed sacrifices and religious observances. This was the first step in reestablishing worship, and by tradition and necessity, it preceded the repair work on the temple. Later, the restoration of the temple building began, marked by a service of dedication and praise to God.

A Time to Build

I. INTRODUCTION

Back to Basics

*I*n 1958, Vince Lombardi accepted the position of head football coach at Green Bay, Wisconsin. He was not getting the "dream team." The Packers had developed a tradition of losing; it was a team few respected.

Lombardi arrived in Green Bay firm in the belief that he could turn the pitiful Packers around. He brought to the shores of Lake Michigan the lessons he learned as assistant coach under Earl "Colonel Red" Blaik of West Point Military Academy: stick with simple blocking and tackling, execute plays perfectly, and behave respectfully on the field. Lombardi expected strict obedience, dedication, and total effort from everyone. Long hours were the custom, intensive training the rule.

Legend has it that, after a particularly humiliating defeat, Lombardi stood before his tired and dirty football players in the locker room with the intense look they had come to recognize. The room was silent. Lombardi held up a football. Then he declared, "Gentlemen, this is a football." From then on it was back to basics.

Three years after arriving in Green Bay, Vince Lombardi led his Packers to the National Football League championship. They became the dominant team in pro football, winning five NFL championships and the first two Super Bowls. Their dramatic turnaround resulted from obedience to the coach, hard work, and mastery of the basics.

When the exiles returned to Palestine, the Jews were coming off repeated years of captivity, seventy seasons of defeat. The leaders, prophets, and, to some extent, the citizenry, understood that if the community of faith were to flourish, it would require strict obedience to God and a return to the basics of faith: acceptable worship, adherence to the law, and purity among the people.

II. COMMENTARY

A Time to Build

> **MAIN IDEA:** *Having established the legitimacy of the returned exiles to reinstitute temple worship, the writer of Ezra takes us to holy ground, describing the community's adherence to the law. The people begin again the daily sacrifices, the festivals, and the building of the temple.*

A The Altar (3:1–6)

> **SUPPORTING IDEA:** *The purpose in returning to Palestine was to reestablish legitimate worship at the temple. Before building the temple, however, they repaired the altar and began the prescribed sacrifices.*

3:1. Those who left Babylon and relocated in Judea settled in their ancestral lands and towns. **When the seventh month came . . . the people assembled as one man in Jerusalem.** Some interpreters believe this represents a time early in the exiles' return. Others hold to a later date—after the people had lived in the area for some time.

The seventh month (Tishri) occurred in the fall, around September or October. This was the most sacred month of the Jewish year. In this one month the community observed the Feast of Trumpets, the Day of Atonement, and the Feast of Tabernacles. Though the Day of Atonement could not be observed at this time (since there was no temple), it was, nevertheless, a time of remembrance, sacrifice, and celebration.

3:2. **Then Jeshua son of Jozadak and his fellow priests and Zerubbabel son of Shealtiel and his associates began to build the altar of the God of Israel.** The chronicler picks up his narrative around 522–520 B.C. Once the exiles returned, they became occupied with maintaining their ancestral property, grew intimidated by the hostilities around them, and thus never fully pursued the temple's reconstruction. Sheshbazzar, whom Cyrus sent to accompany the exiles to Judah at the start (Ezra 1:11), and who, according to Persian archives, laid the foundation of the temple (Ezra 5:16), was possibly replaced by Zerubbabel. Through Haggai's urging, Zerubbabel assumed the construction project in earnest.

Jeshua was listed first because he represented the priesthood, coming from the line of the last high priest, Jozadak. This gave divine confirmation for the actions of building and dedicating the altar. Zerubbabel, as the political leader, acted in concert with the religious arm of the nation. But it was not these two men alone who repaired the altar. They were joined by the priests and political officers as well.

The purpose of the altar was **to sacrifice burnt offerings on it. The altar was built in accordance with what is written in the Law of Moses.** Unlike other nations, they were not to chisel the stones with tools (Exod. 20:25), but were to use rocks as they found them (Deut. 27:6). It is possible that the altar was destroyed when Nebuchadnezzar plundered the city. It is also possible that the altar, though standing, was considered defiled since conformity to the law had disintegrated during the exile. If this were the case, the exiles would have felt compelled to rebuild it in strict adherence to Mosaic commands.

By using the term **man of God** for Moses, prophetic and, perhaps, supernatural attributes were attached to him. The Jews viewed Moses as a person through whom God worked; his words were understood as issuing from God himself. The term was later used by Paul of Timothy, and all believers, urging conformity to the path of righteousness and the revealed word of God (1 Tim. 6:11; 2 Tim. 3:17).

3:3a. Even though the returning exiles carried an imperial edict into Palestine, King Cyrus and his authority were far away. Once the exiles arrived in Jerusalem and Judea, tension arose between the returning Jews and the various people of the region. The chronicler explains further the hostile environment in chapter 4; here he simply acknowledged the situation: **Despite their fear of the peoples around them, they built the altar on its foundation.** Because continuity was critical to this community, as well as strict obedience to the law, they repaired or rebuilt the altar on the spot where the altar in Solomon's temple had stood.

3:3b–5. Once the altar was built, they gave **burnt offerings on it to the LORD.** These, too, were in conformity with the law. In accordance with the instructions given on Mount Sinai, the people were to offer daily two one-year-old lambs without defect, along with a grain offering mixed with oil, and a wine offering (Exod. 29:38–41; Num. 28:3–8).

Then **they celebrated the Feast of Tabernacles with the required number of burnt offerings prescribed for each day.** The Feast of Tabernacles was both a harvest celebration and a memorial, recalling the Israelites' nomadic experience in the wilderness (see "Deeper Discoveries"). In keeping with the exiles' passion to follow preexilic form, they celebrated the feast in preparation for temple reconstruction, just as Solomon had celebrated the same feast at the dedication of the temple (Num. 29:12–38).

From that point on, it seems, the exiles observed all the details of the law. **They presented the regular burnt offerings**—which would be the daily sin offerings and the Sabbath sacrifices. They also observed **the New Moon sacrifices,** which were given at the beginning of each month (the Jews followed a lunar calendar), and they offered the **sacrifices for all the appointed sacred feasts of the LORD.** These included Passover, the Day of Atonement (though this was not possible without the temple), the Feast of Trumpets, the Feast of Tabernacles, and Pentecost. In addition, they gave **freewill offerings**. These were not required but were to be given spontaneously as an act of worship and gratitude.

3:6. In the seventh month the exiles **began to offer burnt offerings to the LORD**. Worship and sacrifice to God began before the rebuilding of the temple: **though the foundation of the LORD's temple had not yet been laid**. It is perhaps more appropriate to translate this, "before the LORD's temple had been repaired." This fits more properly with the historical events, with Sheshbazzar laying the foundation (Ezra 5:16). Reconstruction was halted until later. Even when Zerubbabel became governor, the temple project had not progressed, even though worship ritual was followed.

B The Temple (3:7–13)

> **SUPPORTING IDEA:** *Worship was reintroduced at the site of Solomon's altar. Skipping ahead, the chronicler next described the beginning efforts of temple restoration.*

1. The leaders initiate repairs (3:7–10)

3:7. They gave money to the masons and carpenters. Much of the narrative parallels the original temple preparation and construction during the reigns of David and Solomon. Both masons and carpenters were conscripted by David in the original temple preparations (1 Chr. 22:15). The exiles also gave **food and drink and oil to the people of Sidon and Tyre**, just as Solomon had done (2 Chr. 2:10), in payment for cedar logs.

3:8. The temple repair began **in the second month of the second year**; Solomon also started construction in the second month (2 Chr. 3:2). The building program began not after the exiles' initial arrival under Cyrus but later **after their arrival at the house of God in Jerusalem**. The years between their arrival and the actual construction project were spent in preparation: assembling the workmen, the supplies, and shipping the timber from Lebanon.

It was spring, and Zerubbabel and Jeshua, along with the priests and Levites who had come with them from the captivity, began the supervision and work of repairing the temple. The leaders appointed **Levites twenty years of age and older to supervise the building of the house of the LORD**. David also appointed Levites to supervise the temple building, though he designated those men thirty years of age and older.

Jeshua and Zerubbabel enlisted those younger perhaps because of the few Levites who returned, giving them a smaller population from which to recruit. They may also have based their selection process on David's model of

(handwritten margin note) Maybe because there just weren't enough.

appointing Levites twenty years and older for temple work (1 Chr. 23:24–27).

3:9. In general terms, the Levites of qualified age supervised the construction. The chronicler again validated these Levites by iterating the Levitical families from among the exiles. With the exception of **the sons of Henadad and their sons and brothers**, the families of **Jeshua** and **Kadmiel (descendants of Hodaviah)** are mentioned in Ezra 2:40.

3:10. The thrust of this chapter is worship. Very little space is given to the actual repair. Worship and religious practice were the focus. The building project began **when the builders laid the foundation of the temple**. After that it was all about the priests, the celebration, the Levites, and the response of the people. Even so, it is unlikely that the foundation was laid so much as repaired; the stones of the original temple were too massive to have been demolished.

The initiation of repairing the temple was marked by a sacred ceremony, much as what had occurred at the dedication of the temple by Solomon. The priests, dressed in their official finery, called the people to worship with silver trumpets. The Levites, specifically the sons of Asaph, offered the sound of cymbals in worship (1 Chr. 25:1,6). Everything was carried out with precise purpose and a keen awareness of tradition, **as prescribed by David king of Israel**.

2. The people respond (3:11–13)

3:11. The priests and Levites led the worship service as the temple rebuilding began. Those gathered at the temple site responded: **with praise and thanksgiving they sang to the LORD**. The people sang, **He is good; his love to Israel endures forever**. This confident and grateful approach to God is found in several of the psalms. The reaction seemed heartfelt as **all the people gave a great shout of praise to the LORD, because the foundation of the house of the LORD was laid**. The people offered thanksgiving not only for what God had done but in anticipation of what he would do in the future.

3:12–13. Despite the excitement of the day and the anticipation of their future, **many of the older priests and Levites and family heads, who had seen the former temple, wept aloud**. A dual response spread through the congregation. The older priests, who had seen Solomon's temple and, perhaps, served within its courts, wept at the contrast between the old and the new.

At the same time the younger exiles **shouted for joy.** They were excited at the prospect of the temple's reconstruction. The combined voices **made so much noise** that **the sound was heard far away.**

MAIN IDEA REVIEW: *Having established the legitimacy of the returned exiles to reinstitute temple worship, the writer takes us to holy ground, describing the community's adherence to the law. They begin again the daily sacrifices, the festivals, and the building of the temple.*

III. CONCLUSION

Out of Order

For over seventy years, an "Out of Order" placard could have hung on the gates of Jerusalem. Behind the captivity and destruction that the Babylonians wrought, an internal breakdown in the spiritual life of the people had led the nation to malfunction. Betraying God's exclusive claims, the people compromised the integrity of Judah's distinctive laws and relationship to the one true God, resulting in disorder and community failure. God's intended ordering, his sovereign arrangement of life, was disregarded, and the entire system almost shuddered to a halt.

Then the exiles returned. They followed the original plans for worship prescribed by King David and King Solomon. Like an intricate network, each aspect of worship traced its way back to the original mandates given by God through his chosen messengers, whether king, prophet, or priest. Each element of the system was to model the integrity of what God had revealed. The exiles returned with the full intention of putting Judah in order, of getting the nation working again in proper relationship to God.

It was, perhaps, the proper place to start. But as the author of Ezra later hints (and Haggai specifically reveals), reconnecting to traditional practices addressed only part of the disorder. As always, the internal condition of individuals remained the critical component for spiritual rightness. The outward forms of worship exist to draw us to the person and presence of God. The condition of the heart and soul before God is the critical element in acceptable worship and maturity in faith.

PRINCIPLES

- God has exclusive claim on all creation.
- God expects obedience expressed from a heart of devotion.
- In dealing with people, nations, and communities, God demonstrates exceptional patience.

- Joy results from proper obedience.
- Because of God's creativity, depth of being, and energy, freedom of form and expression in worship exist within prescribed parameters.

APPLICATIONS

- In the pursuit of biblical truth, follow through with actions of obedience. This is where you find the joy of Christ.
- Remember God's mercy toward you. It protects you from the deceits of pride.
- In worship, be sure to follow the biblical guidelines for worship while at the same time allowing freedom in personal and cultural expressions of reverence.
- Obey God and Christ, and do not compromise for your own personal acceptance or safety.

IV. LIFE APPLICATION

The Business of Fear

Henri J. M. Nouwen wrote, "The Spirit of God is a creative spirit, always expressing itself in new life. When that spirit is extinguished by fear, we cling to what we have and thus stop moving and growing" (Nouwen, p. 59).

Fear is one of the strongest dynamics in society today. It is the persistent "what if." This was no more apparent than after the World Trade Towers in New York City were demolished by hijacked airliners on September 11, 2001. Fear paralyzed the national airways. People stayed home. Fear crippled business and sent the stock market plummeting. People who were generally resistant to governmental interference in personal affairs were willing to relinquish individual rights and constitutional protections in order to attain a sense of safety. While the flag fluttered from buildings and cars, the national demeanor reflected uneasiness.

Fear's playground is not only international politics, of course. Fear works its way into businesses, neighborhoods, families, even the church. In every case the result is a constriction of life, a strangling of energy. Fear turns in on itself in morbid self-absorption, redefining reality. Fear makes us tentative. We hesitate, reconsider, wait, and withdraw.

Ezra 3:3 states, "Despite their fear of the peoples around them, they built the altar on its foundation and sacrificed burnt offerings on it to the LORD, both the morning and evening sacrifices." Fear fluttered in their chests, it weighted their footsteps, and it sighed in their thoughts to rationalize their timidity. Even so, they built and sacrificed both in the morning and evening—the day circumscribed by obedience.

Courage is born of trust and confidence. Courage is expansive and charged with power. Courage makes us approach, offer, act, and embrace. From the assurances given to Joshua (Josh. 1:9), to the instructions offered by Paul (2 Tim. 1:7), people of faith are to live courageously because their confidence, energy, and destiny are secured in the loving grip of God.

V. PRAYER

God of order and creativity, of law and mercy, help us escape the suffocating atmosphere of fear so that we may breath the fresh air of freedom that comes to those who trust and obey you. Amen.

VI. DEEPER DISCOVERIES

A. Feast of Tabernacles (3:4)

The Feast of Tabernacles or, as it is sometimes called, the Feast of Booths, was the last sacred celebration of the year. It represented two important events.

The first was the celebration of harvest time and God's provision. This feast marked the conclusion of a year's labor—the grain was harvested, the wine pressed. Second, the feast commemorated Israel's wilderness wanderings. The Jewish feasts and sacred gatherings were meant to fix in their memory the actions and love of God for Israel. During this feast they were to "live in booths for seven days . . . so your descendants will know that I had the Israelites live in booths when I brought them out of Egypt. I am the LORD your God" (Lev. 23:42–43).

These were the humble beginnings of God's special interaction with the nation. The booths, or shelters, represented the deliverance of the Jews from Egypt, God's presence with them, and the giving of the law. Every seventh year, at the Feast of Tabernacles, the entire law was read before the people. The law ordered Jewish life, their politics, worship, and social structures. It was God's great gift to the nation, and it was given while they wandered in the desert with only God as their refuge and protector.

During the feast each family was to build a booth, or shelter, made of branches. They were to live in this temporary hut during the celebration. Each day a sin offering was sacrificed as well as varying numbers of rams, lambs, and bullocks as an expression of God's generosity toward his people and the people's gratitude toward God.

B. New Moon Sacrifices (3:5)

The Israelites followed a lunar calendar with each month consisting of the moon's full revolution. At the presentation of each new moon, special offerings were given and trumpets were blown. These were the New Moon sacrifices referred to in Ezra 3:5.

The Feast of Trumpets was closely tied to the New Moon sacrifices, and it may be this feast to which Ezra 3 actually refers. The people observed the first day of the seventh month (around October), as a Sabbath day. As at the New Moon sacrifices, the trumpets were sounded, but this time louder and longer, since this marked the beginning of the most sacred month of the year. Ten days later the people would observe the Day of Atonement—that one day of the year when the high priest entered the Holy of Holies; this was followed by the Feast of Tabernacles. The trumpets signaled the excitement to come, the voice of God to his people, the days of remembrance to be celebrated.

VII. TEACHING OUTLINE

A. INTRODUCTION
1. Lead Story: Back to Basics
2. Context: Several waves of exiles returned to Palestine in order to claim family lands and reinstitute lawful worship at the temple in Jerusalem. They began with good intentions but, over time, the work dropped off. Hostilities also developed with neighboring people, creating a fearful atmosphere.
3. Transition: Despite the difficult conditions, Jeshua the priest and Zerubbabel the governor headed up a renewed effort to rebuild the altar.

B. COMMENTARY
1. The Altar (3:1–6)
2. The Temple (3:7–13)
   a. The leaders initiate repairs (3:7–10)
   b. The people respond (3:11–13)

C. CONCLUSION: OUT OF ORDER

VIII. ISSUES FOR DISCUSSION
1. Discuss fears that hold people back from obedience to God or from ministry. Write down steps you can take to overcome obstacles to your obedience.

2. Discuss different forms of worship. Are there unacceptable modes? Are there ways in which new expressions can be discovered?
3. What is worship? Why are we commanded to worship? How does private worship prepare us for corporate worship?
4. What are the benefits of adhering to church traditions? Are there problems?

Ezra 4

A History of Opposition

I. **INTRODUCTION**
Lessons from Screwtape

II. **COMMENTARY**
A verse-by-verse explanation of the chapter.

III. **CONCLUSION**
Mathematical Musings

An overview of the principles and applications from the chapter.

IV. **LIFE APPLICATION**
Ecology 101

Melding the chapter to life.

V. **PRAYER**
Tying the chapter to life with God.

VI. **DEEPER DISCOVERIES**
Historical, geographical, and grammatical enrichment of the commentary.

VII. **TEACHING OUTLINE**
Suggested step-by-step group study of the chapter.

VIII. **ISSUES FOR DISCUSSION**
Zeroing the chapter in on daily life.

Misery inclines a man to fear all things, and then to believe all that he fears.

Philippe-Paul de Segur

IN A NUTSHELL

Jerusalem experienced a joyous celebration as the altar and temple reconstruction projects began. But along with hopeful anticipation, the chronicler admitted to persistent opposition encountered by the community of faith. Evidence entered the record from the reign of Darius, and the later administrations of Xerxes and Artaxerxes, of individuals and groups who disrupted and delayed the work.

A History of Opposition

I. INTRODUCTION

Lessons from Screwtape

C. S. Lewis penned a small book titled *The Screwtape Letters,* a compilation of fictional letters between the managerial devil, Screwtape, and his underling, Wormwood. The correspondence between the two fiends revolves around Wormwood's efforts to draw a young Christian away from the faith. Lewis wanted to illuminate the perils and vicissitudes of the human condition, particularly that of the Christian.

Throughout the narrative, Screwtape advises Wormwood on effective strategies for rendering the Christian's faith useless. He assures Wormwood that "a moderated religion is as good for us as no religion at all." He understands that restrained Christianity, full of ideas and talk but demonstrating little change, was a contradiction in terms. Theological compromise and acquiescence to social pressure undercut and destroy the essence of faith; they render it a parody.

When the Jews began reconstructing the temple, they were confronted with an offer of help from some neighbors who, by their own testimony, had been sacrificing to the Lord for a number of years. Zerubbabel and the other leaders faced a choice. They could lighten their own workload by accepting assistance and, at the same time, assure peaceable relations with their neighbors. Or they could stick to the original mandate given by Cyrus and, they believed, by God.

Zerubbabel decided to refuse all help. This initiated years of hostility between Judah and the surrounding people. However, Zerubbabel understood that these people had amalgamated the worship of the one true God with their devotion to other gods. To allow these people a hand in the work of temple restoration would compromise the integrity of the project and of worship. Perhaps they understood what earlier generations had not, that, as Screwtape said, "The safest road to Hell is the gradual one—the gentle slope, soft underfoot, without sudden turnings, without milestones, without signposts."

II. COMMENTARY

A History of Opposition

MAIN IDEA: *The Jews returned to Palestine with a clear call from God to reestablish worship, rebuild the temple, and reaffirm the nation's relationship with God; but the assignment was not easy. From the start, opposition formed against the exiles and continued through successive Persian monarchs.*

A An Offer of Help (4:1–5)

SUPPORTING IDEA: *Judah's leaders rejected an offer of help, seeing it as a proposal of compromise. The offer was rejected, and opposition to the project mounted.*

1. The offer (4:1–2)

4:1–2. For almost twenty years the temple project lay silent, its rubble a perpetual reminder of abandoned dreams. Then, prompted by the prophetic voices of Haggai and Zechariah, a new sense of divine purpose energized Zerubbabel, Jeshua, and all the people to reclaim the national mission. The shouts of excitement and joy that concluded chapter 3 reverberated throughout the Judean hills. Something was happening in Jerusalem.

When the enemies of Judah and Benjamin heard . . . they came to Zerubbabel and to the heads of the families. Those who met with Zerubbabel and the other leaders represented people who had been relocated to areas within the former Northern Kingdom by **Esarhaddon king of Assyria.** Though not ethnic Jews, these men offered to help restore the temple because, as they explained to Zerubbabel, **like you, we seek your God and have been sacrificing to him** since arriving in the area.

Since their earliest imperial days, the Assyrians forcibly relocated conquered peoples. As described in 2 Kings 17, exiles of the Northern Kingdom were replaced with people from Babylonia and other regions, each bringing their pagan religious practices. Since gods were considered territorial, these people, on their arrival in Palestine, included the worship of God in their religious duties: "They worshiped the LORD, but they also served their own gods in accordance with the customs of the nations from which they had been brought" (2 Kgs. 17:33).

The offer to help rebuild the temple came not from devotion to the one true God but from a cosmopolitan view of religion. It may have contained political overtones as well. The offer suggested a power struggle between the old order of amalgamation and the new effort to observe the law's exclusive claims.

Why purity?

Explain who these people were . . .

2. *The response (4:3)*

4:3. Zerubbabel, Jeshua, and the other leaders refused to allow their participation. Adherence to the exclusive claims of God and the specific commands of King Cyrus of Persia allowed no compromise. Perhaps the memory of Judah's exile, caused mostly from embracing foreign gods, compelled their response: **You have no part with us in building a temple to our God.** They may also have understood the political implications of turning from the imperial edict.

3. *The reaction (4:4–5)*

4:4–5. Rejection begets antagonism. The offer of help was withdrawn, and the surrounding people **set out to discourage the people of Judah** and disrupt their work.

Historical evidence does not pinpoint the precise time during which opposition was encountered and counselors were **hired to work against them and frustrate their plans.** But it is likely that unrest and contention boiled just beneath the surface of Judean life. Through the lens of a historian, the chronicler perceived subversive elements interfering with the national purpose, causing progress on the temple to lag for twenty years. Haggai presented a different perspective, describing the failure in terms of spiritual abandonment and self-absorption (see Hag. 1:2–11).

𝔹 Historical Divergence (4:6–23)

SUPPORTING IDEA: *The chronicler set large a parenthesis in the midst of his narrative. Having mentioned the issue of outside opposition to the temple, he inserted accounts of hostilities that occurred later.*

4. *The reign of Xerxes (4:6)*

4:6. The chronicler interrupted his story of Zerubbabel to illustrate the persistent opposition faced by the Jews as they tried to establish a community under God and the law. The first example came from the reign of Xerxes, better known for his court intrigues during the era of Esther. By this time the temple was restored and dedicated. But the event was included to further indict the non-Jews of the area.

Xerxes came to the throne at the end of 486 B.C. Soon after, the people of the area **lodged an accusation against the people of Judah and Jerusalem.** "They" were neighbors, those transplanted by the Assyrians. Here was the chronicler's proof that they were "enemies" (4:1). What form this complaint took, and what specific charges were leveled, remains unknown. For the purposes of the writer of Ezra, however, it was enough to know that these surrounding people desired to undermine the holy enterprise.

5. The reign of Artaxerxes (4:7–23)

4:7. Twenty-one years later Artaxerxes assumed the Persian throne. Some time during his reign another charge against the Jews entered the official records. Bishlam, Mithredath, Tabeel, and the rest of his associates wrote a letter to Artaxerxes. The contents of the letter were omitted from the biblical text. At some point another complaint was lodged. In this case the writer included excerpts from official documents, noting that **the letter was written in Aramaic**, the language of the court.

4:8. Two men **wrote a letter against Jerusalem to Artaxerxes the king.** These two, **Rehum the commanding officer and Shimshai the secretary,** represented a much larger group that is described more fully in Ezra 4:9–10.

4:9–10. The chronicler wanted his readers to know who instigated the false accusations against the Jews: the **judges and officials over the men from Tripolis, Persia, Erech and Babylon, the Elamites of Susa, and the other people.** These were captive peoples whom King Ashurbanipal of Assyria had **deported and settled in the city of Samaria and elsewhere in Trans-Euphrates**—a large area extending to the Mediterranean Sea.

4:11. After digressing to identify those who sent the letter, the writer began again: (**This is a copy of the letter they sent him**), indicating **King Artaxerxes**, and the general area from which the letter issued, **the men of Trans-Euphrates**. This pulled the reader back on track.

4:12–16. The letter pointed out to King Artaxerxes that **the Jews who came up to us from you** had gone to Jerusalem and were **rebuilding that rebellious and wicked city.** This may refer to the Jews allowed to accompany Ezra back to Jerusalem by the edict and good will of Artaxerxes himself. Ezra returned, along with a new wave of exiles, in the seventh year of Artaxerxes's reign. No doubt this disturbed the surrounding neighbors. The letter contained inflammatory language intended to bias the king.

They are restoring the walls and repairing the foundations. The claim was exaggerated, since no grand reconstruction project existed—only assumptions and accusations. The work on the walls was, most likely, simply an effort to use rubble fill in order to obtain a proper substructure for the building of homes.

The writers of the letter then constructed fantasies they hoped would incite the king. They claimed that if the walls were rebuilt, **no more taxes, tribute or duty will be paid, and the royal revenues will suffer.** However, the group of Jews living in Judea had few resources, and even less power, to make such a defiant stance against the Persian government. The authors of the letter merely capitalized on recurring problems the Persians had on their frontiers (revolts in Trans-Euphrates and Egypt), knowing that possibilities contain as much persuasion as realities.

The authors affirmed their loyalty to Artaxerxes and the Persian Empire, being **under obligation to the palace** and not wishing **to see the king dishonored**. In fact, they went a step further by inviting the king to search the archives about the history of Jerusalem and its relationship to previous rulers. The records would confirm that Jerusalem was **a rebellious city, troublesome to kings and provinces, a place of rebellion from ancient times**. The enemies of the Jews preyed on the king's fears, suggesting that if nothing were done to stop the activity in Jerusalem, he would **be left with nothing in Trans-Euphrates**.

4:17–20. Artaxerxes's reply was clear. He greeted **Rehum** and **Shimshai** and acknowledged their letter. He noted that, in accord with their suggestion, he had searched the historical records about Jerusalem. He agreed that the city had, in fact, experienced **a long history of revolt against kings**. In addition, **powerful kings** had ruled from Jerusalem **and taxes, tribute and duty were paid to them**—perhaps referring to David or Solomon. Generally, Jerusalem did not command a great empire such as would threaten Persia. But for kings whose rule was secured by force, even remote possibilities were treated seriously.

4:21–22. Artaxerxes concluded his letter by telling Rehum and Shimshai to **issue an order to these men to stop work**. However, the king allowed himself some flexibility by adding the escape clause, **until I so order**. The decree was in force until Artaxerxes decided to change his mind.

4:23. Rehum, Shimshai, and company lost no time in obeying the king's order; after all, the work stoppage had been their idea from the beginning. In fact, these men **compelled** the Jews **by force to stop** the work. Military force is implicit in the language. Soldiers entering Jerusalem in a display of force may have been all that was needed. Or it may be that Rehum destroyed what had been built, ordering his military to tear down and burn the walls. If so, it would fit that Nehemiah's anguish over the state of affairs in Jerusalem came from this more recent act of violence rather than from the destruction by Nebuchadnezzar of Babylon.

C The Story Resumed (4:24)

SUPPORTING IDEA: *The chronicler reminded his readers of the story of Zerubbabel and Jeshua.*

4:24. The writer of Ezra used a literary device at this point by repeating the essence of verse 5, thereby reconnecting the reader to the story of Zerubbabel and Jeshua: the work on the house of God in Jerusalem came to a standstill until the second year of the reign of Darius king of Persia.

MAIN IDEA REVIEW: *The Jews returned to Palestine with a clear call from God to reestablish worship, rebuild the temple, and reaffirm the nation's relationship with God—but the assignment was not easy. From the start, opposition formed against the exiles and continued through successive Persian monarchs.*

III. CONCLUSION

Mathematical Musings

A number of years ago a new mathematical system was introduced into the public schools that educators dubbed "new math." Some thought it a great advance, others felt bewildered, and some deemed it a retreat into confusion. Of course the math was not new at all, only the method. The sum of 8 and 7 remained predictably 15, and the square root of 9 held steadfastly at 3. That, say those who enjoy numbers, is the beauty of math—each function, equation, and formula can be repeated with identical results. If one follows the process properly, the same solution can be anticipated each time a similar problem is faced. It is the bliss of reliability.

We often approach our relationship with God with the same mathematical expectations. We reason that the sum of God's nature and our obedience should equal positive results. When the power of God changed the heart of a king and inspired the exiles to return to Jerusalem and they obeyed, then the temple should be rebuilt, worship should be instituted, and life should flow sweetly from this. Instead, the work lagged, the neighbors proved hostile, crops failed, and life became hard. It became tempting to shrug and declare life unpredictable and God a mystery.

Admittedly, God's ways are far beyond our understanding. But if revelation teaches anything, it teaches God's consistent and unchanging nature. Yet, when life becomes confusing or bewildering, we shake our heads in wonderment at how God works, forgetting about the innumerable variables of the human heart that get tossed into the equation. So we adjust our understanding of God based on experience, rather than analyzing our experience by the standard of God's unalterable disposition.

God is forever and always what he has declared and demonstrated himself to be—utterly steadfast. The returned exiles experienced difficulties not because of God's failure, absence, or inexplicable behavior, but because petty pride, hurt feelings, power struggles, selfishness, and a host of other human tendencies were added to the problem. Even so, God remained the one constant, faithfully pursuing his people through discipline and godly messengers, patiently offering grace, reconciliation, and hope.

PRINCIPLES

- God remains utterly dependable and unchanging.
- The world is a hostile environment for Christians and the gospel.
- God remains sovereign over nations.
- Those who obey God experience his strength and help.
- Obedience to God centers on pleasing and honoring him.
- Obedience to God does not guarantee that life will be fair or even just.

APPLICATIONS

- Do not pursue hardship for its own sake, assuming God takes pleasure in adversity. By the same token, do not flee from difficulties that may come from following Christ. Faithfulness is what counts.
- When you take a position on an issue, remember to stand on biblical principle and not just personal opinion.
- Do not be surprised when society misunderstands and works against you, the church, or Christian mission.
- Form your views of God from his revelation, not from your limited understanding of life.

IV. LIFE APPLICATION

Ecology 101

In 1872, President Ulysses S. Grant signed the Yellowstone Park Act, creating the first national park in the United States. Congress and the president intended to preserve an unspoiled ecological sanctuary that would escape the changes and degeneration that civilization was causing in the surrounding countryside.

But throughout the years it became apparent that the task was more ambitious than first reckoned. The history of Yellowstone Park exhibits a faltering and conflicting attempt to manage a wilderness.

By the turn of the twentieth century, elk and bison were hunted to near extinction. In Yellowstone Park, however, a great effort was made to protect as well as increase herd populations. Hunting was not allowed; elk were fed and tended; wolves and coyote were eliminated. In time, the elk thrived . . . but at a cost. The ecological balance was destroyed. Elk overgrazed the land and drove away other animals; rejuvenating fires subsided for lack of grasses;

erosion and silt runoff increased, harming fish and beaver. The park was a disaster. Without purifying opposition, the "unmarred" beauty that captivated its first visitors lay spoiled and struggling for survival (Chase, pp. 3–37, 371–75).

At present we live a wilderness experience, surrounded by hostility, confronted with evil. The history of faith remains consistent in this regard: "In this world you will have trouble" (John 16:33). During the years in which sporadic effort was made to rebuild the temple, the Jews' surrounding neighbors frustrated their work, sometimes by intimidation, sometimes by force. Even later, after the temple was completed, plots were hatched to keep Jerusalem in disrepair. Kings wavered between good will and malevolence toward the Jewish community.

The response to religious opposition has remained consistent as well: amalgamation, retreat, or engagement. Some abandon the faith. More often, we retreat to the protective environment of the church. There we can avoid the counterbalancing effort of interacting with society where we may face misunderstanding, disagreement, or persecution. Supposing spiritual advance, we seek a place untroubled, where comfort and spiritual bliss coexist. But rather than nurturing strength, it proves debilitating. In the process, the environment of society shifts dangerously out of balance.

History has demonstrated that God often uses the natural enemies of the gospel to advance his purposes and purify his people. God is the great caretaker of our soul and life, and we must leave to him the management of our time and experience. Rather than grasp for paradise lost, may we instead engage the present moment. In this world we will have trouble—guaranteed. But Jesus didn't stop there. He reminded his disciples to take heart because "*I have overcome the world*" (John 16:33, emphasis added).

V. PRAYER

Father, help us to live well in this world. May we not seek suffering, and so increase our pride and taint the joy of your gospel. May we not seek comfort, and so compromise your truth and forfeit the treasures of eternity. Assist us so we seek only you and, in so doing, follow wherever you lead. Amen.

VI. DEEPER DISCOVERIES

A. The Enemies of Judah (4:1–2)

The writer began Ezra 4 with a strong accusation against a group of people that, from all appearances, simply wanted to help the resettled Jews rebuild the temple. He called them "the enemies of Judah."

Hundreds of years before the encounter between Zerubbabel and his northern neighbors, Israel, upon the death of Solomon, splintered into two kingdoms. Each was ruled by one of Solomon's sons. Rehoboam ruled Judah from Jerusalem; Jeroboam ruled Israel from Shechem.

Twenty years after the split, Judah finally enjoyed stability under the godly king Asa. Meanwhile, Israel floundered under a series of kings who "did evil in the eyes of the Lord." One of these kings, Omri, bought a hill and built a city upon it. He called the city Samaria and made it the seat of Israel's government.

Eventually, the northern kingdom of Israel fell to Assyria. The land was divided into Assyrian provinces except for the small region around the city of Samaria. The upper classes of Israel were deported to other towns within the empire, and people from Babylonia and various conquered lands were relocated to Samaria.

The writer of 2 Kings declared

> Each national group made its own gods in the several towns where they settled. . . . To this day they persist in their former practices. They neither worship the LORD nor adhere to the decrees and ordinances, the laws and commands that the LORD gave the descendants of Jacob, whom he named Israel. When the LORD made a covenant with the Israelites, he commanded them: "Do not worship any other gods or bow down to them, serve them or sacrifice to them. But the LORD, who brought you up out of Egypt with mighty power and outstretched arm, is the one you must worship." . . . They would not listen, however, but persisted in their former practices. Even while these people were worshiping the LORD, they were serving their idols (2 Kgs. 17:29,34–36,40).

These were the Samaritans, the northern neighbors of Judah. At the time of Zerubbabel, they were distrusted, seen politically as foreigners and spiritually as pagans. By Jesus' time, these Samaritans were despised, deemed racially impure and religiously corrupt.

B. A Chronology of Major Events

- 586 B.C.: Fall of Jerusalem
- 559–530 B.C.: Cyrus II (The Great) rules Persia
- 539 B.C.: Cyrus defeats Babylon
- 538 B.C.: First return of exiles to Jerusalem
- 530–522 B.C.: Cambyses rules Persia
- 522–486 B.C.: Darius I rules Persia
- 520–480 B.C.: The prophets Haggai and Zechariah minister
- 516 B.C.: Temple restoration completed

- 486–465 B.C.: Xerxes I rules Persia
- 479–465 B.C.: Esther reigns with Xerxes
- 465–424 B.C.: Artaxerxes I rules Persia
- 458 B.C.: Ezra journeys to Jerusalem
- 445 B.C.: Nehemiah returns and city walls are built

VII. TEACHING OUTLINE

A. INTRODUCTION

1. Lead Story: Lessons from Screwtape
2. Context: As the people started rebuilding the temple, they drew the attention of their neighbors. Something was going on in Jerusalem. Neighboring Samaritans saw in the building project an opportunity to advance their own power.
3. Transition: Sometimes looks can be deceiving. Zerubbabel and the Jewish leaders were confronted with offers of help from their neighbors; however, these friendly advances were merely guises for control and selfish pursuits.

B. COMMENTARY

1. An Offer of Help (4:1–5)
   a. The offer (4:1–2)
   b. The response (4:3)
   c. The reaction (4:4–5)
2. Historical Divergence (4:6–23)
   a. The reign of Xerxes (4:6)
   b. The reign of Artaxerxes (4:7–23)
3. The Story Resumed (4:24)

C. CONCLUSION: MATHEMATICAL MUSINGS

VIII. ISSUES FOR DISCUSSION

1. How does a person determine when to compromise for the sake of peace and when to remain firm on issues?
2. Why is religious commitment often interpreted as political opposition?
3. How should a Christian respond to false accusations and opposition? Provide biblical examples or references.

Christ in ~~principles~~ final hours being accused

Ezra 5

Walking in Truth

*K*eep one thing forever in view—the truth; and if you do this, though it may seem to lead you away from the opinion of men, it will assuredly conduct you to the throne of God.

H o r a c e   M a n n

 I N   A   N U T S H E L L

*E*arly in the reign of Darius, under the inspiration of the prophets Haggai and Zechariah, the resettled Jews in Jerusalem began again the rebuilding of the temple. The king's officials, watchful of Persian frontiers, investigated the project and sent a letter to the king asking his ruling on whether the temple reconstruction should continue or be stopped.

Walking in Truth

I. INTRODUCTION

Road Maps

*O*ne summer our family took a road trip. At the beginning it wasn't difficult to navigate our way. We pointed our car west, merged with traffic on Interstate 90, and drove. We buzzed along the tops of Ohio and Indiana, followed the curve of Lake Michigan through Chicago, veered northwest through Wisconsin, and bore a straight line across Minnesota, South Dakota, and Wyoming. We entered Yellowstone Park and spent a day watching bison and elk, skipping rocks across Yellowstone Lake, and observing geologic curiosities like paint pots, sulfur springs, and geysers. We left the park as the sun slipped from the hillsides, pulling the amber of late afternoon westward. In half an hour we would be at our cabin in Ennis, Montana. I unfolded the map.

On a horizontal line, we were probably thirty miles from our destination. But no direct road linked where we were to where we wanted to be. We had exited the park at the wrong place. In order to travel thirty miles west, we had to drive over one hundred miles out of our way. I had waited too long to consult the map . . . and it cost us. Instead of settling into our cabin, we were winding our way through the mountains in the dark.

The Jews had spent a number of years on a costly detour, both politically and spiritually. The nation had yet to recover, but the community of faith had wound its way back through the Judean hills, arriving in Jerusalem. Critical to their faith was the reconstruction of the temple. But in the process of resettlement, they had veered off course. The temple wreckage lay in the dust like a forgotten idea.

It was at this point that God spoke through two prophets, Haggai and Zechariah. They called the people back to their original purpose; they unfolded the map of God's design and pointed them in the right direction—the completion of the temple. But as the people got back on track and began to work, they discovered they had to navigate uncharted territory; they needed to establish working relations with the new Persian monarch and his officials. Yet, as they held their course, even these new twists and turns brought them closer to their objective.

II. COMMENTARY

Walking in Truth

> **MAIN IDEA:** *Inspired by God's prophets, the Jews started afresh the temple reconstruction. As work commenced, Persian officials investigated the project, questioned the leaders, and sent a letter to King Darius asking his ruling on the validity of the restoration.*

A Renewed Effort (5:1–2)

> **SUPPORTING IDEA:** *The voice of God came to his people through the prophets Haggai and Zechariah. Awakened and inspired by their message, the people began again the temple's repair.*

5:1–2. "Is it a time for you yourselves to be living in your paneled houses, while this house remains a ruin?" (Hag. 1:3). So began the message of God through **Haggai the prophet**. He told the Jews to consider their ways because their neglect of the temple symbolized their neglect of God. Because of their misplaced priorities, life was hard. Drought plagued the area, crops were meager, and the people were disappointed and frustrated.

A few months after the message of Haggai, **Zechariah the prophet, a descendant of Iddo, prophesied**. Iddo was the head of a priestly family, and Zechariah traced his ancestry to this line. Zechariah began his prophecy, "'Return to me,' declares the LORD Almighty, 'and I will return to you'" (Zech. 1:3). The prophet also announced God's intention to show mercy to Jerusalem, and he assured the people that Zerubbabel would rebuild the temple (Zech. 4:9).

These reprimands, as well as encouragements of God's favor and presence, were given by the prophets **to the Jews in Judah and Jerusalem**. About a month after the first message from Haggai, under the leadership of Zerubbabel and Jeshua, the people began in earnest the restoration of the temple. **The prophets of God were with them**, and they continued to deliver God's encouragement and direction.

B The Investigation (5:3–17)

> **SUPPORTING IDEA:** *The governor of the area launched an investigation into the temple work, questioned the Jewish leaders, and sent an inquiry to King Darius.*

1. On-site inspection (5:3–6)

5:3–4. About the same time as the Jews began their work, **Tattenai, governor of Trans-Euphrates, and Shethar-Bozenai and their associates** approached those in charge of the temple reconstruction. Tattenai was a Persian-appointed official governing over an area referred to as "Beyond the River." The title of governor was used flexibly. Zerubbabel, also a governor, held responsibility over a smaller area under Tattenai. Many scholars believe Shethar-Bozenai served as secretary. Those called "associates" were official inspectors who made periodic checks throughout the empire in the interest of the king. These men were known as "the king's eyes and ears," since they watched the far reaches of the kingdom on his behalf.

Most likely these officials came to Jerusalem on a routine inspection. These were the early years of a new monarch, and there were rebellions flaring in other parts of the realm. Tattenai showed no alarm at the temple construction. Nonetheless, the visiting officials posed a couple of questions to the Jewish leaders: **Who authorized you to rebuild this temple?** and **What are the names of the men constructing this building?** The questions indicated no hostility or suspicion. In fact, they were routine, civil inquiries that assumed legal justification for the building.

5:5. While "the king's eyes" traveled throughout the Persian Empire, assessing the territories and activities of the people, the eye of Judah's God was **watching over the elders of the Jews**. The writer of Ezra inserted a strong contrast between the protectors of Darius and Judah's God, who ruled over all the earth. Darius had his inspectors, but God watched and reigned over everyone. Because of this, the temple reconstruction was not halted **until a report could go to Darius and his written reply be received**.

The confluence of God's purpose and a government's disposition created a favorable environment for the temple work to continue. Tattenai and his associates obviously did not suspect the Jews of treachery or insurrection. If they had, the temple work would have stopped immediately. Instead, they allowed the building to continue while correspondence between the governor and the king traveled back and forth.

5:6. The chronicler again lists all the Persian officials responsible at the inspection, adding that these men then wrote a formal letter to the king. In this way he prefaced the next section, writing: **This is a copy of the letter that Tattenai, governor of Trans-Euphrates . . . and their associates . . . sent to King Darius**.

2. Tattenai's letter to Darius (5:7–17)

5:7–10. Tattenai recounted in his letter to the king the progress of a typical inspection tour. He apparently believed what the Jews had told him, and he did not suspect them of sedition. He reported that the Jews were building the temple **with large stones and placing the timbers in the walls**. Timbers were often used structurally, suggesting that the temple construction was making significant progress. He added, **the work is being carried on with diligence and is making rapid progress**.

Tattenai further summarized what occurred on the inspection and the questions they posed: **We questioned the elders, "Who authorized you to rebuild this temple?". . . . We also asked them their names . . . for your information.** Reference to the Jewish leaders as "elders" was Tattenai's preference and not a Jewish designation. Community leadership was structured around "heads of families."

5:11–16. Tattenai reported to the king that the Jews identified themselves as **servants of the God of heaven and earth.** They claimed that God was not simply a local or nationalistic deity, but one who ruled over all the created order. Because of this, he deserved a temple. In fact, he already had a temple, built years before by **a great king of Israel.** The Jews did not specifically name Solomon, but by including this historical link, they maintained continuity with the former temple.

The community understood that the ruins at their feet came not from the capricious act of a monarch but from their own unfaithfulness and disobedience to God. It was this that allowed **Nebuchadnezzar the Chaldean, king of Babylon,** to destroy the temple and deport the people to Babylon. By identifying their relatives as deportees, they identified themselves as returned exiles.

But now, under the administration of Cyrus, positive changes were taking place. In the very first year of his kingship, he had **issued a decree to rebuild this house of God.** The Jews made the obvious point that their current effort had historical precedence as well as Persian support. This was neither a new project nor a purely local concern. Cyrus was committed to the temple's restoration, and he proved it by returning to Jerusalem all **the gold and silver articles of the house of God, which Nebuchadnezzar had taken from the temple.**

The Jewish leadership acknowledged Cyrus's appointment of **Sheshbazzar** as governor. Cyrus had told Sheshbazzar to take the gold and silver temple articles and **deposit them in the temple in Jerusalem.** Furthermore, the people were commanded to **rebuild the house of God on its site.** Sheshbazzar, not Zerubbabel, was mentioned in the historical Persian records, and Darius would note this. The return of the temple articles and the emphasis on rebuilding the temple on its former site underscored the connection between the original temple and its reconstruction.

The Jews also claimed that **from that day to the present it has been under construction but is not yet finished.** Construction was not continuous but suffered neglect—as the prophets candidly pointed out. But again, the leadership wanted to emphasize the continuity of the project, especially under Persian authority.

5:17. Tattenai ended his letter in a fashion typical of government correspondence for that period: **Now if it pleases the king, let a search be made in the royal archives of Babylon to see if King Cyrus did in fact issue a**

decree. Tattenai knew Darius had access to legal documents and assumed they would be found in Babylon (though they were actually located in Media; Ezra 6:2). Confident that the archives would support the Jews' testimony, yet knowing only Darius could rule on such a matter, Tattenai concluded, **let the king send us his decision in this matter.**

> **MAIN IDEA REVIEW:** *Inspired by God's prophets, the Jews started afresh the temple reconstruction. As work commenced, Persian officials investigated the project, questioned the leaders, and sent a letter to King Darius asking his ruling on the validity of the restoration.*

III. CONCLUSION

The Problem of Guilt

The well-known psychiatrist Karl Menninger once wrote a book titled *Whatever Became of Sin?* Our modern era redefined sin as guilt, and guilt became a psychological hindrance, mere baggage to be discarded on the road to good health and well-being. Our society has tried to do away with guilt. But psychology, sociology, education, and even religion have succeeded only in weakening the conscience. Rather than freeing us from debilitating guilt brought about by sin and shame, our culture has become terrorized by a psychology that rationalizes transgression.

For thousands of years, we as human beings have tried to disassociate ourselves from sin and guilt. From Adam and Eve to the most recent crime, we weave stories, point fingers, deny involvement, and rationalize actions. As a consequence, we become caught in a cycle of repeat offenses, unable to grasp the freedom of salvation. Committed to lies, we fail to experience the liberty of truth.

After several years living in Palestine, the Jewish exiles experienced drought, crop failure, hostile neighbors, and a growing apathy about the temple reconstruction. But when the prophets Haggai and Zechariah pointed out their sin, the people acknowledged their guilt and recommitted themselves to the worship of God: "The whole remnant of the people obeyed the voice of the LORD their God. . . . And the people feared the LORD" (Hag. 1:12). In addition, the exiles acknowledged sin as the cause for Nebuchadnezzar's victory over Judah almost one hundred years earlier: "Our fathers angered the God of heaven" (Ezra 5:12).

By adhering to the truth, confessing it, and committing themselves to it, the Jews found salvation. God declared himself to be present with them. Their guilt was absolved not by denial but by the grace of God's righteousness.

PRINCIPLES

- God faithfully pursues his creation.
- Confession is an admission of guilt and an acknowledged need for change; it always precedes salvation.
- Truth guides those who bring about positive change in the world.
- Nations, rulers, and the world in general express themselves in ways consistent with their natures—some for good, some for evil—but God determines their limits.

APPLICATIONS

- When people ask about your faith or circumstances in your life, answer truthfully, even acknowledging difficulties and failures when appropriate.
- When you realize you have offended another person, or recognize sin in your life, confess the wrong. In this way you rescue the situation and build stronger relationships.
- Don't give in to despair or retreat when faced with hardship. God sets limits on the powers of this world.
- Remember your past. Keep a journal or establish celebrations to mark God's faithfulness in your life.

IV. LIFE APPLICATION

Glad You Asked

Question marks wave at the reader and demand a pause. A question assumes possibilities; it may even invite doubt. It represents the essence of inquiry. We can't seem to progress through a day without a gaggle of them, from mundane to profound.

Early on, children learn the inherent power of the question. It stops conversations. It confuses. Sometimes it embarrasses or produces frustrated outbursts. Most often, however, it transports a person to new knowledge. Questions signal an investigation, and investigation precedes understanding.

A question mark shadows the opening words of Ezra 5. We are told that the prophets Haggai and Zechariah prophesied to the Jews in Judah and Jerusalem. Suddenly, it seems, everyone pitched in to complete the temple, displaying a determination unmatched in the previous twenty years. Why?

God used these two men to pose some pointed questions to his people. "Is it a time for you yourselves to be living in your paneled houses, while this house remains a ruin?" (Hag. 1:4). This made them pause. "You expected much, but see, it turned out to be little. What you brought home, I blew away. Why?" (Hag. 1:9). One suspects there are other possibilities here beyond the positioning of the jet stream, or the current instability of the stock market. Questions make us think. They urge us to investigate further.

With God's questions hanging in the air, the people reconsidered their lives; they reevaluated their priorities. Then "the people obeyed the voice of the LORD their God and the message of the prophet Haggai. . . . And the people feared the LORD" (Hag. 1:12). As a result, God declared, "I am with you" (Hag. 1:13). It was the honest response to God's forthright questions that restarted the temple restoration.

V. PRAYER

Father, full of perfect knowledge, the one who knows us better than we know ourselves—you hold out the continual invitation for us to follow you. Empower our will, change us within, so that we will listen to your word and obey with joy. Amen.

VI. DEEPER DISCOVERIES

A. Persian Governmental Organization (5:3–6)

Darius divided his vast empire into twenty regions known as satrapies. Each of these was administered by a satrap, or governor. Tattenai was satrap over the Trans-Euphrates satrapy. Since loyal men were needed to govern Darius's far-flung empire, satraps were chosen from Persian nobility. These governors, responsible for security, justice, economic development, and governmental management in their region, lived comfortable and luxurious lives.

Darius knew these governors could establish mini-kingdoms—potentially ruinous to any empire. As a precaution, secretaries were appointed to oversee activities within a satrapy. These secretaries reported directly to the king. Quite likely Shethar-Bozenai was one of these. Darius also appointed inspectors, popularly known as "the king's eyes and ears." They, in turn, kept watch on the secretaries to make sure officials were properly fulfilling their jobs. These inspectors or "associates" accompanied Tattenai and Shethar-Bozenai to Jerusalem.

What made this political organization effective was the communication system created by Darius. Darius established a network of highways, chief of which was the stone-paved Royal Road. It stretched over sixteen hundred miles from Susa, off the Persian Gulf, to Sardis near the Mediterranean Sea. From this main artery branched a road to modern Pakistan and another to Babylon and Egypt. Dotting the thoroughfare were 111 stations where travelers could refresh their horses and themselves and stay the night. It was possible for mail to travel quickly from Susa to all sections of the empire It was along this road system that Tattenai's letter to Darius traveled.

B. Darius, King of Persia (5:5–6,17)

Darius came to the throne amid a swirl of mystery and controversy. After the death of Cyrus the Great, the throne was assumed by his son Cambyses. As was the habit of kings, Cambyses worked to broaden the empire, initiating a military campaign against Egypt. He was accompanied by Darius who, at that time, seems to have served in the military. While the king was busy in Egypt, back in Persia a man named Gaumata, from the Magi tribe, claimed to be the rightful heir to the throne. He gained a significant popular following. In addition, he took from many Persian nobles their lands, slaves, and houses; this pleased the common people.

Hearing of the unrest, Cambyses left Egypt. Differing accounts are given about the circumstances of his death, but most agree he died from a thigh wound suffered on his return. Upon his death rebellions flared in various parts of the empire.

Darius, along with the nobles from six other clans, forcibly overthrew the Magi usurpers. Then, in a questionable figuring of genealogy, Darius traced himself to the royal family of Cyrus—thus bestowing legitimacy on his claim of kingship. With the support of the most powerful nobles, Darius spent the early part of his reign quelling uprisings.

In this climate of sedition and intrigue, it was reasonable for the satrap in Trans-Euphrates, during the second year of Darius's reign, to question and investigate the temple reconstruction. Though the officials did not seem to suspect disloyalty, the climate of Darius's early years called for vigilance.

VII. TEACHING OUTLINE

A. INTRODUCTION

1. Lead Story: Road Maps

2. Context: After Cyrus's dynamic reign his son Cambyses ruled for a brief eight-year period. His unexpected death sparked a grab for power. Through the strength of clan loyalties and brute force, Darius gained the Persian throne. It was at this time that the Jews returned to work on the temple.

3. Transition: Inspired by the convicting messages of the prophets Haggai and Zechariah, the temple work resumed.

B. COMMENTARY
1. Renewed Effort (5:1–2)
2. The Investigation (5:3–17)
   a. On-site inspection (5:3–6)
   b. Tattenai's letter to Darius (5:7–17)

C. CONCLUSION: THE PROBLEM OF GUILT

VIII. ISSUES FOR DISCUSSION

1. Discuss ways in which the questions of unbelievers can be gateways for presenting the gospel.
2. Is confession always necessary for salvation or the restoration of a broken relationship?
3. Share times from your past when you have recognized God's faithfulness.
4. Investigate the Gospels and find instances when Jesus asked questions. What did he ask? How would you answer his questions today?

Ezra 6

In the Service of God

I. INTRODUCTION
Symbiosis

II. COMMENTARY
A verse-by-verse explanation of the chapter.

III. CONCLUSION
And the Band Plays On

An overview of the principles and applications from the chapter.

IV. LIFE APPLICATION
Sleeping Giants

Melding the chapter to life.

V. PRAYER
Tying the chapter to life with God.

VI. DEEPER DISCOVERIES
Historical, geographical, and grammatical enrichment of the commentary.

VII. TEACHING OUTLINE
Suggested step-by-step group study of the chapter.

VIII. ISSUES FOR DISCUSSION
Zeroing the chapter in on daily life.

The great thing in this world is not so much where we are, but in what direction we are moving.

Oliver Wendell Holmes

 IN A NUTSHELL

King Darius searched the governmental archives and found the royal memorandum of Cyrus decreeing the temple's reconstruction. Darius wrote back to Tattenai instructing him not only to allow the temple to progress but to pay building expenses out of the royal treasury. Four years later the temple was finished. The Jews celebrated, installed priests and Levites, and observed the Passover Feast.

In the Service of God

I. INTRODUCTION

Symbiosis

*T*hroughout the Bible spiritual realities are often explained in terms of nature. From Solomon to Isaiah to Jesus, God's representatives spoke of trees, ants, vines, flowers, and even badgers. Some say this penchant for the organic was rooted in the agrarian society in which they lived. But God created all of nature after a particular design—including people. Nature offers not just clever metaphors but true reflections of the way the created world works.

Nature displays a high degree of interconnectedness. In the Amazon rain forest a particular water lily opens only at night. Large bright white petals spread themselves in the dark. This dazzling light attracts a particular kind of beetle that then spends the night crawling around on the flower eating its nectar. In the morning, as the sun tops the horizon, the flower closes, trapping the beetles. All day the beetles scrub around in the blossom. At dark the petals open once again, releasing the beetles.

Now the beetles are coated in pollen. They will carry this golden powder to other flowers in an obliging act of fertilization. The original flower, having released its pollen to the beetles, turns a flushed pink. This color holds no allure for the insects, and they will not return to that flower again, assuring the process of pollination.

Peoples and nations also exist in greater or lesser degrees of interconnectedness. These relationships can prove parasitic or mutually helpful.

After an official governmental inquiry into the temple work in Jerusalem, the Jews continued working as they waited for a response from King Darius. The king's ruling would dictate what kind of relationship would exist between Judah and its Persian overlords. When he replied, the Jews not only found that they were allowed to complete the temple but also that the Persian Empire would help them achieve their goal.

Much like the water lily and the beetle, both would benefit from the alliance. Judah would gain its temple, and Persia would secure the support of the Jews and (the king hoped) the benevolence of Judah's God.

II. COMMENTARY

In the Service of God

> **MAIN IDEA:** *Within God's sovereign design, two dissimilar peoples—the ruler and the ruled—found mutual benefit at the temple altar. Darius financed the temple project to its completion, hoping to secure God's favor. The Jews celebrated by installing temple officials and observing the Passover Feast.*

A The Persian Response to the Temple (6:1–12)

> **SUPPORTING IDEA:** *The Persian court investigated the Jews' historical claims for reconstructing the temple. Satisfied of its legitimacy, King Darius decreed full support for the project.*

1. The archival search (6:1–2)

6:1–2. Tattenai instructed Darius in his letter, "Let a search be made in the royal archives of Babylon" (Ezra 5:17); that was where he expected to find Cyrus's memorandum since the Jerusalem Jews had returned from Babylonian regions. So a search was first made **in the archives stored in the treasury at Babylon.** Darius's scribes found no records in Babylon, so they searched next in **the citadel of Ecbatana in the province of Media.** A scroll was found, and the chronicler excerpted a portion of it.

2. The memorandum (6:3–5)

6:3–5. In the first year of King Cyrus, the king issued a decree concerning the temple of God in Jerusalem. This dates the memorandum to 539 B.C.—the first year in which Cyrus was king of Babylonian lands. He had been recognized as king of Media and Persia several years before that.

Specifically, the temple was to **be rebuilt as a place to present sacrifices.** The decrees further specified the dimensions of the temple: **ninety feet high and ninety feet wide, with three courses of large stones and one of timbers.** In all probability, the size of the temple replicated that of Solomon's, as did the location. Detailing the measurements as well as the number of courses of stones and timbers set limits on what the Jews were allowed to do.

The Persian government needed to define carefully the scope of the repairs since the financing was **to be paid by the royal treasury.** As a way of promoting good will among subject peoples, imperial funding was given for various cultic centers and temples throughout the empire. However, even though Cyrus had committed royal funds for the temple, the resources would actually have come from revenue collected throughout the satrapy of Trans-Euphrates.

Cyrus also specified within the decree that **the gold and silver articles of the house of God . . . are to be returned to their places in the temple in Jerusalem**. By ordering the return of the temple articles that Nebuchadnezzar had confiscated, Cyrus acknowledged the continuity between the two structures. Unlike the temple built by expatriate Jews in Egypt, the building in Jerusalem was honored as the legitimate house of God where the temple treasures and articles belonged

3. Darius's reply (6:6–12)

6:6–7. Darius gave instructions to Tattenai the governor, Shethar-Bozenai the secretary, and all the other officials involved in the original inquiry. He wrote: **Stay away from there. Do not interfere with the work on this temple of God**. He did not mean that the officials of the region must never enter Jerusalem. The king wanted his ministers to understand that nothing must hinder the temple's completion. The actual work and supervision of the project, however, remained with **the governor of the Jews and the Jewish elders**.

6:8–10. Darius further endorsed the original decree by extending financial and material support to the project. He added his own pronouncement, specifying what Tattenai and the others were to do **for these elders of the Jews in the construction of this house of God**. Temple-related expenses were **to be fully paid out of the royal treasury, from the revenues of Trans-Euphrates**. As satrap over the territory that included Judea, Tattenai was responsible for paying construction expenses from his region's income. These officials should ensure that work on the temple would not stop because of financial needs.

Darius next provided a list of supplies necessary for the daily sacrifices. Tattenai and his men were to supply the Jews with **young bulls, rams, male lambs for burnt offerings to the God of heaven**. How did a Persian monarch know the exacting Judaic laws governing animal sacrifice? It was common for the court to secure the advice of religious experts, and most likely, this list was compiled with the help of Jewish advisors.

In addition, they were to supply **wheat, salt, wine and oil, as requested by the priests in Jerusalem**. All these were elements of the daily sacrifices, and Darius commanded the fresh resupply of these items day after day. The king's interest in the daily sacrifices was to enable the Jews to **pray for the well-being of the king and his sons**. The Persian kings viewed the gods within their realm as tribal deities, and it was in their best interest to win the favor of all the various gods.

6:11–12. Darius concluded his decree with stern warnings: **if anyone changes this edict, a beam is to be pulled from his house and he is to be lifted up and impaled on it**. This seems harsh and incongruous with the degree of the crime. But the edict of the king was inviolate: "in accordance with the laws of the Medes and Persians, which cannot be repealed" (Dan. 6:8). To disregard such an edict was a major offense.

May God, who has caused his Name to dwell there. This points to Jewish influence in the substance and wording of the decree. The phrase was used before in reference to the temple, as yet not built, when the Israelites stood on the threshold of entering the promised land (Deut. 12:11). The Persians assumed God would protect his parochial interests and **overthrow any king or people** who might **destroy this temple in Jerusalem**.

Ⓑ Completion and Dedication of the Temple (6:13–18)

SUPPORTING IDEA: *By the command of God, the help of the Persian government, and the work of the Jews, the temple was completed. Offerings of dedication were given according to the law.*

4. Finishing the temple (6:13–15)

6:13–15. Tattenai, Shethar-Bozenai, and the other regional officials appropriated funds; administered the supply of animals, wine, grain, oil, and salt; and coordinated with the Jewish leaders the delivery and implementation of these resources. These men performed their duties **with diligence**. And the Jews built and prospered under the preaching and teaching of the prophets Haggai and Zechariah.

The temple was eventually completed **according to the command of the God of Israel and the decrees of Cyrus, Darius and Artaxerxes, kings of Persia**. Once again divine providence and the will of man intersected. Revelation permits a glimpse of the cosmic dimensions of what appear as chance, fate, or political maneuvering. It is God who "changes times and seasons; he sets up kings and deposes them" (Dan. 2:21).

One problematic element does occur in this sentence—the inclusion of Artaxerxes. Artaxerxes reigned well after the completion of the temple. Most likely the writer simply took this occasion to pay tribute to the Persian kings who positively affected temple worship, remembering the supportive position that Artaxerxes later assumed when he sent Ezra to Jerusalem.

The temple was completed **in the sixth year of the reign of King Darius**, March 515 B.C., seventy-two years after the destruction of Solomon's temple: "These nations will serve the king of Babylon seventy years" (Jer. 25:11). "When seventy years are completed for Babylon, I will come to you and fulfill my gracious promise to bring you back to this place" (Jer. 29:10).

5. Dedicating the temple (6:16–18)

6:16–18. Then the people of Israel—the priests, the Levites and the rest of the exiles—celebrated. The last stone was laid, and the people gathered to dedicate the new building. The writer viewed only the returned exiles as constituting the true Israel.

Modeled upon Solomon's dedication, though with far fewer animals, they offered bulls, rams, and male lambs. Then, **as a sin offering for all Israel, twelve male goats, one for each of the tribes of Israel.** To purify the altar and atone for sins, the exiles stood as representatives of the nation. Although only members of the tribes of Benjamin, Judah, and Levi were present, they sacrificed on behalf of all the tribes, thereby associating this temple once again with Solomon's and its jurisdiction over a unified Israel. Completing the dedication was the installation of the priests and Levites according to **the Book of Moses.**

Celebrating Passover (6:19–22)

SUPPORTING IDEA: *In keeping with historical precedent, Passover was celebrated shortly after the temple's dedication, marking the renewal of religious life.*

6:19–21. In keeping with the original Passover mandated by Moses, the people gathered **on the fourteenth day of the first month.** Passover was what set the Jewish calendar; it signaled the beginning of a new year. It represented new life, since the Israelites were rescued from Egyptian slavery and passed over by God's judgment. Passover symbolized God's salvation (Exod. 12:1–14).

With the second temple completed, **the priests and Levites . . . purified themselves and were all ceremonially clean.** At this point the historical model appears to come from King Josiah's reinstitution of the law and covenant (2 Chr. 35:1–19). From the time of the kings, the festival had evolved from a family observance to a priestly duty. In the writings of Moses, each family was to prepare and offer a sacrifice. However, as the nation became more organized and centralized, the responsibility passed to the priests and Levites: the **Levites slaughtered the Passover lamb for all the exiles.**

When Judah and Israel disintegrated politically and the Jews were scattered, religious observances and attitudes changed. Stripped of national leadership and cut off from the temple, religious practice lost its cohesion. When the exiles returned to Jerusalem, the Jews, lacking political institutions, turned again to the temple and its hierarchy and to ceremonial standards as their sources for communal identity. During this time temple worship, ceremonial cleanness, and ecclesiastical governance grew in importance. Without a king or kingdom, Israel emerged as a predominantly religious community.

6:22. For seven days they celebrated with joy the Feast of Unleavened Bread. This festival immediately followed Passover. Whereas Passover spoke mainly of God's mercy and of judgment passed over, the Feast of Unleavened Bread reminded the people of deliverance. It was to continue as a lasting ordinance marking the day God brought the Jews out of Egypt (Exod. 12:17–20). When the exiles gathered in Jerusalem, they observed the feast **with joy** because God had changed the attitude of the king of Assyria, **so that he assisted them in the work on the house of God.**

Calling Darius **king of Assyria** appears odd, but it may merely designate him as a foreign ruler. Because each new empire assimilated the last, the Persian kings were viewed as rulers of Babylon and, because Babylon absorbed Assyria, as rulers of Assyria as well.

The proposal of the temple's reconstruction in Ezra 1 began with God moving the heart of a pagan king; the temple was completed with God exercising his sovereignty over the world's dominant ruler of the time. From start to finish, God ruled, implementing his purposes.

MAIN IDEA REVIEW: *Within God's sovereign design, two dissimilar peoples—the ruler and the ruled—found mutual benefit at the temple altar. Darius financed the temple project to its completion, hoping to secure God's favor. The Jews celebrated by installing temple officials and observing the Passover Feast.*

III. CONCLUSION

And the Band Plays On

> If ponies rode men,
> And grass ate the cow;
> If cats should be chased
> Into holes by the mouse . . .
> If summer were spring
> And the other way round;
> Then all the world would be upside down.

These simple, silly words formed the lyrics of a popular song of the eighteenth century. Yet their absurdity seemed fitting one bright October day in 1781 as Cornwallis's army surrendered to George Washington. While the Redcoats relinquished their weapons, the British band played on; the lilting song sharpened the irony as the most powerful nation in Europe succumbed to a ragtag group of American patriots.

The same song could easily play in the background through centuries of Jewish history—a slave nation that plundered Egypt before they departed; Gideon who, with pottery jars and torches, defeated a massive army; a shepherd who killed a giant.

But unfaithfulness to God caused Israel and Judah to stumble, until each fell beneath the heel of invading armies. First the Assyrians, then the Babylonians trampled and bludgeoned Israel and Judah. The narrow corridor between the Mediterranean Sea and the Dead Sea was ransacked, its leaders captured or killed, and large numbers of its citizens forced into exile. Thus began a wave of domination and displacement for the Jews that continued into the twentieth century.

Even so the song could be heard as groups of Jews reoccupied the Judean countryside with plans to rebuild the temple. Few would have heard it. The contrast between the power of Darius, the Persian monarch, and the small enclave of Jews scattered around the environs of Jerusalem appeared almost comical. But through that community of faith, God preserved his law and temple, the symbols of his love, faithfulness, and mercy.

The Persian Empire was eventually overrun by Alexander the Great. The Greek Empire was splintered by factions and finally absorbed by Rome. The Roman Empire decayed and was swept away by invading barbarians. Marduk, Ahur-Mazda, and Jupiter are relics of antiquity, dusty deities who interest only the occasional scholar. Only the God of Israel remains. He displays his power through the weak, his glory through the ordinary. Faith in God accomplished what empires and pantheons of deities could not—a realm of influence that spread beyond the confines of the Judean hills and extended across the centuries.

And the band plays on.

PRINCIPLES

- God works through secular governments and institutions to accomplish his will.
- Cooperation should exist between government and the community of faith as long as righteousness is not compromised.
- People of faith should act with openness and honesty.
- Celebrations within the church provide opportunities to offer thanks and acknowledge God's goodness.

APPLICATIONS

- Pray for civic and national leaders.
- Get involved in your local government and community.
- In your home acknowledge God's love, mercy, and grace. Your words can be offerings given to God, and they pass on encouragement to others.
- Study the Bible and learn its principles so you can live in faithful obedience to God's will.
- Give generously to God and his work around the world.

IV. LIFE APPLICATION

Sleeping Giants

A Canadian friend once told me that living next to the United States was like living beside a sleeping giant—you never knew when it might roll over.

The Jews of Judea and Jerusalem probably felt the same about Persia. Each time the imperial colossus stretched into new territory, or adjusted following the ascension of a new king, a sense of uncertainty probably settled upon the people. How would the government regard Judea and Jerusalem? What policies would they enforce or ignore? What special interests might they pursue?

The Jews had kept a low profile since their arrival in Judea. From time to time there was activity around the temple, but it was inconsequential. Then prophetic messages ignited the will of the people to complete the temple, and they launched into a flurry of activity. It caught the attention of the government. So after an inspection by the regional authorities, the Jewish community waited to see how the government would respond to their construction project. They waited to see if the giant would shift its position, if it would roll over and crush their efforts.

True faith gets noticed; a community of faith draws attention. Consequently, there will come times when the church encounters the "giant" of government. But whatever the position of government, the church pursues kingdom objectives, persisting in the quiet habits of religious life and working to offer grace to society through Jesus Christ.

Every human institution and each political system has been damaged by fallen human nature. Even so, circumstances arise when the community of faith can work amicably with the government. Great mutual benefit results when such cooperation occurs. The privilege falls to us to pray for our government "and all those in authority, that we may live peaceful and quiet lives in all godliness and holiness. This is good, and pleases God our Savior, who wants all men to be saved and to come to a knowledge of the truth" (1 Tim. 2:2–4).

V. PRAYER

You who formed the earth, who sets the boundaries of nations and determines the length of life, we submit to your wise rule. We ask that your grace and mercy be exercised through those who govern so that your people may tell others about your love and salvation. Amen.

VI. DEEPER DISCOVERIES

Babylon and Ecbatana (6:1–2)

The city of Babylon was situated in modern-day Iraq. Its name means "Gate of God." It was a large city with perhaps over two hundred thousand people. Surrounding it were two thick walls with rubble fill in between. The outer wall was over thirty-six feet wide and allowed two chariots to pass each other. Outside was a moat. Inside, cutting through the center of the city, ran the Euphrates River, supplying fresh water to the inhabitants.

Eight magnificent gates allowed entry to the city, each named for a god within the Babylonian pantheon. The Ishtar Gate was paneled with blue glazed bricks upon which figures of bulls, flowers, and dragons were painted. Not far inside this gate was Nebuchadnezzar's famed citadel. Here were the "hanging gardens," terraced plantings of flowers and trees.

In the center of the city stood an enormous ziggurat, a pyramid-shaped square tower. Rising tower upon tower, each successive level decreased in size until at its apex stood a terrace and temple. The ziggurat commanded the center of Babylon and rose probably three hundred feet. In direct line with the ziggurat was the temple of Marduk, supreme god of the Babylonians. This temple contained silver, gold, bronze, precious stones, lapis lazuli, and alabaster.

The city of Ecbatana was located in present-day central Iran. It was a royal fortress built by the Medes in the foothills of the Zagros Mountains. It came under Persian control when Cyrus conquered Media in 550 B.C. The Persian monarchs used Ecbatana as a summer residence in order to escape the heat of the central plains. It was here that Cyrus's decree about the Jews' temple reconstruction was found.

VII. TEACHING OUTLINE

A. INTRODUCTION

1. Lead Story: Symbiosis
2. Context: The beginning of Darius's reign was marked by provincial rebellion and unrest. Consequently, his regents were vigilant in tracking and investigating conditions within the empire. This led to an on-site inspection of the temple project and a request for Darius's endorsement.
3. Transition: King Darius searched the royal archives to discover if the temple reconstruction had been previously authorized by Persian edict.

B. COMMENTARY

C. CONCLUSION: AND THE BAND PLAYS ON

VIII. ISSUES FOR DISCUSSION

1. How should we as believers pray for government, business, and church leaders?
2. What are the Christian's responsibilities to government? Should a Christian ever participate in "civil disobedience"?
3. Should churches or Christian organizations partner with government in civic projects or activities? If so, are there times when such cooperation would not be appropriate?
4. Discuss ways in which your church could celebrate God's goodness. Think beyond "fun, food, and fellowship" to find creative ways of expressing thanksgiving and worship.

Ezra 7

The Hand of God

Character is much easier kept than recovered.

T h o m a s   P a i n e

Ezra 7

I N   A   N U T S H E L L

Almost sixty years lapsed between the completion of the temple and the journey to Jerusalem by Ezra, the priest and scribe. Like those before him, the new Persian king, Artaxerxes, responded favorably to Jewish religious interests.

The Hand of God

I. INTRODUCTION

The Wrong Neighborhood

*L*ocation, location, location.

Success, we are told, depends on it. Whether one wants to start a business, advance a career, raise a family, or sell a house—location tops the list of critical considerations. The experts, armed with charts and statistics, point to business visibility, traffic patterns, purchasing habits, networking, safety—and the list goes on. This may explain why so many Christians equate finding God's will with where they should live, work, or attend school. After all, it's all about location.

Or is it?

In 516 B.C., when the temple in Jerusalem was completed, priests and Levites were installed in their duties, and the rituals of the law were inaugurated. The environment for spiritual development couldn't have been better. The holy city was reoccupied by consecrated priests and Levites. They served in the temple courts, offered the daily sacrifices, safeguarded the golden vessels, and conducted the annual feasts; these were men who were well-positioned. Yet, in less than sixty years, the community developed spiritual problems.

In spite of their prime location, the Jerusalem priests remained a peripheral element in the coming spiritual renewal. Instead, it was Ezra who initiated reform—a man trained and sharpened for service not in Jerusalem but in Babylon.

But, of course, the issue was not *where* Ezra lived but *how* he lived. Known for his devotion and integrity, Ezra understood the heart of God and was prepared to serve him anywhere. He knew that God's will was resolved not in a particular location but in holiness and faithfulness. These could be practiced anywhere. Ezra's "success" was rooted not in the neighborhood but in piety.

II. COMMENTARY

The Hand of God

MAIN IDEA: *God's grace flows perpetually; he works from an economy of generosity and renewed opportunities. Once again a group of Jews prepared to leave Babylonia and journey to Jerusalem, led this time by Ezra, a priest and devout teacher of the Mosaic Law.*

A Ezra the Man and the Mission (7:1–10)

SUPPORTING IDEA: *Ezra's priestly heritage served as a backdrop for presenting his devotion and integrity. Recounting his lineage also connected him in history to other great priests and validated his authority.*

1. Ezra's background (7:1–6)

7:1–5. The writer's aim was to track the Jews' spiritual history, not to trace the tides of social or political change. Consequently, the concluding years of Darius and the entire reign of Xerxes (nearly sixty years) were relegated to silence. The narrative fast-forwards to **the reign of Artaxerxes king of Persia**.

It was imperative for the Persian government to solidify Jerusalem and Judea as a temple state. For this task Ezra was commissioned. But to the Jewish mind, the next essential step after completing the temple was religious purity as prescribed by the Mosaic Law. In order to establish Ezra's qualifications, a genealogical sketch was amended to the text. Though incomplete compared to 1 Chronicles 6, the genealogy in Ezra is accurate. The main purpose of the record was to establish connecting points of authority, going back to **Phinehas . . . Eleazar . . .** and **Aaron the chief priest**.

7:6. Ezra was **a teacher well versed in the Law of Moses, which the LORD, the God of Israel, had given**. The term *teacher* can also translate as "scribe," denoting a person skilled in the study, practice, and teaching of the Torah. It was a position that gained importance in the postexilic community and increased in influence through the time of Jesus. Ezra's highest commendation was that he was a skilled student of the Pentateuch, an honorable practitioner of its commands, and an effective teacher of its laws.

Ezra stood in favor with God and man: **The king had granted him everything he asked**. It remains uncertain what Ezra requested, but the statement indicates the high regard in which he was held by the Persian court. Even so, the ultimate determination of blessing and judgment rested with God. Ezra was given what he requested because **the hand of the LORD his God was on him**.

2. A summary of the mission (7:7–10)

7:7. Ezra was not alone. In his company were **Israelites—priests, Levites, singers, gatekeepers and temple servants.** Over the years several waves of Jews had returned to Jerusalem. Yet, for whatever reasons, many faithful, obedient Jews remained in Babylon. Some returned now, with Ezra, but other faithful Jews stayed behind.

7:8–9. Ezra and his caravan arrived in Jerusalem in August (**the fifth month**) 458 B.C. (**the seventh year of the king**), having left their Babylonian homes in April (**the first month**). Leaving on **the first day of the first month** may have been the plan, but as recorded in Ezra 8:31, they left for Jerusalem "on the twelfth day of the first month," having spent twelve days by "the canal that flows toward Ahava" (Ezra 8:15). Ezra's journey lasted fourteen weeks, and it took the caravan through nine hundred miles of harsh country-side and treacherous lands. Their safe arrival in Jerusalem was attributed to God's guidance and protection.

7:10. Ezra was not only skilled in scholarship and knowledge of the law but in living according to its mandates and spirit. His life was held in balance by a devotion to wisdom, a commitment to righteousness, and a desire to teach others the ways of God.

B The King's Commission (7:11–26)

SUPPORTING IDEA: *King Artaxerxes provided Ezra with a letter of commission, authorization, and support, as well as limitations for his mission to Jerusalem.*

3. Introductions (7:11–12)

7:11. A copy of the letter **King Artaxerxes had given to Ezra the priest and teacher** was inserted in the text. The writer again commends Ezra for his knowledge and integrity, and his duty toward the community, being a man learned in issues of the law and the **decrees of the LORD for Israel**.

7:12. Artaxerxes's decree was copied into the text in Aramaic, the language of the Persian court. It began in typical fashion with a salutation: **Artaxerxes, king of kings, to Ezra the priest . . . Greetings.** "King of kings" was a title conferred by Persian monarchs upon themselves. Artaxerxes addressed Ezra as **a teacher of the Law of the God of heaven**. Most scholars see this as an official title, possibly designating Ezra as scribe of Jewish affairs within the Persian court.

4. Ezra's commission (7:13–20)

7:13. Artaxerxes reaffirmed the decree of Cyrus I by granting permission for Jews within the Persian Empire to return to Jerusalem: Those **who wish to go to Jerusalem with you, may go.** Delineating categories of Israelites, priests, and Levites within the text suggests a particularly Jewish concern and may indicate that the document was prepared with the help of a Jewish advisor, or Ezra himself.

7:14. The king laid upon Ezra a direct commission: **You are sent by the king and his seven advisers.** Whether anyone else chose to journey to Jerusalem, Ezra was given a mission by the king and his most trusted counselors. These men, along with the king, represented the ultimate power of Persia, and it was to them that Ezra was responsible. But the king's commission also provided for Ezra the force of imperial authority as he dealt with satraps, officials, and the people of Judah.

Ezra was to **inquire about Judah and Jerusalem with regard to the Law of your God.** Ezra was afforded some authority in dealing with the people of Judah and Jerusalem; it seems doubtful that he was sent simply to make some investigations and file a report. In context with the rest of the Book of Ezra, it appears he was to determine the condition of religious practice, ascertain who within the region was subject to Jewish law and custom, instruct the people about the law's requirements, and enforce its observance.

Ezra's authority was limited to the Jews of the region and to the maintenance of religious and social codes. The reference to the law, **which is in your hand,** refers not to a scroll Ezra carried but to his expertise.

7:15–16. King Artaxerxes next gave specific instructions about how monetary contributions were to be spent. Artaxerxes and his seven advisers gave **silver and gold . . . to the God of Israel.** The Persian monarchs had displayed a liberal posture toward the gods of their conquered peoples. Historical records show these kings funding temple repairs and cultic traditions in Babylon, Egypt, and India. Artaxerxes believed it was for his personal benefit and the welfare of the empire that all the various religions functioned properly. The gifts of silver and gold were entrusted to Ezra, but the intended recipient was **the God of Israel, whose dwelling is in Jerusalem.**

Ezra was also given permission to raise funds among the people **from the province of Babylon.** Apparently, non-Jews could make donations as well. Ezra was also to gather **freewill offerings of the people and priests.** These were financial gifts of the Jews who remained in Babylon.

7:17. The financial gifts were not given as a blank check; Artaxerxes provided Ezra with a shopping list. With the money he was to buy **bulls, rams and male lambs, together with their grain offerings and drink offerings.** Most likely Artaxerxes was not aware of the requirements of the Judaic sacrificial system. It is reasonable to assume that this section of the decree was issued under the guidance of a Jewish advisor.

The purchase of animals, grains, and wine was for sacrifice **on the altar of the temple . . . in Jerusalem.** Since the maintenance of the daily sacrifices was addressed later in the decree, it seems these particular sacrifices were intended for a one-time celebration.

7:18–20. After purchasing supplies for the celebration, Ezra and the other Jerusalem leaders could use the rest of the money as seemed best, **in accordance with the will of your God**. While this phrase restricted the use of funds to religious purposes, Artaxerxes felt confident in the discretion of Ezra and those who understood the requirements and needs of the temple.

In addition to money, Ezra received "20 bowls of gold . . . and two fine articles of polished bronze" (Ezra 8:27). These were entrusted to Ezra **for worship in the temple**. Artaxerxes concluded the opening section of the decree directed to Ezra by offering funds from the royal treasury for the daily maintenance of the temple and the required sacrifices: **Anything else needed for the temple of your God . . . you may provide from the royal treasury**.

5. Further instructions (7:21–24)

7:21–23. Having pledged governmental assistance, Artaxerxes gave a directive to **all the treasurers of Trans-Euphrates**. These men were responsible for fulfilling the king's edict; they were the treasurers with whom Ezra would have to deal, should additional funds be needed. The king directed these men to provide **whatever Ezra the priest . . . may ask**—but within limits. Artaxerxes's grant contained a ceiling on certain commodities. **Salt** was supplied **without limit** since it was a less costly product.

7:24. It was not uncommon for the Persian monarchs to exempt cultic priests and officials from taxation. Consequently, Artaxerxes warned the treasurers of Trans-Euphrates that they had **no authority to impose taxes, tribute or duty** on any of the priests, Levites, and other temple workers in Jerusalem.

6. Concluding instructions to Ezra (7:25–26)

7:25. Artaxerxes concluded his edict with some final instructions to Ezra. **In accordance with the wisdom** received **of God**, Ezra was to **appoint magistrates and judges to administer justice**. The king extended to Ezra the authority to organize and unify the social structures within Judea. However, his authority applied only to the Jewish communities. The Persian monarch did not envision the establishment of a Jewish state in Trans-Euphrates. However, he was interested in maintaining the ancient laws and traditions of Israel in order to secure harmony, organizational efficiency, and social order.

Artaxerxes gave Ezra the power to organize life in Jerusalem and all the Jewish communities throughout Trans-Euphrates under the Mosaic Law. In the interest of unity, these laws would apply, as appropriate, to non-Jews living in these places. Therefore, Ezra would have to **teach any** who did not know the law.

7:26. A penalty clause completed the royal decree. By endorsing the Mosaic Law as the social and religious authority throughout Judea, Artaxerxes conferred upon it the same civil power as the Persian law. He pronounced **the law of your God and the law of the king** as equal. Because of this, anyone guilty of disobedience was punishable by the Persian justice system. The penalties were listed in order of harshness from **death** to **imprisonment**.

 Ezra's Praise (7:27–28)

SUPPORTING IDEA: *In his memoirs Ezra praised God's provision, care, and goodness. Armed with these, Ezra gained courage for the journey ahead.*

7:27–28. The text of Artaxerxes's decree and the narrative of Ezra's journey were bridged by a declaration of praise taken from Ezra's personal memoirs. He expressed thanksgiving for the grace and kindness of God. Ezra looked upon the events leading to his departure and saw the participation of **the LORD, the God of our fathers**. For him, the flow of events was another instance of God's faithfulness through history, his peculiar care to the Jewish people, and his sovereign work over the nations.

MAIN IDEA REVIEW: *God's grace flows perpetually; he works from an economy of generosity and renewed opportunities. Once again a group of Jews prepared to leave Babylonia and journey to Jerusalem, led this time by Ezra, a priest and devout teacher of the Mosaic Law.*

III. CONCLUSION

Crossings

Hundreds of years before Ezra's time, Joshua stood on the banks of the Jordan River ready to lead the Israelites into the promised land. God called him to act courageously. He knew that Joshua would face danger, difficulties, even uncertainty and loneliness. To persevere he needed courage. Each directive of God—"be strong and courageous"—was founded on one of three critical elements.

First, his courage rested on God's promise that Joshua would "lead these people to inherit the land" (Josh. 1:6). He was participating in God's design; he was a partner in God's work. Joshua could lead confidently because he believed God was trustworthy, and he knew he was centered in the divine will.

Second, Joshua's courage issued from his own obedience (Josh. 1:7). While the foundation for Joshua's courage rested on God's character, he was responsible to act in harmony with God's instructions; he was to obey. Obedience was evidence of trust; it complemented God's guidance and compassion.

Third, a relationship was established. This intimacy armed Joshua with courage because he knew God would never leave him or forsake him (Josh. 1:9). As Joshua headed into the unknown, he was defended and loved by the God who ruled the nations.

In the spring of 458 B.C., Ezra assembled a small group of Jews on the banks of a Babylonian canal (8:15). The return of the people seemed less threatening than similar events from the early pages of Jewish history. But for Ezra and those with him, it was no small mission. Ahead stretched nine hundred miles of hostile territory and uncertainty about how the people would receive them. Even so, according to Ezra's journal, he was filled with courage because "the hand of the LORD my God was on me" (Ezra 7:28).

Ezra rediscovered the truths declared to Joshua. He saw God's sovereign power at work in the heart of Artaxerxes, the supply of materials, and the gathering of exiles. He recognized divine providence and God's faithfulness to his people. Assured of God's nearness, Ezra set his face toward Jerusalem.

PRINCIPLES

- The righteous and unrighteous alike live under God's sovereign rule.
- God's will is not confined to a place or religious form. His will for righteousness, mercy, justice, and love applies to all peoples.
- Courage comes from deepening intimacy with God—being confident in his character and obedient to his commands.
- Christians should be known for their integrity.
- God deserves all praise.

APPLICATIONS

- Guard your heart. Be persistent in seeking God through prayer and Bible study.
- Forge a reputation for integrity and trustworthiness. Speak honestly with others; never gossip or complain.
- Devote yourself to practicing the will of God.
- Act with courage. Rather than allowing circumstances to determine your response, obey God's revealed will.
- Cultivate the habit of praising God. Establish a time each day for private worship, and each week attend a local church to join in praising God with others.

IV. LIFE APPLICATION

Galloping Gertie

In the summer of 1940, a sleek new bridge spanned the Tacoma Narrows, a passage within the inland waterways of Puget Sound. Suspended between two rocky and forested faces, it promised a shorter route to Washington State's Olympic Peninsula and to the naval shipyards at Bremerton. Its slender ribbon of roadway represented the latest in engineering theory and aesthetic design.

Four months later, as a moderate wind blew through the channel, the bridge began to vibrate up and down. Dubbed "Galloping Gertie" because of its propensity for slight oscillations, on November 7 the road's movements grew in magnitude. Alarmed, the authorities closed the bridge. The bridge danced in contorted rhythms until a six-hundred-foot section of pavement jerked free and fell into the water.

Despite its elegant appearance, the bridge's structural integrity was flawed. The engineers used only a fraction of the standard stiffening depth and constructed the road too narrow for its length. The bridge could not withstand even moderate winds. It failed because it was too flexible.

Shaped in the indifferent and at times hostile environment of Babylon, Ezra emerged as a man of exceptional character. Resolute in his study and obedience of the Mosaic Law, his inner spirit and outward practices conformed to the high standards of holiness set by God. But Ezra also stood in the gap between the Jewish community and the Persian world. In such a position, pressured by opposing interests, Ezra embodied a proper balance of grace and strength.

Jesus Christ provides our inner framework for godly character and personal integrity. But without a commitment to God and his standards, a person loses the stabilizing depth that godly character provides. He becomes "blown here and there by every wind of teaching" (Eph. 4:14). Such a person swings dangerously out of control. Without correction he may wrench loose from the cords of faith and take a damaging fall.

Integrity consists of elemental soundness—maintaining enough firmness to withstand outside pressures, while avoiding excessive rigidity that could result in internal buckling and eventual collapse. Christians should be known for their integrity, their complementary balance between principle and forgiveness, justice and mercy.

V. PRAYER

Lord, each day the lure of compromise pushes, pulls, and presses us. Establish us in your truth, strengthen us by your Spirit, and grant us clarity of mind that we may live in unwavering obedience, worthy of your love. Amen.

VI. DEEPER DISCOVERIES

A. Artaxerxes (7:7–8,11–14,21,26–28)

Artaxerxes I, called by the Greeks Longimanus (Long-Hand) because his right hand was longer than his left, signaled the beginning of Persia's decline. Though it would take 135 years before Alexander the Great completed its destruction, the Persian monarchy, inebriated by power and wealth, began producing less noble and capable rulers.

In a trail of blood that would mark the later kings, King Xerxes was murdered by one of his powerful advisors, Artabanus. Xerxes's son, Artaxerxes, installed himself as king, killing his eldest brother, the rightful heir to the throne. Another brother who was satrap of the province of Bactria led a revolt and was defeated in battle and executed by Artaxerxes. Meanwhile, Artabanus, the murderer of Xerxes, was killed by Artaxerxes for plotting to take the throne.

During his forty-one-year sovereignty, Artaxerxes quelled rebellions in Egypt and Syria. Insurgence was a growing problem throughout the empire as satraps gained extensive power, ethnic and cultural interests intensified, and the domination of the Persian kings became more repressive.

Despite the violent beginnings of his reign, Artaxerxes was known as a relatively kind and forgiving king. His interactions with Ezra, and later Nehemiah, show his generous and sympathetic spirit.

VII. TEACHING OUTLINE

A. INTRODUCTION
1. Lead Story: The Wrong Neighborhood
2. Context: Within the Persian Empire, Judea was designated a "temple-state," a community whose laws and organization were based on temple codes and conduct. Like other Persian kings, Artaxerxes's government helped assure the proper administration of religious life among its subject people. Ezra, a Jewish priest known for his integrity and piety, was commissioned by the king to travel to Jerusalem to bring social and religious order.

3. Transition: Since Ezra represented God and king before the Jews, his ancestry was written into the record to show his legitimacy for the tasks ahead.

B. COMMENTARY

1. Ezra the Man and the Mission (7:1–10)
    a. Ezra's background (7:1–6)
    b. A summary of the mission (7:7–10)
2. The King's Commission (7:11–26)
    a. Introductions (7:11–12)
    b. Ezra's commission (7:13–20)
    c. Further instructions (7:21–24)
    d. Concluding instructions to Ezra (7:25–26)
3. Ezra's Praise (7:27–28)

C. CONCLUSION: CROSSINGS

VIII. ISSUES FOR DISCUSSION

1. What are some elements of personal integrity? In what ways might Christian character be distinctive?
2. Define piety. How does our culture view it? How can a Christian develop a proper piety?
3. Artaxerxes expected the Jews to offer sacrifices and prayers for him and the empire. What responsibility does the Christian have to government? How should we pray for leaders and governments?
4. Share experiences in which you believe you have seen the hand of God working through circumstances.

Ezra 8

The Journey

Quote

*G*od will not have his work made manifest by cowards.

R a l p h   W a l d o   E m e r s o n

Ezra 8

IN A NUTSHELL

*E*zra assembled his caravan, reviewed who was present, and called for a fast. A few days later they left Babylon. After traveling for four months, the group arrived in Jerusalem. The financial contributions were given to the temple priests, and the king's orders were delivered to the Persian officials in Trans-Euphrates.

The Journey

I. INTRODUCTION

Dear Diary

*D*iaries, journals, scraps of paper, and napkin scribbles all testify to an inner need to fix in ink a piece of our individual journey. When written, daily routines and personal thoughts and experiences suddenly become significant—either for their commonness or flash of brilliance. By transcribing experiences, we affix some measure of importance to our daily lives.

December 25, 1805. "We would have Spent this day the nativity of Christ in feasting, had we any thing either to raise our Sperits or even gratify our appetites, our Dinner concisted of pore Elk, So much Spoiled that we eate it thro' mear necessity" (Lewis and Clark, *Corps of Discovery*).

August 25, 1989. "The first day of school was very fun. Did you know that the first day of school was mostely math but it was fun. It was so fun that I went home lafing" (Lara, age 8).

This impulse to write and record, to put on paper something of the self belongs to our creative heritage, our need to call into being. In the substance of our words we incarnate thought, and our experiences come alive with the breath of meaning.

The next two chapters of Ezra show us portions of the scribe's personal memoirs. At times they read like a journal with daily on-the-road jottings; other entries came from memory, after time had made some determining inroads into Ezra's recollection, after details had washed away with reflection leaving only the essence or the needful. What remains is a glimpse not only into history but also into a soul—the self's inner editor choosing what held value in that experience.

II. COMMENTARY

The Journey

MAIN IDEA: *Ezra's personal accounts reveal a man of order. He carefully assembled the caravan, assigned tasks to responsible men, and accounted for every person and article under his protection. Yet he avoided the rigidity of legalism because his heart was humble before God.*

A The Caravan (8:1–14)

SUPPORTING IDEA: *Though large groups of Jews had returned to Jerusalem in past years, faithful men and their families still lived in Babylonian territories. Some of these now packed their belongings and assembled with Ezra to journey to Judea.*

1. Introduction (8:1)

8:1. Chapter 7 concluded with Ezra gaining courage from God's involvement in human affairs. Emboldened, he recruited **family heads and those registered with them** to accompany him to Jerusalem. As noted in Ezra 2, Jewish society was organized around men and their extended families.

2. The priests (8:2a)

8:2a. As a scribe Ezra kept careful records. He listed those who went with him on the journey, beginning with the priests. This reflected the increasing importance of the priestly office, as well as Ezra's own station as a priest. Two patriarchal families formed this group: **the descendants of Phinehas** and **Ithamar**. The families of **Gershom** and **Daniel** traced their ancestry through these two descendants of Aaron the high priest (see "Deeper Discoveries").

Ezra, poised on the edge of the desert, had in his company priests descended from those who had crossed the desert in the great exodus from Egypt. Though these families had remained in Babylon during earlier migrations, the invitation to participate in God's work remained open.

3. The royal line (8:2b–3a)

8:2b–3a. The political line of Israel was registered next: **the descendants of David**. The family accompanying Ezra, **Hattush** son of Shecaniah, was a distant relative in the royal line (see 1 Chr. 3:22). The memory of Davidic ancestry continued in the postexilic community.

4. The laity (8:3b–14)

8:3b–14. Ezra next listed the ordinary citizens. These composed the largest portion of the group. Twelve clans were listed, possibly symbolic of Israel's twelve tribes. All of the families listed in Ezra's group were also listed in the earlier exodus of Ezra 2. Since these were sprawling, extended families grouped under one patriarchal head, not everyone within these familial organizations had made the earlier journey.

In fact, it is probable that family members connected to these clans still remained in Babylonian lands after Ezra's caravan left. The only exception to this may be **the descendants of Adonikam, the last ones, whose names were Eliphelet, Jeuel and Shemaiah**. The term *the last ones* may indicate that these were the remaining members of that particular family.

Approximately fifteen hundred men uprooted their families to return to Jerusalem. Including women and children, about five thousand people made the trip. Compared to previous groups, it was a relatively small caravan. Perhaps news of hostile neighbors and agricultural difficulties had filtered back to Babylonia. Pulling up stakes and traveling across the desert to a broken-down city probably held little appeal for most of the Jewish exiles in Persia.

𝕭 Final Preparations (8:15–30)

> **SUPPORTING IDEA:** *Before leaving Babylonia, Ezra enlisted Levites to join the caravan, called for a general fast to petition God's protection, and entrusted the money and valuable articles to consecrated priests.*

5. Recruiting Levites (8:15–20)

8:15. Loaded with their belongings, the people assembled **at the canal that flows toward Ahava** (a place unknown to modern archaeology). The Euphrates River ran through the city of Babylon. Many smaller tributaries as well as man-made channels branched from it. Along one of these the people met. The area probably provided an open plain convenient for gathering a large group. They **camped there three days** in preparation for their departure.

When Ezra went through the camp, checking supplies and noting who had arrived, he **found no Levites**. This was significant to Ezra because, under Pentateuchal law, Levites were responsible for the transport of temple articles.

8:16–17. Unwilling to proceed without some representative Levites, Ezra called together some men **who were leaders**, and a couple of others noted as **men of learning**. These men went **to Iddo, the leader in Casiphia**. One can only conjecture who Iddo was and what his role in the Jewish community might have been. The name Iddo was certainly respectable, having prophetic and priestly precedent. The prophet Zechariah was either the grandson of a man named Iddo or the descendant of an earlier prophet by that name (2 Chr. 13:22).

The purpose of Ezra's envoy was to recruit Levites and temple servants. Ezra instructed the men in how to present their case, telling them **what to say to Iddo and his kinsmen** (his kinsmen being fellow priests).

8:18–20. Considering what was asked of these Levites—to uproot their families and move nine hundred miles away—Ezra was correct in attributing success to **the gracious hand of our God**. It demonstrated God's activity in, and approval of, the journey.

Just as he previously listed the assembly, Ezra recorded the newcomers by family descent. **Sherebiah** seems a particularly prized addition, since Ezra distinguished him as **a capable man** and established his Levitical credentials through **Mahli** to Levi, **the son of Israel**. Also among the group were **descendants of Merari**, the clan traditionally responsible for transporting the tabernacle. In all, thirty-eight Levites joined Ezra.

Along with the Levites came **220 of the temple servants**. These were men of a lower class who assisted the Levites in the temple (see comments on Ezra 2:43–54). Since these temple workers were not mandated in the pentateuchal law, their inclusion was validated because **David and the officials had established** the positions **to assist the Levites**. Like everyone else in the caravan, the servants **were registered by name**—though the list does not appear in the biblical text.

6. Petitioning God (8:21–23)

8:21–23. Finally, the company was complete. Before they left their riverfront campsite, Ezra **proclaimed a fast**. The call went throughout the camp for the people to humble themselves before God. By fasting, the community placed themselves in a vulnerable position, like an afflicted person whose sole deliverer and sustainer is God. In this way the people appealed to God's special protection of the powerless. They asked God **for a safe journey** because of their weak position as well as the reality of traveling with **children** and transporting valuable **possessions**.

The fast was made more critical because, as Ezra admitted, he was **ashamed to ask the king for soldiers and horsemen to protect** the caravan **from enemies on the road**. He had told the king earlier that the Lord would protect them on the trip. He probably thought it would be hypocritical to turn right around and ask for the king's protection. He trusted God to conduct them safely through some very treacherous territory.

7. Consecration of priests and articles (8:24–30)

8:24–27. Before they broke camp, Ezra **set apart twelve of the leading priests**, along with some of the most recent recruits from among the Levites, **Sherebiah** and **Hashabiah** (both mentioned in Ezra 8:18–19) **and ten of their**

brothers. These two groups of twelve were responsible for the transport of the valuable articles. Whether the number twelve held symbolic importance remains uncertain. However, entrusting the safety of temple property to the Levites was solidly within the Mosaic law (Num. 3).

So Ezra weighed out to the selected priests and Levites the **offering of silver and gold** that Artaxerxes, his advisers, and others in Babylon **had donated for the house of our God**. The gifts had been given to God, so it was right that God's servants should assume responsibility for their safety.

Like an accountant, Ezra listed the articles and their weights, or values. Most scholars believe that, though the original accounting by Ezra was accurate, scribal errors and translation difficulties have created inaccuracies. Especially of concern are the **650 talents of silver** (approximately twenty-five tons) and the **100 talents of gold** (just under four tons). The value exceeds reasonableness. As for the **silver articles**, it is generally acknowledged that "100" refers to the number of articles in their possession, not to the combined weight of the pieces.

The other pieces fit well within ancient measures and values—**20 bowls of gold valued at 1,000 darics** (about twenty pounds) and **two fine articles of polished bronze**, probably highly polished brass.

8:28–30. After accounting for all the gold, silver, and valuable articles, Ezra passed them into the care of the priests and Levites, stating, **You as well as these articles are consecrated to the LORD**. Other translations render this statement, "You are holy to the LORD, and the vessels are holy." This captures more clearly the implications and intent of Ezra's commission to the priests. Because God's essence is holiness, anything set apart for his exclusive use must, by necessity, be holy as well.

In addition, the silver and gold **were a freewill offering to the LORD**. Anything consecrated to the Lord, deemed holy, belonged in the perpetual service of God. Offerings, by contrast, were consumed for God's praise and glory. The gold and silver would purchase necessities for temple worship; they would not remain in the temple, but be offered or used for its service.

Ezra commissioned the priests and Levites to keep a careful watch on all the valuables, to **guard them carefully until you weigh them out in the chambers of the house of the LORD in Jerusalem**. The chambers were outer rooms of the temple used for storage. At the end of their journey, they would transfer these sacred pieces into the care of **the leading priests and the Levites and the family heads** in Jerusalem, giving a careful account of what they brought. The priests and Levites accepted the articles, the silver and gold, and the responsibility given them by Ezra.

C The Journey (8:31–32)

> **SUPPORTING IDEA:** *Having made every preparation, Ezra and the caravan embarked on the journey to Jerusalem.*

8:31–32. Ezra wrote that **on the twelfth day of the first month** they finally pulled up stakes, packed the tents, and set out for **Jerusalem**. He devoted little space in his memoirs to the actual trip. The only thing he deemed worthy of note was that **the hand of our God was on us, and he protected us from enemies and bandits along the way.** Their safe passage demonstrated God's grace and faithfulness to his people.

D Taking Care of Business (8:33–36)

> **SUPPORTING IDEA:** *Trustworthy, and always careful to fulfill his responsibilities, Ezra transferred the articles and finances, performed required sacrifices, and delivered the king's edict.*

8:33–34. **On the fourth day,** Ezra and the consecrated priests and Levites took **the silver and gold and the sacred articles** to the temple. Everything was again weighed and noted. Responsibility for the treasures was then transferred to **Meremoth son of Uriah, the priest.** At the transfer of the money and articles, witnesses were on hand to verify what was deposited in the temple treasury: the priest **Eleazar son of Phinehas**, and two Levites, **Jozabad** and **Noadiah**.

Ezra emphasized again the protocol followed: **Everything was accounted for by number and weight** and **was recorded.** These numbers would be matched against the original entries made before the journey.

8:35. The final two verses of the chapter probably come not from Ezra's journal but from the hand of the chronicler since it switches from first-person narrative to third person. After their arrival the members of the caravan **sacrificed burnt offerings to the God of Israel.** This was normal practice. The **twelve bulls for all Israel,** as well as all the sacrifices (offered in multiples of twelve), reinforce the view that the returned exiles represented the entire nation. The **twelve male goats** were given **as a sin offering** in order to achieve ceremonial cleanness after living in a pagan land.

8:36. Ezra and his company completed their responsibilities by delivering **the king's orders to the royal satraps and to the governors of Trans-Euphrates.** The king's decree was distributed, and the officials **gave assistance to the**

people and to the house of God. Appreciation and honor were given to the Persian oligarchy for its continued support of Jewish custom and worship.

MAIN IDEA REVIEW: *Ezra's personal accounts reveal a man of order. He carefully assembled the caravan, assigned tasks to responsible men, and accounted for every person and article under his protection. Yet he avoided the rigidity of legalism because his heart was humble before God.*

III. CONCLUSION

Mirror, Mirror

In the classic tale "Snow White," the evil queen gazes into the looking glass and delivers the famous line, "Mirror, mirror on the wall, who's the fairest of them all?"

The question is rhetorical, of course. We learn that the queen has assumed her own superiority. In fact, lacking rivals, the mirror's answer always comes back in her favor. It says a lot about her self-absorption. It also explains her peevishness when one day the mirror replies, "Snow White." By the end of the story, the queen becomes an evil hag, poisoned by the stale air of her own ego. She demonstrates Edmund Carpenter's observation that we become what we behold.

Who hasn't known a person so preoccupied with hatred or bitterness toward someone that he took on the characteristics of the person he presumed to dislike? The fixation so obstructed his vision that life became his anger, hate, or bitterness. It defined who he was.

Of course the principle works equally for good. It prompted the author of Hebrews to write, "Holy brothers, who share in the heavenly calling, fix your thoughts on Jesus, the apostle and high priest whom we confess" (Heb. 3:1). And again, "Let us fix our eyes on Jesus, the author and perfecter of our faith" (Heb. 12:2a).

Ezra was fascinated with God. He had a holy obsession with his righteousness, power, perfection, and grace. He gazed upon God's excellence in the law. He watched his power demonstrated in the secret places of a king's heart. He observed his mercy in the wilds of the desert. In turn, Ezra's life was defined by his Lord, and his vision encompassed heaven and earth.

PRINCIPLES

- God is involved in the affairs of humankind.
- God responds to the prayers of the righteous.
- Anyone or anything associated with God must be holy.

- Responsibility must be matched by personal integrity.
- Faith and piety can be expressed in various ways.

APPLICATIONS

- Do not judge yourself or anyone else by what other Christians do. We all stand alone before God about our actions, speech, and thoughts.
- Never act out of fear of other people; your life and success depend solely on God.
- Commit yourself to persistent and faithful prayer.
- Whatever responsibility you are given, conduct yourself with openness and honesty.

IV. LIFE APPLICATION

From Russia with Love

When the Soviet Union collapsed under the weight of its own tyranny and corruption, revelations about life under communism spread rapidly westward. Formerly impenetrable borders could not hold back the news as the sins of former generations and leaders were denounced in a national catharsis. But in the chaotic mix of relief and anger, quieter stories emerged.

At a gathering in Moscow, a reserved middle-aged lady told the story of a woman whose husband was exiled because of his faith in Jesus Christ. The woman, left alone to care for their eight children, was herself eventually arrested. She was taken before the interrogation committee. In her arms she cradled her youngest child, a baby girl.

In the isolated room the interrogators pressured the woman to renounce her faith. If she did not, they promised, her children would be killed. For a long time the woman did not speak or move. Then she laid her infant daughter on a bench in the otherwise empty room. She decided she could entrust her child to the God who promised never to leave her or forsake her. Between two guards she walked out the door to prison. Years later she was released. She returned home. Running to meet her was that same little girl.

The woman telling the story paused. "She was my mother," she said. "I was the baby who was left on the bench."

Like Ezra before her, the woman in Russia, through whatever torments her mind passed, based her decision on one thing—God. Against the pressure of circumstance, despite the mind's rationalizations, each chose the immutable. Each felt compelled to wager on God: Ezra chose the invisible God above the armies of Persia; the Russian woman chose the enduring love of God over the fear of man. Each trusted God's revealed character—his love, protection, and sovereign grace.

V. PRAYER

God of heaven and earth, open our eyes so that in looking we may see you; in gazing we may behold your goodness, love, and holiness. Amen.

VI. DEEPER DISCOVERIES

The Descendants of Aaron (8:2a)

Aaron had four sons: Nadab, Abihu, Eleazar, and Ithamar. Of the two priestly families listed by Ezra, Daniel traced his line back to Aaron's son Ithamar; Gershom descended from Eleazar's only son Phinehas.

Aaron's other sons, Nadab and Abihu, died without heirs. In the desert God had given Moses explicit instructions for the various offerings and sacrifices that Israel and its priests were to offer. Following this, in an elaborate ceremony, Aaron and his sons were consecrated to God. At some point following their induction to holy service, Aaron's two sons Nadab and Abihu took their censers, put fire and incense in them, and "offered unauthorized fire before the LORD, contrary to his command" (Lev. 10:1). Because of this, "fire came out from the presence of the LORD and consumed them, and they died before the LORD" (Lev. 10:2).

Those who represent God, who act on his behalf, must live in strict obedience and holiness. If we think God's response seems excessively harsh, perhaps it is because we have become too comfortable with sin and have lost the awe that God's purity should inspire.

VII. TEACHING OUTLINE

A. INTRODUCTION

1. Lead Story: Dear Diary

2. Context: Commissioned by the Persian government to establish religious and civil order in Judea, Ezra gathered a caravan of exiled Jews to travel to Jerusalem.

3. Transition: As a scribe, Ezra kept careful records of everything for which he felt responsible. As a priest, he meticulously followed the rituals and requirements of the law.

B. COMMENTARY

1. The Caravan (8:1–14)
    a. Introduction (8:1)
    b. The priests (8:2a)
    c. The royal line (8:2b–3a)
    d. The laity (8:3b–14)
2. Final Preparations (8:15–30)
    a. Recruiting Levites (8:15–20)
    b. Petitioning God (8:21–23)
    c. Consecration of priests and articles (8:24–30)
3. The Journey (8:31–32)
4. Taking Care of Business (8:33–36)

C. CONCLUSION: MIRROR, MIRROR

VIII. ISSUES FOR DISCUSSION

1. What role, if any, can fasting have in the life of the church?
2. What does it mean to be consecrated to God? How might this show in the life of a Christian?
3. What practical steps can believers take to "fix our eyes on Jesus"? What does this mean?
4. Share within your group ways in which God has specifically answered your prayers.

Ezra 9

Between Heaven and Earth

I. INTRODUCTION
Follow the Leader

II. COMMENTARY
A verse-by-verse explanation of the chapter.

III. CONCLUSION
Remembrance

An overview of the principles and applications from the chapter.

IV. LIFE APPLICATION
The Trinary Chant

Melding the chapter to life.

V. PRAYER
Tying the chapter to life with God.

VI. DEEPER DISCOVERIES
Historical, geographical, and grammatical enrichment of the commentary.

VII. TEACHING OUTLINE
Suggested step-by-step group study of the chapter.

VIII. ISSUES FOR DISCUSSION
Zeroing the chapter in on daily life.

| Q u o t e |

A civilization may be wrecked without any spectacular crimes or criminals but by constant petty breaches of faith and minor complicities on the part of men generally considered very nice people.

H e r b e r t   B u t t e r f i e l d

Ezra 9

I N   A   N U T S H E L L

S hortly after Ezra's arrival in Jerusalem, a crisis of culture and faith occurred. It was charged that laws of separation had been compromised. Some of the leaders were among the guilty. On behalf of the people, Ezra publicly humbled himself and offered a prayer of confession to God.

Between Heaven
and Earth

I. INTRODUCTION

Follow the Leader

*I*t was a warm summer evening, and our family sat at the table relaxing in post-mealtime banter, each tossing in comments and laughter. We were content and so lingered even as the verbal exchanges diminished. In time a lull occurred. For whatever reason everyone's gaze eventually settled on our granddaughter playing happily in her high chair. Though she had been oblivious to our adult conversation, something in that stillness caught her attention, and she looked up.

Her ascension to power dawned slowly as she looked around the table from face to face. Then a smile tugged at the corners of her mouth as she gained a fuller appreciation of the situation. Tentatively, she raised her hand. Everyone raised a hand. She laughed. We laughed. She clapped. The whole family clapped. She was on a roll.

Leadership confers power. By virtue of position alone, men and women in leadership affect circumstances and people within their domain. Older children to younger, parent to child, president to nation, pastor to church—the force of one person spreads outward in concentric rings of influence. Even when perceived as weak, the leader remains the agent of change, his passivity or dullness creating voids others must fill or precipitating new crises that bring revision or alteration.

When Ezra arrived in Jerusalem, an established hierarchy of priests, Levites, and civic officials directed the affairs of Jerusalem and Judea. Through candid dialogue Ezra was made aware of misconduct among certain leaders. Their actions had created a permissive atmosphere so that their lifestyle was replicated throughout the community.

Ezra confronted the situation with wisdom. His concern for God's nation and his commitment to God's character compelled him to respond in confession and repentance on behalf of the people. Ezra was dedicated to serving under the authority of God, and his leadership provoked positive change.

II. COMMENTARY

Between Heaven and Earth

> **MAIN IDEA:** *Spiritual leaders stand between heaven and earth. While they represent God's authority, they also identify with the needs and failings of the people. Ezra fulfilled this dual role as he helped direct the community of faith back to fellowship with God.*

A The Report (9:1–2)

> **SUPPORTING IDEA:** *Certain Jewish leaders in Jerusalem confided in Ezra about misconduct of various leaders and members of the community.*

9:1–2. The chapter begins: **After these things had been done.** This phrase bridges the time gap between Ezra's arrival in Jerusalem and the episode about to unfold. While some scholars are uncertain about the time frame of the event, it seems reasonable that it fits into the broader context of the reading of the law described in Nehemiah 8.

At this time a small group of leaders, probably village chiefs, met with Ezra. They were not tattling but giving Ezra an official report out of respect for the law which, in accordance with Artaxerxes's decree, served as both religious and civil authority (Ezra 7:25–26). These chiefs reported that **the people of Israel** had not **kept themselves separate from the neighboring peoples with their detestable practices**.

With Exodus 34:11–16 and Deuteronomy 7:1–4 as their starting points, Ezra and the officials interpreted the law outside its literal, historical setting and connected its principles to their current situation. Before Israel entered the promised land, God instructed them not to intermarry with the Canaanites whose land they were about to occupy. The reason was purely religious, not racial (Jews had married non-Jews before without divine judgment—Moses and Joseph to name two). The emphasis was on the "detestable practices" of the surrounding peoples, specifically their idol worship: "Do not intermarry with them . . . for they will turn your sons away from following me to serve other gods" (Deut. 7:3–4).

The officials told Ezra that the surrounding people lived like **the Canaanites, Hittites, Perizzites, Jebusites, Ammonites, Moabites, Egyptians and Amorites**—ancient people representative of heathenism who were expressly judged by God. As societies, they were not the Jews' neighbors at the time of Ezra, but they were illustrative of pagan practices and God's disapproval of such (Exod. 3:8,17). It was in this sense that the officials mentioned them.

The people had married foreign wives, and **mingled the holy race with the peoples around them**. The word *race* is better translated as "seed," carrying the idea of offspring, or sprout. The concern of everyone was not ethnicity but holiness (Ezra 9:6–15). The chiefs' summation that the marriages were acts of **unfaithfulness** further reflects on their religious sensitivities as opposed to any racial superiority. And what made the situation worse was that the leaders and officials had **led the way** in this sinning.

B The Response (9:3–5)

SUPPORTING IDEA: *After hearing the official report, Ezra responded as the official representative of the community with public acts of contrition.*

9:3. Most likely Ezra was aware of the problem before the delegation's visit. But once the issue became official, he responded formally as well. He wrote: **I tore my tunic and cloak**. In Eastern cultures, the tearing of one's garment was a symbol of humility, anguish, or mourning. That Ezra tore not only his cloak (outer garment) but also his tunic (under garment) indicates the strong emotion and deep distress he felt on behalf of the community. He viewed the sins of the individuals as reflective of the nation; he mourned that the spiritual fabric of the community had unraveled to such an extent that God's holiness was treated with contempt.

He also **pulled hair** from his head and beard. Shaving one's hair and beard were also rituals of mourning. But because these acts were popular among the pagan cultures surrounding Israel, the law forbade them (Deut. 14:1–2). So the Jews made it lawful by restricting the practice to pulling out hairs from the head and beard. Finally, Ezra **sat down appalled**. Sitting in silence expressed his utter shock at what had occurred.

9:4. Through his public demonstration of grief, Ezra brought the issue of mixed marriages into the open. In response, **everyone who trembled at the words of the God of Israel** gathered around him. These Jews, fully aware of the situation, gathered around Ezra in solidarity with him. The issue was the **unfaithfulness of the exiles**. The questionable marriages were viewed as violations of divine command and affronts to God and his exclusive claims on all the people of Israel. The gathering of silent mourners remained in the temple area **until the evening sacrifice**, around 3:00 p.m.

9:5. Then, at the evening sacrifice, Ezra wrote, **I rose from my self-abasement**. He broke his silence in order to pray. He fell on his knees with his hands **spread out to the LORD his God**. His kneeling further emphasized an attitude of humility. As a person before a potentate, Ezra bowed before God with his hands spread out in admission of the people's unworthiness and great need.

⬛ The Prayer (9:6–15)

SUPPORTING IDEA: *As a leader, Ezra offered a public prayer of confession on behalf of the community. It was sincere and personal, emotional and forthright.*

9:6. Ezra did not distance himself from the community. He identified with the people, including those who had sinned and produced the crisis. **O my God**, he prayed, **I am too ashamed and disgraced to lift up my face to you**. Ezra was embarrassed. Though innocent of wrongdoing, he felt mortified by those who had affronted God. His soul's sensitivity was such that he understood the implications of God's holiness and the demands such holiness placed on his people. Their sins, with which Ezra identified, had **reached to the heavens**.

9:7. Ezra viewed the present plight as part of Israel's historical pattern: **From the days of our forefathers until now, our guilt has been great**. The current offense was part of a greater tendency. Over and over the community had indulged itself, testing God's goodness and trivializing his grace.

Ezra associated himself not only with the Judean community but also with the Jews' historical past. He interpreted history according to the relationship between God and Israel. Prosperity resulted from obedience while disaster was the natural consequence of sin: **Because of our sins, we . . . have been subjected to the sword and captivity . . . at the hand of foreign kings, as it is today**. Politics were driven by divine will in concert with human tendencies and passions.

9:8–9. The years of Israel's history were littered with spiritual and political failures which resulted in oppression by conquering empires and the destruction of the temple. **But now, for a brief moment, the LORD our God has been gracious**. The conciliatory policies of the Persians brought a reprieve, and this came about because of God's sovereignty. Compared with the accumulated years of foreign domination, the current situation seemed a brief moment.

Ezra acknowledged God's grace as evidenced by the **remnant** of Jews living in Judea and by the restoration of the temple, **his sanctuary**. The "remnant" refers to those among God's people whom he preserves and protects as his representatives. The remnant provided proof of God's promises and the people's hope for the future.

Ezra claimed that these two realities—Jews living in Judea, and the restoration of the temple in Jerusalem—gave **light to our eyes and a little relief in our bondage**. In their long night of exile and domination, the community found refreshment in these signs of hope. Though they were still **slaves**, in that Israel had not regained political autonomy, God's preservation of a community and the rebuilding of the temple were evidence that **our God has not** deserted us. . . . He has shown us kindness. . . . He has granted us new life. He had given them a wall of protection in Judah and Jerusalem.

The central element of God's goodness was found in the restoration of the temple and the reestablishment of traditional worship. The "wall of protection" referred not to the walls of Jerusalem but to the restored relationship between the Lord and Israel.

9:10–12. But now, O our God, what can we say after this? Ezra acknowledged God's grace, mercy, and faithfulness; he contrasted these with the community's acts of disobedience: we have disregarded the commands you gave through your servants the prophets.

Ezra repeatedly returned to the law as the basis for life and conduct. The current crisis resulted not from conflicting opinions or differences in culture and tradition but from violations of God's expressed will. In his public prayer Ezra extracted the commands that had suffered abuse and offered them as incriminating evidence against the community.

Ezra stitched together phrases from several pentateuchal books. Together they formed a scriptural principle which the current community was violating: The land you are entering to possess is a land polluted by the corruption of its peoples. As Israel stood poised to enter the promised land, they were told, "Do not learn to imitate the detestable ways of the nations" (Deut. 18:9).

The main point of Ezra's prayer came from Deuteronomy 7. Here was found the injunction against intermarrying with people of the surrounding nations. Ezra recited, Do not give your daughters in marriage to their sons or take their daughters for your sons, though he did not include Deuteronomy 7:4, which contained the explanatory ending: "for they will turn your sons away from following me to serve other gods, and the LORD's anger will burn against you."

Ezra then melded various Scriptures. From Deuteronomy 7:2 came the instruction: Do not seek a treaty of friendship with them at any time. The remaining sentiments recurred throughout prophetic writings and the law. From Genesis to Isaiah the nation was told that obedience to the commands of God resulted in prosperity in the land and an enduring inheritance throughout the generations.

9:13. Ezra returned to his opening theme: the habitual disobedience of Israel and God's enduring mercy. Ezra acknowledged that the exile was a result of . . . evil deeds and great guilt. But as harsh and difficult as the exile was, God had punished them less than our sins have deserved. God still preserved a remnant. Ezra saw the severity of God's holiness and understood that love and mercy tempered his response.

9:14. In light of God's goodness and mercy, Ezra wondered, Shall we again break your commands and intermarry with the peoples . . . ? Would you not be angry enough . . . to destroy us, leaving us no remnant or survivor? This was not hyperbole or dramatic rhetoric. He felt disturbed and convicted over the people's sins and their presumption. Like Moses he felt shame, confusion, and amazement that God had been treated so indifferently. He understood that God's justice could annihilate every one of them.

9:15. Ezra concluded his prayer with declarations of God's righteousness and the people's guilt, but he stopped short of asking for forgiveness. He bowed before the Lord in confession. The admission of guilt was all he dared at this time. Though God had graciously shown mercy throughout Israel's history, Ezra would have felt it impertinent to assume divine acquittal: **not one of us can stand in your presence**.

> **MAIN IDEA REVIEW:** *Spiritual leaders stand between heaven and earth. While they represent God's authority, they also identify with the needs and failings of the people. Ezra fulfilled this dual role as he helped direct the community of faith back to fellowship with God.*

III. CONCLUSION

Remembrance

Historian Arthur M. Schlesinger Jr. wrote: "History is to the nation rather as memory is to the individual. As an individual deprived of memory becomes disoriented and lost, not knowing where he has been or where he is going, so a nation denied a conception of its past will be disabled in dealing with its present and its future" (Schlesinger, p. 46).

To some extent the Jews seem to have suffered this disorientation as they resettled in Judea. Like the expatriate, or even the missionary who has spent the greater portion of his life away from home, the exiles had spent all or most of their lives in a mix of Jewish tradition and Babylonian custom.

For seventy years Judah's history was interrupted and daily life was fragmented by the loss of nationhood and the domination of a foreign culture. The years of exile accomplished a longing for home, but they also necessitated a search for identity. The children of the exiles knew the distant stories of the nation, but they had few personal recollections.

In his public prayer of confession, Ezra connected the past to the present. He sketched for the people a bit of who they were, and it was not particularly flattering. He made no mention of past spectacles: crossing the Red Sea, manna in the desert, toppling Jericho. He excluded the nation's heroes: Abraham, Isaac, Jacob, Moses, David, and Solomon. Instead, Ezra appealed to a history based not on nationalism but on divine grace. In this way he prepared them to face the present crisis with hope and to look to the future with resolve.

PRINCIPLES

- Leaders have a greater responsibility for conduct since they have a wider range of influence.
- God's people are expected to be holy as God is holy.
- Sin results in destructive consequences.
- God is faithful, righteous, just, and merciful.
- True confession proceeds from an honest heart that acknowledges God's righteousness.
- Every person is responsible at two levels—individually before God and corporately with other believers.

APPLICATIONS

- In all your relationships, act faithfully and properly with love, justice, and mercy; in this way you demonstrate the life of God to others.
- When you sin, confess it to God. Look within your heart and ask God's Spirit to show you the depth of your offense so you will not become callous and insensitive to wrong.
- Learn prudence. Train yourself to look ahead to the consequences of your decisions.
- Identify yourself with the local church. Accept accountability among other believers.

IV. LIFE APPLICATION

The Trinary Chant

God blazes in the white light of purity, untouched by anything that can diminish or detract. He exists in completeness, with nothing greater to which he must aspire, nothing missing for which he must seek. Day and night the chant of praise fills the heavens: "Holy, holy, holy is the Lord God Almighty, who was, and is, and is to come" (Rev. 4:8). Voices resound in unending echoes declaring God's essence—perfection, purity, and completeness. He is holy.

What in our experience leads us to understand this core distinctive of God? Only God's revelation of himself to us. A. W. Tozer says that God's holiness is unique and can't be imagined from anything in human experience. God's holiness "stands apart, unique, unapproachable, incomprehensible and unattainable. The natural man is blind to it. He may fear God's power and admire His wisdom, but His holiness he cannot even imagine" (*Knowledge of the Holy,* p. 111).

So holiness is never required of unbelievers; they are called to repentance. But holiness is expected of those who enter into relationship with God. His people are told, "Be holy because I . . . am holy" (Lev. 19:2; 1 Pet. 1:16). Not because sin's proximity threatens God's perfection but because it cannot have its home there.

God's essence, then, is the starting point and the ending point for every other facet of Christian obedience. It also becomes the target of all sin. In sinning we join the profane to the pure. We betray God and ourselves.

Yet sin happens—sometimes willfully, sometimes because of the weakness of our present human condition. When it does occur, the only appropriate response is that expressed by Ezra: "Not one of us can stand in your presence" (Ezra 9:15). Yet in Christ we gain this confidence that "if we confess our sins, he is faithful and just and will forgive us our sins and purify us from all unrighteousness" (1 John 1:9). This promise does not minimize sin; it magnifies God's grace.

V. PRAYER

Lord, show us our sin that we may fly to you for cleansing; show us our offense so we will not be blinded by pride. Leave us not with the mind's excuses, but show us the truth that we may live free. Amen.

VI. DEEPER DISCOVERIES

Sin

In Hebrew the word for "sin" was commonly applied to the archer missing his target or to someone's foot missing a step or stumbling. Biblically *sin* is an inclusive term expressing moral digression, however slight.

Whether tagged as wickedness, iniquity, wrong, or unrighteousness, sin surfaces as a response to a moral standard. In Scripture it at times refers to a specific act; at other times it explains a principle around which life organizes itself—a condition or a lifestyle. In either case sin fails to attain the perfection of God's holiness or to achieve the purpose of God's design.

The world works under the condition of sin; it regulates and arranges life based on faulty premises, misdirected goals, inept philosophies, and a disregard for God. Even those societies and cultures that are ostensibly "Christian" or religious operate outside the realm of God's rule and revelation, attempting to achieve what can only be realized in the nature and dominion of God. It explains why John wrote, "If anyone loves the world, the love of the Father is not in him" (1 John 2:15b). James concurred, adding, "Anyone who chooses to be a friend of the world becomes an enemy of God" (Jas. 4:4b). The world constantly drifts away from God.

But people, too, operate under a condition of sin, a pervasive mentality separated from God. From this damaged frame of reference, this unbelief, springs the acts and inactions of sin.

In belief and practice sin is a refusal. As insidious as a thought, or as brazen as an act, sin rejects truth. God alone defines truth and reality, so any departure from his completeness plunges a person into the fallacious realm of sin. No one living in the truth can sin; no one departing from truth can be complete, or holy.

Because sin departs from God's perfection, sin always results in diminishment—a promise unrealized, a desire never granted; it is half pleasures and missing pieces—death in the guise of life. It always mocks what it intends to fulfill because sin's core quality is perpetual deficiency.

VII. TEACHING OUTLINE

A. INTRODUCTION
1. Lead Story: Follow the Leader
2. Context: Since the return of the first exiles under Cyrus, the people of Judea fluctuated between observance and neglect of Judaic law. Ezra's arrival in Jerusalem brought him face-to-face with a community whose religious life was compromised and whose understanding of God's revelation proved inadequate.
3. Transition: As magistrate for Persian as well as Judaic law, Ezra received a report from village leaders about unchecked disobedience in Judea.

B. COMMENTARY
1. The Report (9:1–2)
2. The Response (9:3–5)
3. The Prayer (9:6–15)

C. CONCLUSION: REMEMBRANCE

VIII. ISSUES FOR DISCUSSION

1. To what extent is the local church responsible for the actions of its individual members?
2. God calls all believers to be holy. Discuss the implications of 2 Timothy 1:9 and 1 Peter 1:15–16 in the daily life of a Christian.
3. Is confession necessary for forgiveness?

Ezra 10

Crisis of Faith

Quote

You cannot change character or behavior

and leave beliefs intact.

D a l l a s   W i l l a r d

Ezra 10

 I N   A   N U T S H E L L

Ezra and the Jewish leaders called for a national assembly. The people confessed their sin and agreed that appointed leaders would investigate and judge each case of intermarriage separately; they also pledged to abide by their leaders' decisions.

Crisis of Faith

I. INTRODUCTION

Yet I Sin

*I*n the late sixteenth and early seventeenth centuries, the Puritans tried to rid the Church of England of what they considered abuses and blasphemies. Their desire was to purify the church, to purge it of sin and reclaim it for God's holy purposes. As often happens, their zealous response to legitimate concerns led to a radicalism that resulted in wrongs. Even so, the Puritans gave to the church a rich heritage of biblical understanding. As they revered God and understood his holiness, they became acutely aware of their own failings.

The following selection comes from that tradition. It is a confession of human nature, as well as a declaration of God's beauty and his compelling perfection.

> Thou art good beyond all thought, but I am vile, wretched, miserable, blind; my lips are ready to confess, but my heart is slow to feel, and my ways reluctant to amend.
>
> Give me grace to bewail my insensate folly, grant me to know that the way of transgressors is hard, that evil paths are wretched paths, that to depart from thee is to lose all good.
>
> I have seen the purity and beauty of thy perfect law, the happiness of those in whose heart it reigns, the calm dignity of the walk to which it calls, yet I daily violate and condemn its precepts.
>
> All these sins I mourn, lament, and for them cry pardon. Work in me more profound and abiding repentance; give me the fullness of a godly grief that trembles and fears, yet ever trusts and loves, which is ever powerful, and ever confident; grant that through the tears of repentance I may see more clearly the brightness and glories of the saving cross (Bennett, p. 70).

Sin always develops from a root of disrespect. By comparison, confession and its accompanying repentance always spring from a high view of God and an awe of his holiness. In response to Ezra's public prayer contrasting God's faithfulness with Israel's habitual waywardness, many people within the Jewish community joined him in mourning their sins. Their brokenness before God became the first step in restoring the community to its calling as God's people.

II. COMMENTARY

Crisis of Faith

> **MAIN IDEA:** *In a community of faith, the behavior of its members, even if a minority, profoundly influences the character of the group. Sin always destroys. To ignore its presence is to fuel its power.*

A A Consensus (10:1–6)

> **SUPPORTING IDEA:** *A group gathered around Ezra during his public humiliation and prayer. These people joined in demonstrations of sorrow over the sins of Israel. As a result, they agreed upon the next step of action.*

1. A crowd gathers (10:1)

10:1. The written record switches from Ezra's personal journal to third-person narration. Clearly Ezra was troubled because certain Jews had married women from the pagan cultures of the area. He viewed these marriages as a breach of Israel's covenant to remain separate and holy unto God.

It seems that Ezra recognized the power of a public action. He prostrated himself **before the house of God** in an outer court of the temple. Rather than dealing with the situation in private, either by himself or with a few select leaders, Ezra brought the issue into the open. As a result, a cross-section of the public responded, including women and children, and **they too wept bitterly**. It became a matter of concern for the community, especially the devout: those "who trembled at the words of the God of Israel" (Ezra 9:4). Ezra gained support for his following actions.

2. A plan proposed (10:2–4)

10:2–3. From the crowd stepped **Shecaniah**, acting as official spokesman for those gathered in the temple court. It was probably not as spontaneous as it might appear. In his speech to Ezra, he indicated that discussions preceded the formal public acknowledgment.

Shecaniah was the **son of Jehiel, one of the descendants of Elam**. The clan of Elam was among the first exiles to leave Babylon at the time of King Cyrus (Ezra 2:7). Some interpreters conjecture that Shecaniah's father was the same Jehiel mentioned in Ezra 10:26. This is doubtful since he would have come from a forbidden mixed marriage. Both names were common at that time and probably had no connection to the Jehiel found guilty of intermarriage.

Like Ezra, Shecaniah identified with the misdeeds of the minority and publicly acknowledged, **We have been unfaithful to our God by marrying**

foreign women. The term for "unfaithful" refers to the breaking of a covenant. Covenantal pledges formed the bonds of relationship between Israel and God; on the basis of these sacred agreements promises were fulfilled or curses enacted. Shecaniah also saw the prospect of amelioration through a new covenant: **there is still hope for Israel. Now let us make a covenant before our God**. That which indicted them might also free them.

So Shecaniah offered a plan **to send away all these women and their children**. Plainly, for those living with pagan wives, this meant divorce. The plan was not constructed quickly or in the emotion of the moment. It seems to have evolved through deliberations between Ezra (**the counsel of my lord**) and community leaders (**those who fear the commands of our God**). Shecaniah ended his proposal by stating, **Let it be done according to the Law**.

The law, in this case, may refer to the concessions of Deuteronomy 24:1–4 in which a man could divorce his wife if he found "something indecent about her." Since the foreign women were now deemed "unclean," a formal divorce would then be "lawful." Shecaniah might, however, simply have meant that the people should proceed according to the spirit of the law that prohibited marriage outside the faith.

10:4. Shecaniah told Ezra, **Rise up; this matter is in your hands**. He acknowledged Ezra's authority to deal with the situation. The first step of public admission was complete. Backed by the leadership—**we will support you, so take courage and do it**—Ezra was encouraged to take the next step. Rather than forced compliance, Ezra desired willing change.

3. The oath (10:5–6)

10:5. Ezra ended his public mourning by putting **the leading priests and Levites and all Israel under oath to do what had been suggested**. As chief magistrate, Ezra took Shecaniah's proposal and offered it publicly. If the process was to continue to resolution, all those involved needed firm commitment to the end. An oath bound them to follow through. In this instance, "all Israel" applied only to those representatives of the nation who were in the temple area at the time. These **took the oath**. The occasion for the collective community to respond came later.

10:6. Then **Ezra withdrew** from the crowd and the temple court and retired to **the room of Jehohanan son of Eliashib**. Some interpreters contend these two men represent a high priestly line, others that they came from a family of temple caretakers. Since no further clarification is offered by the author, it seems a fine point to argue. No doubt Jehohanan served the temple in some office.

A person's private life reveals inner character far more accurately than public performance. Ezra's civic mourning was not mere formality. Away from the crowd, he maintained a fast before God: **he ate no food and drank no** water. His anguish was genuine and deeply felt, and he **continued to mourn over the unfaithfulness of the exiles**. The "exiles" refers to the whole nation, not only those who returned from captive lands.

🄱 The Assembly (10:7–15)

> **SUPPORTING IDEA:** *Change proves far more effective if it comes from personal conviction rather than outside imposition. The nation was assembled to confront the intermarriage issue and to decide on the divorce proposal.*

4. The proclamation (10:7–8)

10:7–8. Ezra preferred to administer justice through communal consensus. Having secured an oath of agreement from the Jewish leaders, he next had a verbal **proclamation** sent by heralds throughout Judea **for all the exiles to assemble**.

Official assemblies such as this had precedent in Jewish history and served as a type of mandatory conference during which opinions could be voiced between the people and their leaders. The assembly was required, and **anyone who failed to appear within three days would forfeit all his property**. Community life and character were at stake, and this required the involvement of everyone.

As chief magistrate under commission by Artaxerxes, Ezra had the legal authority to punish those who did not comply with decrees and laws. Among the penalties allowed by the Persian king (Ezra 7:26), confiscation of property and banishment seemed most suited to Ezra's methods. Anyone found in contempt of the order would lose his property; it would transfer to the temple as property belonging to the Lord. In addition, he would **be expelled from the assembly of the exiles**. Those who disobeyed the proclamation would be excommunicated from the holy nation.

5. The gathering (10:9–15)

10:9. Ezra never had to exact any punishment; everyone showed up: **Within the three days, all the men of Judah and Benjamin had gathered in Jerusalem**. If these events occurred within the larger context of Ezra's reading of the law (Neh. 8), then the people's sensitivity to God's commands was already heightened, creating a desire for obedience.

It was the **ninth month**, some time in December, and the winter rains were frequent and, at times, quite heavy. After traveling along the muddy routes to Jerusalem, the people sat **in the square before the house of God, greatly distressed by the occasion and because of the rain**. One can envision a great mass of men, rain soaked and cold, waiting to discuss a depressing and weighty matter. To add to the solemnity, they assembled at the same spot where Ezra had voiced his public prayer and performed his acts of mourning; it was also the place where, a couple of months before, they had stood to hear him read the law.

10:10. Once again, **Ezra the priest stood up**. No doubt they thought back to his reading of the law; they must have recalled how that former day ended in great celebration and praise to God. But two months later the scene was one of dreary foreboding.

Ezra explained the situation: **You have been unfaithful; you have married foreign women**. Of the thousands gathered, only a relative handful was guilty as charged (a little over one hundred). Even so, Ezra indicted the whole community. Sin always has a long reach of culpability because sin rarely indulges itself alone. The people were guilty of communal negligence.

10:11. Ezra charged the people, **Now make confession to the LORD**—literally, praise the Lord. Confession, admitting and mourning sin's subversion and wrongness, becomes a declaration of praise because it acknowledges God as true and just. In admitting guilt a person admits the worthiness of God's law. But words of confession mark only the beginning. Beyond that, the will must be redirected because sin, at its root, rejects God's will. So Ezra urged the people to do God's will. Actions in harmony with God's revelation and nature confirm repentance.

Ezra concluded his remarks by emphasizing the need for spiritual distinctiveness; the marriage issue resulted from a larger problem of compromise. The crisis had developed from relaxed attitudes toward the cultures around them. Therefore, Ezra aimed his directive at the entire assembly, telling them to **separate . . . from the peoples around you**. Ezra and the leaders urged the people to divorce their **foreign wives**.

This decision stands in marked contrast to the teachings of the New Testament. Jesus clearly prohibited divorce except in instances of immorality (Matt. 5:32); Paul, within the framework of certain concessions, instructed Christians to refrain from divorce, even if married to an unbeliever (1 Cor. 7:12–17). However, to Ezra and the other leaders, the survival of the Jewish faith and community seemed at risk. Drastic measures were needed to purify the community from a growing corruption.

10:12–14. The response of the assembly was a resounding, **We must do as you say**. Rather than make hasty decisions that would disrupt lives, the assembly offered a proposal of their own: **Let our officials act for the whole assembly**. They transferred the power of decision from the collective to their established leaders. In effect, they proposed a commission, or grand jury. From each town these men would summon to Jerusalem anyone who had **married a foreign woman**. The commission would review each case individually, assisted by the village **elders and judges** who could testify about those under investigation.

The assembly concluded with the hope that the plan would prove sufficient to turn away **the fierce anger of our God in this matter.** God's anger was assumed because of the breaking of covenantal faith.

10:15. From the assembly came two dissenting voices: **Jonathan son of Asahel and Jahzeiah son of Tikvah.** These laymen, supported by **Meshullam and Shabbethai the Levite,** opposed the proposal. Meshullam had traveled to Jerusalem with Ezra and had been instrumental in recruiting Levites to join the caravan (Ezra 8:16). He remained a strong leader among the exiles and was supportive of Ezra at the public reading of the law (Neh. 8:4). Shabbethai was a well-regarded Levite. He, too, had assisted during Ezra's reading of the law by instructing the people in its meaning (Neh. 8:7–8).

Most scholars believe that these four men opposed not the divorces but the proposed method by which a commission would decide each case. These men wanted an immediate ruling rather than a prolonged process.

The Commission (10:16–17)

> **SUPPORTING IDEA:** *Ezra appointed a commission to investigate the cases of intermarriage.*

10:16–17. The majority opinion was followed. Consequently, **Ezra the priest selected men who were family heads** to form the official investigative group. He placed the decision-making authority in the hands of community leaders. Each appointee headed a family, and each family was represented.

Ezra lost little time in forming the commission and putting it to work: **On the first day of the tenth month they sat down to investigate the cases.** The first case was brought before the group approximately ten days after the national assembly. It took about three months for them to complete their work, ending **on the first day of the first month.**

The Guilty (10:18–44)

> **SUPPORTING IDEA:** *With completion of the commission's work, an official listing was entered into the record of those found guilty of marrying pagan women.*

10:18–24. The results of the commission's investigation were listed. Those found guilty were recorded by family, starting with officials of the temple and continuing in descending order to the laity. The list begins with **the descendants of Jeshua son of Jozadak**—the high priestly clan—and continues through the clans of priests, Levites, singers, and gatekeepers.

They all gave their hands in pledge to put away their wives. Though the statement occurs only after the high priestly line, most likely it refers to all those found guilty.

Each also **presented a ram from the flock as a guilt offering**. Leviticus 5:17–18 states, "If a person sins and does what is forbidden in any of the Lord's commands, even though he does not know it, he is guilty and will be held responsible. He is to bring to the priest as a guilt offering a ram from the flock." These marriages were not acts of defiance, rebellion, or willful disregard of God's commands. Because these men violated no specific law, they sinned "unintentionally" (Lev. 5:15).

10:25–43. The other Israelites were listed after the temple leaders. These were common citizens within Judea. Many of the family names found here also appear in the list of Ezra 2 and were among the first exiles to leave Babylon. One expects such a similarity because enough time would have to elapse for these men to settle in the region and marry.

10:44. The Book of Ezra concludes abruptly yet poignantly. Having penned the last name, the author added, **all these had married foreign women, and some of them had children by these wives**. The community was purified, but at the price of severed relationships and "fatherless" children.

> **MAIN IDEA REVIEW:** *In a community of faith, the behavior of its members, even if a minority, profoundly influences the character of the group. Sin always destroys. To ignore its presence is to fuel its power.*

III. CONCLUSION

Buried Treasure

The Book of Ezra narrates the spiritual development and reorganization of the postexilic Jews under the Mosaic law. It spreads before the reader a history, complete with principal and minor players, dates, and events; it includes daring, cowardice, opposition, and intrigue. The book ends in cultural and spiritual confrontation as the issues of Jewish identity, sin, and righteousness demand communal and personal decisions.

But the people had to resolve their questions without the aid of a miraculous twist of nature, or a thunderous voice from the mountain, or a fire to illuminate their way. Instead these people were left with a book. So they read of distant times and of people who, even to them, were known as ancients. They opened the histories and early law books to help them navigate the spiritual and social issues involved. But this led to a new set of difficulties because they lived in a context different from that described in their holy writings. The nation no longer existed. Their neighbors originated from nations not mentioned in the Mosaic commands. Their specific situation was not addressed.

Ezra, however, believed firmly in the adequacy of God's revelation. Consequently, he practiced scriptural interpretation. From the stories he extracted principles that reached across the years and epochs; he looked to historical specifics to discover ageless, universal doctrines. Then he returned to the particular, applying what he understood to daily life.

The practice has continued through the centuries to this day. It requires caution and prayer and the counsel of the complete Scriptures in light of the context. But through divine wisdom we, too, must dig beneath the details of biblical texts and expose the eternal so that, like Ezra, we can bring it back to earth through practical use.

PRINCIPLES

- God's values often conflict with culture.
- Christian distinction results from an inner change and requires new habits of thought and behavior.
- Sin's consequences often continue even though forgiven.
- Obedience to God requires more than following religious forms, rituals, or duties.
- Scripture addresses the needs of life; it is our source for knowing how to live well.

APPLICATIONS

- When other Christians fail or sin, treat them with understanding and fairness but also with a love that holds them to the high call of following Christ.
- Confession of sin opens the door to forgiveness, but remember that authentic repentance involves acts of obedience and change.
- Remember that it is never too late to obey God.
- Study the Bible; it will make you wise and equip you for life (2 Tim. 3:16–17).

IV. LIFE APPLICATION

Warnings and Guideposts

Ezra's primary achievement in his day was restoring the law as the standard for life and conduct within the community. His example of scriptural application and understanding remains timeless. As Paul wrote, "All Scripture is God-breathed and is useful for teaching, rebuking, correcting and training in righteousness, so that the man of God may be thoroughly equipped for every good work" (2 Tim. 3:16–17). In our own efforts to understand biblical truth and apply its principles to daily life, basic methods and standards must be followed in order to guard against error.

First, since men wrote the Bible, we should seek the meaning of the text in the same way we would any other piece of writing. The tools of language and literature follow conventional processes, and we should not discard them when looking at the Bible. As David L. Cooper of the Biblical Research Society wrote: "When the plain sense of Scripture makes common sense, seek no other sense. Take every word at its primary, ordinary, usual, literal meaning unless the facts of the immediate context, studied in the light of related passages and axiomatic and fundamental truths, indicate clearly otherwise."

In other words, unless Scripture indicates otherwise, the words used by the Bible should be understood in their common, accepted meanings. Scripture interprets Scripture, and if neither the author nor any other biblical text qualifies, interprets, or points to secondary meanings, we should not either.

Second, context controls interpretation. The intent of the author regulates our understanding. There are three main contexts to consider:

1. *The context of the whole book.* To whom was it written, and what was the author's purpose in writing? For instance, the intent of Romans is very different from that of James. Paul wrote to proclaim salvation as a work of grace through faith in Christ; James wrote in order to combat particular heresies and to defend salvation as inseparable from works. Both authors had particular audiences in mind, and both addressed specific needs. Even so, both writers presented harmonious truth. It is critical to understand the perspective and purpose of the author, and then relate it to other clear teachings in Scripture on the same subject.

2. *The context of the paragraph or immediate passage.* What do the surrounding verses say? What is the issue or event current to the time in which it was written? Often word studies prove beneficial when interpreting a particular text. But historical background and social context can aid understanding, too.

3. *The context of the Bible itself.* Scripture will never contradict itself.

Ezra was devoted to knowing and practicing the law, as well as instructing the Jewish people in its meaning and requirements (Ezra 7:10). Though particular stipulations of the law no longer apply since their fulfillment was completed in Christ, the Word of God continues as the basis for life and godliness. To study the Bible carefully and then to apply its message diligently is essential for all believers.

V. PRAYER

Father, your commands are beautiful. Give us discernment so that we can detect the subtle entrapments of sin. Then form your will in ours so that we lovingly embrace the goodness of your ways. Amen.

VI. DEEPER DISCOVERIES

Covenant (10:3)

The word *covenant* comes from the Hebrew root word *berith,* meaning "to cut or cleave." It probably evolved from the covenant of Genesis 15 in which Abraham was instructed to cut some animals in two after which fire, representing the presence of God, passed between the parts. By this God's covenant with Abraham was ratified. It was later expanded with additional requirements, first of circumcision and then the law.

The first recorded covenant, however, was with Noah. This was not so much a contract as a disclosure of God's intent, a promise made by God to humanity. In this covenant God assured mankind that he would not again destroy life through a great flood (Gen. 9:11). It was sealed by the display of a rainbow, not an animal sacrifice.

With the increasing complexity of society and the formalizing of religious practice, biblical covenants between God and man acquired stronger contractual elements. With God's faithfulness proven, increasingly the integrity of the agreement depended on the people's adherence and faithfulness to particular stipulations. Disobedience broke the agreement and revoked its blessings.

The new covenant established through the sacrificial blood of Christ depends on a type of contractual agreement too, because the blessing of God comes into effect by the corresponding faith of an individual. And while obedience does not attain the covenantal blessing, obedience is expected as evidence of good faith. The remembrance meal of bread and wine symbolizes the flesh and blood of Christ, and our eating it symbolizes the acceptance of this covenant.

VII. TEACHING OUTLINE

A. INTRODUCTION

1. Lead Story: Yet I Sin
2. Context: Shortly after Ezra's arrival in Jerusalem, a national assembly convened for the reading of the law. This was a necessary precursor

for establishing the law in social and religious life. The people responded with contrition as they were taught God's Word and its meaning.

3. Transition: Two months after the public reading of the law, the issue of intermarriage with pagan peoples required another national assembly. This time the community was faced with the practical implication of the law's principles.

B. COMMENTARY

1. A Consensus (10:1–6)
   a. A crowd gathers (10:1)
   b. A plan proposed (10:2–4)
   c. The oath (10:5–6)
2. The Assembly (10:7–15)
   a. The proclamation (10:7–8)
   b. The gathering (10:9–15)
3. The Commission (10:16–17)
4. The Guilty (10:18–44)

C. CONCLUSION: BURIED TREASURE

VIII. ISSUES FOR DISCUSSION

1. What are proper steps for restoration after sin, and what is the role of the church?
2. Is community, or whole-church, confession of sin useful? Why or why not?
3. Discuss some practical ways Christians can be distinctive from the surrounding culture.
4. How can the church and individual believers safeguard against legalism?

Introduction to

Nehemiah

AUTHORSHIP

- Taken primarily from Nehemiah's memoirs, though additional texts are inserted (chs. 8–10).
- Nehemiah was a Jewish leader who had attained status in the Persian court as cupbearer to King Artaxerxes.
- Written about events around 446 B.C.
- Written to the returned exiles and citizens of Judah and Jerusalem.

THEMES

- A history of God's faithfulness and the emerging religious character of Judah and Jerusalem.
- A handbook for leadership.
- A great picture of teamwork by the people of Judah as they followed the leadership of Nehemiah.
- Nehemiah demonstrates a careful and righteous response to opposition.
- The book repeatedly highlights God's sovereignty as he works together with his people.
- Prayer and hard work are not mutually exclusive but cooperative elements in serving God.

Nehemiah 1

CR 𝒥

A Worthy Pursuit

Quote

*N*othing in this world is so powerful

as an idea whose time has come.

V i c t o r   H u g o

Nehemiah 1

I N   A   N U T S H E L L

*N*ehemiah was a servant in the intimate circle of King Artaxerxes. As such, he knew that the Persian government had sanctioned actions against Jerusalem. When he learned the full extent of the violence
the Judean Jews had suffered, he was grieved for his people. He sought
God's grace for devising a plan to restore the holy city.

A Worthy Pursuit

I. INTRODUCTION

A Good Question

*T*hey were getting on my nerves. I was a freshman in college, and about seven other students kept asking their friends and classmates (me included), "What's your dominant purpose in life?"

I was just trying to make the basketball team and maybe have a few dates and get my studies done. Sometimes my purpose was to get through the next test, or to play a decent game, or to be liked by my peers. I remember retorting something like, "You guys should get a life." But even though their question was way too philosophical for a freshman, it kept echoing in my head and heart.

The more I have lived, and the more choices I have made and watched others make, the more I realize how important their question is. Unless we have a dominant purpose to glorify God and do his will as revealed in Scripture, we will make some terrible decisions and never achieve the true purpose for which we were made.

Nehemiah is a great example of someone whose desire was to please God and glorify him. His intentions and aspirations were God-focused rather than self-focused. God defined his dominant purpose. When he heard that the walls of Jerusalem were broken down and God's people were living in distress, that driving purpose kicked in. Nehemiah prayed a profound prayer of praise, adoration, submission, and request.

Read this first chapter of Nehemiah and watch what stirred Nehemiah's passions; follow his prayer and notice whom he identified with. Read his prayer out loud and see if it resonates with your own sympathies and concerns. Then ask yourself, "What is my dominant purpose in life?"

II. COMMENTARY

A Worthy Pursuit

> **MAIN IDEA:** *Though he lived in Persia, Nehemiah identified with his fellow Jews, particularly those living in Jerusalem. Passionate for God's glory and driven by empathy, Nehemiah turned to God.*

A The Report (1:1–3)

> **SUPPORTING IDEA:** *Nehemiah took the initiative by asking some recently returned travelers about the welfare of the Jews living in Jerusalem.*

1:1. From the start the reader gains access to the memoirs of an ancient court official and embarks on a journey into the world of Persia and Judea in the mid-fifth century B.C.; we study **the words of Nehemiah son of Hacaliah**.

Nehemiah provided no further family history. Instead, his story began **in the month of Kislev in the twentieth year**. Nehemiah 2:1 makes clear that it was the twentieth year of King Artaxerxes's reign, or about 446 B.C. Since Nehemiah noted that he **was in the citadel of Susa**, the winter residence of the Persian kings, we understand immediately that he held some official position in the Persian court. Most probably, then, Nehemiah calculated his dates based on the Persian royal calendar rather than the calendar year. The Persian court system placed Kislev as the fifth month and Nisan as the ninth.

1:2–3. Nehemiah received some visitors: **Hanani, one of my brothers . . . with some other men**. These travelers had come **from Judah**. It remains uncertain whether Hanani was a resident of Judah or was returning from a trip to the region. If Hanani did live near Jerusalem, then Nehemiah's interests were deeply personal, further explaining his intense emotions and concern.

Evidently Nehemiah took the initiative and **questioned them about the Jewish remnant that survived the exile**. His eager concern extended to all the Jews, those who had remained in Judah during the exile period, and those who had returned by the various caravans throughout the Persian period. Nehemiah asked **also about Jerusalem**.

It seems apparent that Nehemiah had reason for his inquiry—perhaps rumor or official knowledge of imperial activity in the region. As a member of the king's personal staff, Nehemiah probably knew about Artaxerxes's judgment against Jerusalem and his capitulation to hostile forces around Judea (Ezra 4). Consequently, he was anxious to know how the people and the city were doing.

He was told that the Jews were **in great trouble and disgrace. The wall of Jerusalem is broken down, and its gates have been burned with fire.** This describes the strong response effected by Jerusalem's neighbors after they persuaded Artaxerxes to stop restoration work in Jerusalem: "They went immediately to the Jews in Jerusalem and compelled them by force to stop" (Ezra 4:23).

⃟ Nehemiah Prays (1:4–11)

SUPPORTING IDEA: *Before formulating a plan or recruiting support, Nehemiah's first response was to go before God in prayer.*

1:4. After hearing about Jerusalem and the firsthand report of its ruin, Nehemiah **sat down and wept.** His sympathy for the Jews was deep and his emotion was intense when he learned of their suffering. Accordingly, he **mourned and fasted and prayed before the God of heaven,** making his appeal to the one who rules over the affairs of all people. And while Nehemiah's response followed a predictable and orthodox pattern—fasting and prayer—his expressions of grief and concern were sincere. Nehemiah's genuine anxiety for his people was demonstrated by his persistence, seeking God's favor and help for more than four months before an opportunity opened for him to speak or act (Neh. 2:1).

1:5–11b. Though Nehemiah prayed for more than four months, he wrote in his journal a prayer representative of all he offered before God's throne. He began with adoration: **O LORD, God of heaven, the great and awesome God.** He lifted his heart in worship, acknowledging God's greatness. In prayer we speak to the God who rules over all the heavens and, therefore, over all the earth. God **keeps his covenant of love with those who love him and obey his commands.** A covenantal relationship binds both parties; the promises apply to those who live in loving conformity to the pledge.

In prayer we approach the unapproachable because God exists in perfect faithfulness and love. Yet these very qualities give hope, and they gave Nehemiah the courage to ask God to listen and respond: **Let your ear be attentive and your eyes open to hear the prayer your servant is praying.** He asked not only that God listen but that he act.

Nehemiah offered confession for **the sins we Israelites, including myself and my father's house, have committed against you.** In full identification with the Jews, and in full recognition of sin's insidious grip upon the human heart, Nehemiah acknowledged his own guilt and that of his family. His prayer confessed no particular sins but the tendency toward disobedience of which all people are guilty.

Nehemiah embraced God's judgments as just: **We have acted very wickedly toward you. We have not obeyed the commands, decrees and laws you**

He waited for the right opportunity. Leaders need patience

gave your servant Moses. Nehemiah had the whole Deuteronomic law in view, and he indicted himself and the Jewish people for breaching the law's intents, commands, and spirit.

Remember the instruction you gave your servant Moses. Nehemiah did not suppose that God had forgotten or that his memory needed rousing. Instead, in a condensed version of Deuteronomy 30, he affirmed God's power and dependability by placing the Jews' waywardness against the light of what God declared through Moses long ago: **If you are unfaithful, I will scatter you among the nations**. God was, indeed, true to his word, and the seventy-year exile was proof.

However, along with Moses' warnings were blessings, and Nehemiah recalled these as a means of transitioning to his prayerful petition: **But if you return to me and obey my commands, then even if your exiled people are at the farthest horizon, I will gather them from there**. Nehemiah implied that the return had begun, evidenced by the resettlement of Judah and Jerusalem. The revival of religious worship in the rebuilt temple was also underway.

Based on God's proven power and faithfulness to his word, to punish and bless, Nehemiah asked God to act on the people's behalf: **They are your servants and your people, whom you redeemed by your great strength and your mighty hand**. Nehemiah asked God to take action in conformity with his word, his character, and his past grace.

Eight times the term *servant* appears in Nehemiah's prayer, in reference either to himself, the Jewish people, or Moses. Those who served the Lord were equal in privilege and position before the great sovereign ruler of the universe. Nehemiah concluded his prayer as he began it, acknowledging himself as God's **servant**, and asking God to attend to the **prayer of your servants who delight in revering your name**. It was the one thing he could offer—a servant's heart and willingness. With reverential submission he asked God to **give your servant success . . . by granting him favor in the presence of this man**.

Nehemiah was willing to wait, knowing that God alone could move the heart and spirit of "this man"—King Artaxerxes. It required the reversal of a previous edict and a sympathetic audience with a powerful potentate. Only the God of heaven could bring the players of the drama together at the proper time and in the proper way.

1:11c. The concluding portion of verse 11—**I was cupbearer to the king**—sits like a footnote at the chapter's end and seems to belong more appropriately to Nehemiah 2:1. Even so, this simple line leads the reader into the subsequent action and explains Nehemiah's access to the king. Royal cupbearers were responsible for choosing and serving the king's wine and tasting it in order to safeguard the king from conspiratorial poisonings.

In addition, because he was close to the king, the cupbearer was expected to provide cheerful company. Some interpreters believe the ancient cupbearer had considerable influence with the king by way of his unofficial conversation and counsel.

> **MAIN IDEA REVIEW:** *Though he lived in Persia, Nehemiah identified with his fellow Jews, particularly those living in Jerusalem. Passionate for God's glory and driven by empathy, Nehemiah turned to God.*

III. CONCLUSION

Tears

What makes us cry?

I've watched championship football or basketball games where, as the final seconds ticked down and the players realized their defeat, they cried. I've seen a game show where the winning contestant burst into tears because he or she won!

People cry during movies or while listening to a song. They cry for profound reasons or for no apparent reason at all. It can be simple or complex, sorrowful or petty. Or perhaps we are among those who don't believe in showing our feelings. Perhaps nothing moves us to tears.

Nehemiah sat down and cried because the wall of Jerusalem was broken down and its gates were burned. He suffered in his soul because God's city and his people were treated with contempt. The hardships of his countrymen moved him. He was troubled by the sins of his people and his own implication in all that Israel had endured.

Human emotions are rich, and they reflect part of the image of God that we bear. But it might do us well to consider what bothers us, what stirs the deep well of our emotions.

How many times do our sins, or the failures of others, unsettle us to the point of such caring? Are we passionate for God's reputation and that of his church? Are we distressed and driven to prayer on behalf of our brothers and sisters in Christ around the world who suffer for their faith?

What, indeed, makes us cry?

PRINCIPLES

- God is faithful, constant, and unchanging.
- God forgives over and over again.
- True worship leads to obedience.
- Only God can change a person's heart.

APPLICATIONS

- While you can boldly approach God in prayer, take time to acknowledge God's glory, his thoughts and wisdom, and the wonder of his love and grace.
- Don't be afraid to worship God through silence, fasting, and extended times of prayer.
- Read through one of the Gospels, or the Psalms, writing down God's promises.
- Write down one thing in which you need to obey God, then commit to doing it in God's strength.

IV. LIFE APPLICATION

Do You Know Whom You're Talking To?

Whom do you talk to when you pray?

C. S. Lewis once observed that a great many Christians pray not to the God who is but to a "composite object containing many quite ridiculous ingredients." The "composite object," as he termed it, might be constructed from bits and pieces of our own imagination and biblical fact; or it might be a synthesis of medieval art, bookish opinion, and television. We may even pray to some hazy notion because we have never truly come to terms with his revelation.

Nehemiah's prayer was strong because he knew who God is: "O LORD, God of heaven, the great and awesome God, who keeps his covenant of love with those who love him and obey his commands" (Neh. 1:5).

How do we begin?

Nehemiah also understood his own position, and that of all the Jews: "hear the prayer your *servant* is praying before you day and night for your *servants,* the people of Israel" (Neh. 1:6, emphasis added). Nehemiah understood his humble standing before the reigning sovereign of the universe. He knew that he and all God's people lived for God's service.

Then, because he recognized the vast difference between the Creator and the created, Nehemiah confessed his sins and those of his people. God's holiness was not to be ignored; it formed the essence of his being.

Nehemiah's accurate understanding of God led him from confession to request. Though Israel had sinned, and though God was great and powerful, Nehemiah lived in hope. He recalled God's promise to his people—to bring them back to the land of his covenant. He recounted God's faithfulness in the past. He depended on God's continued love for the people he had redeemed by his great strength (Neh. 1:10).

In our modern world, it is easy to become bored—to yawn at sunsets, to miss the wonder of a new baby, to barely notice the stars above our heads. Even the emotions and joys of love can be taken for granted. But there is in all of us a great need to turn to God in worship—to stand in awe and adoration of the one who is greater than ourselves, to understand the truth of his supremacy and his condescension. An acceptance of God as he is leads us to willing obedience and a compelling drive to do his will.

V. PRAYER

Oh Lord, the God of heaven, the great and awesome God, who keeps his covenant of love with those who love him and obey his commands, let your ear be attentive and your eyes open to hear the prayer your servants are praying before you. God, please grant us your favor. We have needs. We have burdens. We seek to care about what you care about. Amen.

VI. DEEPER DISCOVERIES

A. Vision (1:4–11)

Adolph Hitler reportedly said, "What luck for rulers that men do not think."

Sadly, even if not overtly expressed, many leaders hold that same attitude. But such a condescending outlook creates a dangerous arrogance that will eventually drive the leader to assume more control than lies within his prerogatives. Eventually he undermines his own ability to lead effectively, destroying the vision he proclaimed so passionately.

Nehemiah was a thoughtful man, ignited by a vision for God's glory. But his objectives were not self-determined; they rose out of God's law and purposes. Because of this, Nehemiah prayed for and cared for the people he sought to help. As Nehemiah's story develops, it becomes apparent that he wanted people to think and to carefully and purposefully consider their lives and choices. While he led with strength and resolve, he desired that the citizens of Jerusalem and Judah turn their thoughts and hearts back to God and his eternal designs for them. They had become enmeshed in the daily business and busyness of life; Nehemiah wanted to point them to a future founded on God's sovereign love and holiness.

Living intentionally, with thought and purpose in all we do, is hard work for most of us. We become focused on immediacy rather than assuming a "long-sighted" view of life. Yet the life of purpose is designed to "live for the line instead of the dot," as Randy Alcorn states in *The Treasure Principle*. It is the eternal, not the transitory, that truly matters. Godly leaders ignite a vision for these profound truths in others; they provoke people to question and think and to return to the truths of God.

B. History (1:1)

People sometimes wonder why there are so many details in the Bible that, to our modern thinking, seem so unimportant. Why all the listings of names and genealogical records? Why the naming of cities and small towns that have long since disappeared? Why did Nehemiah write down in his memoirs that his story began "in the month of Kislev"? We don't even use the same calendar any more. After all, do you know someone with a birthday in Kislev?

Most importantly for us, reading over two thousand years later—this is history. These are facts, real events, recorded times.

Many treat the Scriptures as so many nice stories or mythology. We have so-called biblical scholars debating what to accept as true and what to regard as legends or Jewish propaganda. But the Bible is primarily a historical record that reveals the sinfulness of humankind and God's gracious response and plan. We are warned against overly spiritualizing biblical texts by the stark reminder that these stories were not allegories. Nehemiah sat down to write about real events that began in the twentieth year of King Artaxerxes's reign over the Persian Empire, in the month of Kislev.

VII. TEACHING OUTLINE

A. INTRODUCTION

1. Lead Story: A Good Question
2. Context: At some point in Artaxerxes's reign, agitators from Samaria and other parts of Trans-Euphrates wrote letters against the reconstruction efforts in Jerusalem. Convinced that Jerusalem posed a potential political threat, the king enlisted the disgruntled neighbors around Judea to halt the Jews' work, destroying the walls and torching the gates.
3. Transition: In the aftermath of this military repression, Nehemiah's brother, along with other Jewish companions, traveled from Jerusalem to Persia. Upon their arrival at the royal citadel in Susa, Nehemiah inquired about the welfare of the Jews and conditions in Judea.

B. COMMENTARY

1. The Report (1:1–3)
2. Nehemiah Prays (1:4–11)

C. CONCLUSION: TEARS

VIII. ISSUES FOR DISCUSSION

1. Is fasting a useful or beneficial counterpart to prayer today? If so, what purpose does it serve?

2. Does God's response to our prayers depend upon us in any way? What about his promises? Can we negate his promises by the way we live?

3. Review Nehemiah's prayer, and see if you can identify three or four essential elements that would help you in your own praying.

4. Discuss the relationship between waiting on God and taking responsibility for planning and acting in accordance with good sense. Are they mutually exclusive? Can both approaches be combined to arrive at a wise decision or action? Explain.

Nehemiah 2

Preparation

I. INTRODUCTION
What Lies Beneath

II. COMMENTARY
A verse-by-verse explanation of the chapter.

III. CONCLUSION
When You're Down

An overview of the pinciples and applications from the chapter.

IV. LIFE APPLICATION
Roads to Nowhere

Melding the chapter to life.

V. PRAYER
Tying the chapter to life with God.

VI. DEEPER DISCOVERIES
Historical, geographical, and grammatical enrichment of the commentary.

VII. TEACHING OUTLINE
Suggested step-by-step group study of the chapter.

VIII. ISSUES FOR DISCUSSION
Zeroing the chapter in on daily life.

*O*pportunity is missed by most people because it is dressed in overalls and looks like work.

Thomas A. Edison

Nehemiah 2

IN A NUTSHELL

*N*ehemiah stood before King Artaxerxes with a sad face—a capital offense in ancient Persia. But God granted him favor, and the king not only listened to Nehemiah but also allowed him a leave of absence in order to rebuild Jerusalem's walls. When Nehemiah arrived in Judah, he inspected the walls at night to assess the work that lay ahead. He then called the Jewish leaders together to present his plan.

Preparation

I. INTRODUCTION

What Lies Beneath

*S*pringtime is amazing. And it's all the more fascinating because, in the Midwest, it grows out of one of the dreariest times of the year.

Late winter in Ohio can be a bit bleak. The sky is overcast, the snow has turned sooty, the black-barked trees streak the horizon, and the roadways are clogged with slush. It's not good for snowmen or skiing.

But during this idle time, when by all appearances nothing much is happening, a dynamic energy roars underground. Chemical changes begin, cells reproduce, an outer covering splits, and a shoot pushes against the soil. Who would suspect it? On the surface everything remains colorless and cold. But beneath, the spark of life, change, and renewal agitates. Then, one day, it breaks through, and a field blossoms in yellows, pinks, and purples.

Nehemiah, distressed by the report of Jerusalem's broken and miserable condition, approached God on behalf of the Judean Jews. He fasted, he prayed, he sought God's mercy and help. For four months he prayed and waited. All that time the walls of Jerusalem remained piles of rubble, and the gates remained scorched and burned. All that time he continued his service to King Artaxerxes, waiting upon the king in the court at Susa. Life on the surface remained unchanged.

But below the surface, where no one could see, the power of God was at work in the heart of the king, and Nehemiah was at work on a plan. In all his waiting, Nehemiah was never idle. He used those four months to calculate what he would do when he arrived in Jerusalem. He took advantage of the time to determine what supplies he would need. And at just the right time, God's power and Nehemiah's preparation converged, and a wall was eventually built around Jerusalem.

When we wait on God, it is a time of expectation that, despite appearances, God's power goes out to effect change. While we wait, we get ready. Together, a world, a nation, a life can be transformed.

II. COMMENTARY

Preparation

> **MAIN IDEA:** *Prayer and planning complement each other in working out God's will. While we depend on God's power and sovereign rule, we carefully organize plans that can further his purposes; while we wait we prepare.*

A Before the King (2:1–8)

When the opportunity opened for Nehemiah to speak to the king, he was ready with a proposal and a strategy for implementing his plans.

1. The opportunity (2:1–4)

2:1–2. Four months passed between Hanani's visit and Nehemiah's encounter with King Artaxerxes **in the month of Nisan in the twentieth year** of the king's reign. During the intervening winter days, Nehemiah had patiently but persistently prayed for God's favor on Jerusalem and on his own designs to rebuild the city's wall. He had vigilantly sought God while silently calculating his plan.

As a cupbearer, Nehemiah was responsible for serving wine to the king to assure its goodness and safety. Nehemiah's position within the royal court allowed him privileged access to the king. On such an occasion, perhaps at a banquet, Nehemiah **took the wine and gave it to the king**.

In his memoirs Nehemiah noted that he had not been sad in the king's presence before. Evidently, during his four months of fasting and prayer, Nehemiah had carefully maintained his composure and cheerful disposition; he had not revealed any anxiety or shown any mood change. Because of his evident control, many believe that Nehemiah purposely chose this particular time to lower his guard before the king, even though it meant great risk. Traditionally, the month of Nisan marked the beginning of the Persian year. New Year's celebrations were often accompanied by special favors and generosity from the king. Nehemiah may have decided that a festive time like this presented the best opportunity for him to ask a favor of the king.

The king, who immediately noticed Nehemiah's changed expression, asked, **Why does your face look so sad when you are not ill?** Such words from an Oriental potentate were not particularly comforting. Persian monarchs required that those who served them were not to bring personal troubles into their presence. Such a breach of protocol could signal conspiracy or disrespect. But Artaxerxes's next comment signaled a little hope for

Nehemiah because the king rightly interpreted his servant's disposition: **This can be nothing but sadness of heart**. Even so, Nehemiah **was very much afraid**.

2:3–4. Despite his fears, Nehemiah knew such an opportunity would not return. He addressed the king with ritual courtesy, **May the king live forever!** Then he answered the king with a rhetorical question: **Why should my face not look sad when the city where my fathers are buried lies in ruins, and its gates have been destroyed by fire?** He expected the king to understand the gravity of such a situation, as indeed he did. Respect for ancestral burial sites was of great concern to ancient peoples, particularly imperial rulers.

Mindful that Artaxerxes distrusted Jerusalem and the intentions of its inhabitants and that the king had authorized the destruction of its walls, Nehemiah avoided mentioning Jerusalem by name, referring to it only in general terms. He omitted reference to the walls of the city as well and spoke only about its gates. Nehemiah understood his audience, and he phrased his concern in terms most likely to gain a favorable response.

King Artaxerxes understood that Nehemiah was not simply venting his feelings or getting something "off his chest." The king knew that, in the language of the court, Nehemiah had something in mind, so he asked, **What is it you want?**

Nehemiah realized the critical stage of their interchange had arrived. Before another word was uttered, he **prayed to the God of heaven**. This is one of the few instances of silent prayer in the Old Testament. It was, perhaps, one of those urgent calls for help and mercy. It was only after speaking to the King of kings that he was prepared to answer the king of Persia.

2. Nehemiah's requests (2:5–8)

2:5. Nehemiah began with the formulaic phrases of court etiquette: **If it pleases the king and if your servant has found favor in his sight**. Nehemiah then quickly advanced to his request: **Send me to the city in Judah where my fathers are buried so that I can rebuild it**. Again, Jerusalem was not mentioned by name, nor did he refer to the walls of the city. Nehemiah petitioned the king in general terms and kept the focus on his personal desire to restore the city of his ancestors.

2:6. It is possible that a time gap occurred between Nehemiah's request and the king's response. Nehemiah wrote, **then the king, with the queen sitting beside him, asked me**. The action may have shifted to a more private and intimate setting, indicated by the presence of the queen. Did the king require time to think about Nehemiah's request? Or to consult his counselors? We cannot know, but Nehemiah may have thought it was important for the queen to be in attendance. Historians agree that Artaxerxes was greatly

[handwritten margin note: Nehemiah used the burial ground verbage to his advantage. He used carefully worded request. He didn't say the city of my God.]

influenced by women, and Damaspia's presence may have worked in Nehemiah's favor.

So the king asked, **How long will your journey take, and when will you get back?** Artaxerxes expected Nehemiah to complete his task and then return to his duties in the court. The king's question confirmed in Nehemiah's mind that **it pleased the king to send me; so I set a time.** In his own calculations and projections, it is doubtful that Nehemiah expected to be absent for twelve years, as he in fact was.

2:7–8. Nehemiah had not spent the last four months only in prayer. In anticipation of that moment before the king, he had carefully analyzed what he would need to carry out his plan; he had devised a proposal. Consequently, Nehemiah made further request of the king, asking for **letters to the governors of Trans-Euphrates, so that they will provide me safe-conduct until I arrive in Judah.**

Nehemiah was aware of the political situation in the regions through which he would travel. Though the governors, satraps, and lower officials were in service to the king, these same bureaucrats often exercised a great deal of personal power in their regions and were known to act independently at times. Nehemiah knew that officials from Trans-Euphrates had previously agitated for the destruction of Jerusalem's walls (Ezra 4) and had won the king's consent.

In addition, Nehemiah asked the king for supplies: **May I have a letter to Asaph, keeper of the king's forest, so he will give me timber?** Asaph is a Hebrew name. Quite possibly the steward of the royal forest was a Jew who, like Nehemiah, had risen to high rank. Nehemiah needed timber for three distinct projects.

First, he needed wood **to make beams for the gates of the citadel by the temple.** This was actually a fortress built slightly north of the temple by the returned exiles in order to guard the approach to the temple mount. Second, timber was required **for the city wall;** this was the first mention of the controversial wall that lay in ruins because of Artaxerxes's command. Perhaps Nehemiah quietly slipped it into the middle of his list in order not to draw attention. Third, he needed lumber **for the residence** he would occupy. Since Nehemiah did not anticipate a lengthy stay, he probably foresaw needed repair to his ancestral home based on the report of his brother, Hanani.

Nehemiah concluded that **because the gracious hand of my God was upon me, the king granted my requests.** He was convinced that none other than God himself could have moved the pagan monarch to reverse his previous decree, ruling in favor of every petition presented by his cupbearer.

Ⅱ The Plan Unfolds (2:9–20)

SUPPORTING IDEA: *With the king's full support, Nehemiah, with few details of the journey, arrived in Jerusalem to begin his ambitious project.*

3. From Persia to Judea (2:9–10)

2:9–10. Nehemiah left Persia and headed toward Jerusalem. Along the way he delivered the king's letters to the various governors through whose territory he passed. Almost as an aside, Nehemiah added that **the king had also sent army officers and cavalry.** Perhaps Artaxerxes understood the independent tendencies of his governors in the provinces and felt the show of military strength would persuade where mere letters might not.

As Nehemiah passed through the regions of Trans-Euphrates, he seems to have encountered his future adversaries. With each presentation of the king's letters, Nehemiah's plans became public, at least among ruling officials. In a foreshadowing, Nehemiah wrote, **When Sanballat the Horonite and Tobiah the Ammonite official heard about this, they were very much disturbed that someone had come to promote the welfare of the Israelites.**

Sanballat had a Babylonian name, though he may have come from Hebrew ancestry. He served as governor of Samaria, the province that generated a great deal of opposition to Jewish activity in the area. Nehemiah referred to him as "the Horonite," a contemptuous referent to the insignificant town from which Sanballat came. Tobiah had a Jewish name. He probably served in Samaria under Sanballat in some capacity. Nehemiah's term, "the Ammonite," was likely a condescending comment similar to "half-breed." Tobiah had mixed parentage.

While the antagonism of these two men was directed primarily against Nehemiah, he viewed their animosity as an attack against God's people, the "Israelites." Probably what rankled Sanballat and Tobiah most was a feeling that Nehemiah posed a threat to their power.

4. Nehemiah inspects the walls (2:11–16)

2:11–12. Nehemiah arrived in **Jerusalem**; after staying there **three days** he set out **during the night with a few men.** A three-day rest after a long journey seems to have been traditional among the Jews (Ezra 8:32).

Sanballat and Tobiah probably had allies in Jerusalem, and Nehemiah was aware that he was probably being watched. The Jews had powerful opponents, and his plans for rebuilding Jerusalem were not universally embraced. Though the general scheme for reconstruction was known, because of imperial mandate and the entourage that accompanied him, Nehemiah's plan for rebuilding the fortifications was still a secret. He confided in his journal: **I had not told anyone what my God had put in my heart to do for Jerusalem**.

He made a late-night tour of the wall with a few carefully chosen men in order to assess the job that lay before him. But Nehemiah retained a bold confidence because God had given him the passion to complete the work. Since he had only been in the city for three days, it is likely that his companions were either relatives or the same men who had met with him in Susa and informed him about conditions in Judea. The small scouting party made its way quietly around the broken walls of Jerusalem.

2:13. Nehemiah and his small party, under cover of darkness, went out of the city **through the Valley Gate**. This gate was located in the western wall and provided access to the Tyropoean Valley below. They apparently made their way along the wall in a counter-clockwise direction, in the direction of the **Jackal Well** until they reached the **Dung Gate**, so named because people passed through it to dump garbage and refuse into the valley. This wooden gate, **which had been destroyed by fire**, was situated at the southern end of Jerusalem. All along the way Nehemiah inspected every portion of the wall.

2:14–15. Nehemiah **then . . . moved on toward the Fountain Gate and the King's Pool**. The Fountain Gate presumably led to a water spring. From this point Nehemiah was forced to make a slight detour away from the wall toward the King's Pool because of the rubble or the steepness of the hill. From there he proceeded on foot because **there was not enough room for my mount to get through**. He continued on foot, inspecting the eastern side of the wall as he made his way along the Kidron Valley. He either turned back and retraced his way or turned away from the valley and **reentered through the Valley Gate**, thus completing the circumference of the wall.

2:16. Nehemiah again emphasized that the project was entirely on his instigation, because **the officials did not know where I had gone or what I was doing**. The officials may have been Persians who accompanied him, or perhaps they were part of the regional political establishment in the area. It seemed inappropriate to Nehemiah to discuss his plans with Persian authorities since he **had said nothing to the Jews or the priests or nobles or officials or any others who would be doing the work**.

Nehemiah sensed his first obligation was with the Jewish community. Priests represented the religious and social life of the community; nobles were family or clan heads; officials represented local political leaders; and "others" was an all-inclusive term for those who would later put their backs to the task.

5. Nehemiah reveals the plan (2:17–18)

2:17–18. Nehemiah did not reveal the audience to whom he next spoke. It is not clear whether he called a large assembly of the citizenry or gathered only the rulers. He did, however, finally divulge his intentions to a significant group of Jews. He said to them, **You see the trouble we are in: Jerusalem lies in ruins, and its gates have been burned with fire.** But Nehemiah wasn't simply telling them what they already knew; his point was, **Come, let us rebuild the wall of Jerusalem.**

He appealed to their national and spiritual heritage. The critical issues were not safety and security but honor and respect. The shambles of Jerusalem reflected badly upon their religious faith.

I also told them about the gracious hand of my God upon me and what the king had said to me. Nehemiah saw divine favor in all that had happened to him; he understood that God was at work. Secondarily, the king had also shown support. The people could join in the purposes of God, and they would have nothing to fear from the Persian government.

Those who heard Nehemiah responded to his report with enthusiasm. **They replied, "Let us start rebuilding." So they began this good work.**

6. Opposition builds (2:19–20)

2:19. Quickly, it seems, opposition to Nehemiah's ambitious plans arose. The speedy reaction suggests that Sanballat and Tobiah had sympathizers in Jerusalem who kept them informed about what was happening. Sanballat and Tobiah were more than disturbed (Neh. 2:10). They, along with **Geshem the Arab**, mocked and ridiculed the Jewish effort.

Geshem was not a Persian official, as were Sanballat and Tobiah; he was the king of Qedar, an extensive area stretching from northern Arabia to the borders of Egypt. Though under Persian control, Geshem exercised a great deal of independent power. It is unclear why he felt compelled to join in the mocking unless he was not pleased with having a new player on the field. Jerusalem posed no threat, yet its strengthening could unsettle the region and provide a firmer Persian presence.

"What is this you are doing?" they asked. "Are you rebelling against the king?" It had been this very accusation that had compelled Artaxerxes to stop the rebuilding of the city not long ago. Sanballat and Tobiah may have intended the taunt as a reminder of what had already happened in order to weaken the resolve of the people and to instill apprehension and fear.

2:20. Nehemiah was not drawn into defending his loyalty to the king; nor was he distracted into producing his royal papers. He knew these men were ambitious and held no particular devotion for Persia or Artaxerxes. He refused to stoop to their level of argument and accusation. Instead, he asserted his confidence in God and his intentions to proceed: **The God of heaven will give us success.** From first to last, Nehemiah's strength and certainty rested in God.

We his servants will start rebuilding. Those who put their hands to the task were working for God; they were his servants. In contrast, **You have no share in Jerusalem or any claim or historic right to it.** Nehemiah, like Zerubbabel before him (Ezra 4:3), declared this was an exclusively Jewish enterprise. These Samaritans had no claim to the city, no legal authority, no part in its religious life or heritage.

> **MAIN IDEA REVIEW:** *Prayer and planning complement each other in working out God's will. While we depend on God's power and sovereign rule, we carefully organize plans that can further his purposes; while we wait, we prepare.*

III. CONCLUSION

When You're Down

When the great linebacker Mike Singletary played for the Chicago Bears, he was known for making tackles anywhere along the gridiron. It didn't matter who was running the football or where he was on the field; somehow Singletary knew where that ball was going to be, and he often got there in time to stop the play.

One time after a game, a CBS reporter asked, "How do you get clobbered by a couple of linemen on one side of the field, then a few seconds later you make a tackle on the other side?"

Singletary replied, "I get up."

Jerusalem was down. Its walls were broken and destroyed, and many had left to live in the countryside. The people were discouraged, the poor were suffering from high taxes, the Persians were taking revenue, and the neighboring groups were dominating in commerce and politics. Then Nehemiah entered town. He pointed them away from life as usual to life as it could be. "Come, let us rebuild the wall of Jerusalem," he told the Jews. "Let's get up!"

There is no other way to do it. If you've been defeated, or discouraged, or have suffered a setback, the only way to change the situation is to "get up." If you stay where you are . . . you'll stay where you are.

PRINCIPLES

- God can work through believers and unbelievers alike.
- The work of God will often encounter opposition.
- Courage means acting in spite of fear.
- Preparation and planning are essential in any enterprise.
- Leadership requires vision and practical implementation of that vision.

APPLICATIONS

- If you have a role as a leader, communicate the group's purpose, then determine specific steps needed to achieve your goals.
- Do not allow fear to govern your actions or decisions; overcome fear by following God's purpose.
- Approach your responsibilities with prayer, a careful consideration of obstacles, and a workable plan.

IV. LIFE APPLICATION

Roads to Nowhere

The Irish novelist George Moore tells a story about Irish peasants who, during the Great Depression, were put to work by the government building roads. For a time the men worked well, and they sang lustily as they worked. They were glad to be employed, and they felt they were contributing to the good of the nation.

But little by little it began to dawn on them that the roads they were building were going nowhere. It became clear that they had been put to work so the government would have an excuse for feeding them. They were doing pointless busywork. It didn't take long before the men grew listless and quit singing their songs.

Moore's insightful conclusion: "The roads to nowhere are difficult to build."

In our own day, when purpose reaches no higher than materialism, sports, or the next television show, we have embarked on roads to nowhere. Listen to the songs on the radio, and you hear little satisfaction or joy. Many popular artists sing of hopelessness or despair, or they rage with violent or lewd lyrics. There are no songs to keep you going, at least not for the spirit.

The story of Nehemiah is the story of resolution and direction because it is a story of living for the purposes of God. After Nehemiah had surveyed the wall and determined the repairs needed, he gathered the leaders of Jerusalem. "Come, let us rebuild the wall of Jerusalem, and we will no longer be in disgrace," he told them. For years the people of Judah had languished, overwhelmed by foreign domination, uncertain about what to do next. Nehemiah arrived with a clear goal in view, one that fit the greater designs of God. As a result, the people replied, "Let us start rebuilding," and they began the work.

We must do the same. We must dare to survey the conditions around us not with the intent of criticizing but with the resolve to rebuild. There are lives that need hope, families that need repairing, and people who need compassion. We serve a God who builds rather than destroys, and he gives direction and meaning to life.

V. PRAYER

God, turn the heart of our president, our governor, and our mayor toward you in all wisdom. Help our leaders care about the things you care about. Teach us to fear you so that we may live wisely and honor you more. Thank you that we can trust in your ultimate control. Amen.

VI. DEEPER DISCOVERIES

A. King Artaxerxes (2:1–6)

Artaxerxes I ruled Persia from 465 to 424 B.C. As the empire expanded and attained great wealth and power, it also began to decline. Opulence has its price tag, and it usually comes in the form of moral decay. Not only did the Persian kings amass great riches; so also did the provincial officials. These satraps at times challenged the authority of the Persian king. Rebellions and bids for independence were continual challenges for the central government in Susa. In addition, the later monarchs were more harsh and repressive than earlier kings. Artaxerxes I came to the throne at the beginning of these troubling and transitional times.

Though he ruled for forty-one years, Artaxerxes's reign marked the beginning of Persia's slow but steady deterioration. Riddled with intrigues, murder, and scandal, each new monarch proved less capable and competent than the one before.

B. Prayer (2:4)

Nehemiah had just come off four months of intensive prayer and fasting. In chapter 1 we were able to listen in on a beautiful and exemplary prayer offered during his time of waiting on God. In that prayer we find the compelling lessons of praising God, thanking him, humbling ourselves in his presence, confessing sin, and making request. In many respects it follows the same approach taught by Jesus to his disciples in Matthew 6, beginning with worship and ending with a request or a call for help.

Prayers of the Bible rarely center on broken bones, financial problems, or upcoming surgeries. While God certainly cares about each situation in our lives, the biblical model focuses on God's sovereign will, spiritual understanding, and the spread of the gospel. Prayers found throughout Scripture also tend to deal with Christian character and one's relationship with God, as in Colossians 1:9–14.

In the Bible there are also short calls for help like Nehemiah offered when facing the questions of King Artaxerxes. In the breath of time between the king's question, "What is it you want?" and Nehemiah's response, he "prayed to the God of heaven." The cry for help can be prayed by anyone. It may not be eloquent, but it comes from the heart which admits its need; that is the starting place of all prayers before the sovereign Lord.

Someone once said that the greatest prayer we can ever learn is, "Help!" It is the simple admittance of personal poverty that is foundational to all prayer. Through obedience, humility, worship, and trust, we must learn to turn to God instinctively.

VII. TEACHING OUTLINE

A. INTRODUCTION
1. Lead Story: What Lies Beneath
2. Context: Nehemiah spent four months praying to God for opportunity and success in speaking to Artaxerxes about rebuilding Jerusalem. His heart was compelled to persist in prayer.
3. Transition: While he was waiting on God, Nehemiah also constructed a workable plan for the renovation project. When the time came for him to speak to the king, he was ready with facts and figures, a timetable, and a materials list.

B. COMMENTARY
1. Before the King (2:1–8)
   a. The opportunity (2:1–4)
   b. Nehemiah's requests (2:5–8)
2. The Plan Unfolds (2:9–20)
   a. From Persia to Judea (2:9–10)
   b. Nehemiah inspects the walls (2:11–16)
   c. Nehemiah reveals the plan (2:17–18)
   d. Opposition builds (2:19–20)

C. CONCLUSION: WHEN YOU'RE DOWN

VIII. ISSUES FOR DISCUSSION

1. What is our part in seeing the will of God fulfilled? What is God's part?
2. Does God work through secular institutions and unbelievers? Should the church ever partner with civic leaders, local governments, or non-faith organizations? Explain your answer.
3. How should the church as well as individual believers respond to opposition?

Nehemiah 3

The Good Work

Nehemiah 3

Quote

*H*ard work spotlights the character of people; some

turn up their sleeves, some turn up their noses,

and some don't turn up at all.

S a m   E w i n g

IN A NUTSHELL

*A*fter the rousing approval of Jerusalem's leaders, the hard work of actually building the wall began. Nehemiah wrote in his journal the names of real people—individuals and families who applied themselves to the project. This was hard, dirty, and sometimes dangerous work, but together they saw it to completion.

The Good Work

What Would God Say?

*H*ave you ever noticed what many people talk about after church on Sunday?

"That was a decent sermon," or "I sure didn't like that one song," or "I wonder why Mrs. Johnson wore that same dress again," or better, "I really felt like I was worshipping today."

If God reviewed a Sunday service at our local church, he would probably write something like this:

The nursery was led by Maureen, with Al and Jenny serving as one of the couples that helped with the babies. The ushering was led by Larry, with Ralph and Harry leading the crews for the first two services. The greeters were organized by Betty, and every door had someone there with a smile. The junior high was taught by Noelle and John, with four sets of parents—the Smiths and the Hansens and the Jibrowskys and the Needlows—leading the small-group discussions. The parking was directed by Charles, with seven volunteers pitching in.

And on and on.

You get the point. God knows how vital every role is, and he notices what everyone is doing. It was the same when Nehemiah and the people of Judah built the wall in Jerusalem.

What will you be doing this Sunday to help build the church?

II. COMMENTARY

The Good Work

> **MAIN IDEA:** *In the work of God, the greatest accomplishments come from a unity of purpose when people of diverse backgrounds, interests, and abilities join together under a compelling vision. Success is achieved not because we are all the same but because our differences are put aside to work for a greater goal.*

Ⓐ The Northern Wall (3:1–5)

> **SUPPORTING IDEA:** *Nehemiah's list began with those who worked on the north wall and its gates.*

3:1–2. The list of builders and the work they completed makes up the whole of this chapter and seems to have been inserted in the memoirs after the fact. Presented as an overview of the work, the actual chronology of events resumes in chapter 4.

One can only conjecture why Nehemiah began as he did, but it seems likely, given his concern for the religious integrity of Jerusalem, that beginning with the work of **Eliashib the high priest and his fellow priests** symbolized the holy and noble task in which everyone was engaged. Additionally, Eliashib, whose grandson was related by marriage to Sanballat (Neh. 13:28), signified the divergent interests that Nehemiah brought together in unified purpose.

The priests **rebuilt the Sheep Gate**. This gate probably provided entry into the city from the Jericho road. It gained its name from the market nearby that sold sheep for use in the ritual sacrifices of the temple. That this gate and others were rebuilt rather than repaired suggests total destruction. **They dedicated it and set its doors in place**. Only in reference to the work of the priests in this particular section does a dedication occur at the time of building. The entire wall was not dedicated until all was complete (Neh. 12:27).

The priests continued building along the wall **as far as the Tower of the Hundred**, probably a preexilic military barracks housing a hundred soldiers. They continued their work **as far as the Tower of Hananel**. This tower is thought to occupy the far northerly portion of the wall and, along with the Tower of the Hundred, served to protect the city along its northwestern side.

Beyond the Tower of Hananel, **the men of Jericho built . . . and Zaccur son of Imri built next to them**. Work crews from different localities are frequently mentioned throughout Nehemiah's list.

3:3. The Fish Gate was rebuilt by the sons of Hassenaah. Again, the gate probably got its name from its associated use. Fish either from the Sea of Galilee or the Mediterranean Sea were brought to market through this gate. Laying **its beams** and putting **its doors and bolts and bars in place** completed the gate.

3:4. Meremoth son of Uriah, the son of Hakkoz, repaired the next section. When Zerubbabel led some of the exiles back to Judea, the clan of Hakkoz accompanied him. At that time the descendants of Hakkoz could not prove their priestly lineage and so were excluded from temple participation (Ezra 2:61–62). Later, however, their ancestry was validated; when Ezra arrived in Jerusalem, he handed over the silver, gold, and sacred articles to Meremoth, son of Uriah. This was the same Meremoth who worked on the wall near the Fish Gate and then helped on another section (Ezra 3:21).

Meshullam son of Berekiah . . . made repairs along this same section of wall and industriously helped on another section (Neh. 3:30). Interestingly, Meshullam's daughter was married to the son of Tobiah (Neh. 6:18).

3:5. The next section was repaired by the men of Tekoa, a town south of Jerusalem. However, **their nobles would not put their shoulders to the work**

under their supervisors. The local rulers in this town refused to cooperate with Nehemiah; it was one of the few instances of Jewish opposition, here demonstrated through passivity. In response, however, the local men threw themselves into the work and finished this section as well as another (Neh. 3:27).

𝔹 The Western Wall (3:6–14)

SUPPORTING IDEA: *Work on the wall around Jerusalem, while explained in sections, occurred simultaneously. As priests and locals from the area worked on the north wall, others built along the western extension.*

3:6. At the northwest corner, **the Jeshanah Gate was repaired by Joiada . . . and Meshullam**. This gate probably got its name from its location in the old, western wall (*Jeshanah* possibly meaning "of the old"). The Meshullam mentioned here was not related to the Meshullam of Nehemiah 3:4.

3:7. The next section of the wall was repaired **by men from Gibeon and Mizpah**. Both of these towns were north of Jerusalem. **Melatiah of Gibeon and Jadon of Meronoth** may have been officials in their respective towns. These areas were **under the authority of the governor of Trans-Euphrates**, or his official seat of government.

3:8. To this point, participants were designated by their clan or their town. In this particular section of the wall, a new group was present—the guilds. **Uzziel** represented **the goldsmiths**, and **Hananiah** represented **the perfume-makers**. This section of the wall may have been near the bazaars where the merchants and guildsmen carried on business. Their desire to secure the city wall may have had its basis in economic interests.

The Bible text next reads, **They restored Jerusalem as far as the Broad Wall**. However, rather than "restored," the more literal translation of this word is: "they left out." In other words, work on the wall continued along a particular line but excluded part of preexilic Jerusalem. The "Broad Wall" enclosed another portion of the city. In fact, over the centuries, Jerusalem became subdivided by walls.

3:9. **Rephaiah son of Hur, ruler of a half-district of Jerusalem, repaired the next section**. Rephaiah was an official in charge of a half district not of the city but of the region around Jerusalem. These larger administrative areas were often subdivided.

3:10. **Jedaiah . . . made repairs opposite his house**. Here, and elsewhere, the workers repaired the wall near or next to their houses. In such instances the workers had a vested interest in doing a good job.

3:11. Malkijah . . . and Hasshub . . . repaired another section and the Tower of the Ovens. Still along the western wall, the tower was probably near the royal palace in an area where bakers operated their ovens.

3:12. Shallum . . . ruler of a half-district of Jerusalem repaired the wall **with the help of his daughters**. Again, this official had administrative responsibilities over a portion of a region outside the city but contiguous to it. Shallum's daughters were mentioned probably because he had no sons; in such a case his daughters would inherit his wealth and property. In light of this, they were recognized as legitimate heirs and partakers in the work.

3:13–14. The Valley Gate (through which Nehemiah had departed to inspect the wall) **was repaired by Hanun and the residents of Zanoah**. These people also **repaired five hundred yards of the wall as far as the Dung Gate**. Nehemiah noted the length because it was exceptionally long. Quite possibly the wall was not as severely damaged in this area, allowing the workers to mend a longer section. **Malkijah . . . ruler of the district of Beth Hakkerem**, repaired the **Dung Gate**.

ⓒ The Eastern Wall (3:15–32)

SUPPORTING IDEA: *The last section described was the east wall. This portion of the wall required more work crews, probably because it was more extensively damaged.*

3:15. The Fountain Gate was repaired by Shallun . . . ruler of the district of Mizpah. This gate probably led to a water spring; it was the only gate along the eastern wall to receive repairs. Shallun was administrator over a district that, while including the city of Mizpah, extended beyond it. The overseer of the actual city of Mizpah was Ezer (Neh. 3:19). It seems the repair of the gate was extensive, with attention given to **roofing it** as well as **putting its doors and bolts and bars in place**.

Shallun also **repaired the wall of the Pool of Siloam, by the King's Garden, as far as the steps going down from the City of David**. Many of these geographical notes present problems for modern archeologists since the features have long been erased and names have changed over the centuries. We do know that the Gihon Spring flowed out of the Kidron Valley and fed the Pool of Siloam, passing under the wall at Hezekiah's Tunnel (2 Chr. 32:30). The "steps" may simply be stairs that led into the original City of David, which was a much smaller enclosure.

3:16. The next section was repaired by Nehemiah son of Azbuk, ruler of a half-district of Beth Zur. His work along the wall was terminated at a point marked by three distinctive features: **the tombs of David . . . the artificial pool and the House of the Heroes**. Some scholars argue that the tombs were the burial sites of the royal line of David. Others maintain that these tombs lay outside the city wall. The House of the Heroes was probably the old military quarters for David's warriors.

3:17–18. The next few sections of wall appear to be handled by **the Levites**, though how far the list of Levites extends is not certain. It is apparent, however, that their Levitical duties did not preclude them from holding civic offices, as in the administration of districts or half districts.

3:19. Ezer, the **ruler of Mizpah**, repaired a section; he was the administrative head of that city. We simply do not know the ancient reference points of **the armory** and **the angle**, although the latter probably refers to a defining projection in the wall.

3:20. The next section of the wall was marked off by private homes. Nehemiah felt compelled to remark on the enthusiasm with which **Baruch** worked, noting that he **zealously repaired** the section that extended **from the angle to the entrance of the house of Eliashib**, the high priest.

3:21. Next to Baruch, we find Meremoth at work again (Neh. 3:4). This time he repaired a very short but symbolically important section. He mended the wall **from the entrance of Eliashib's house to the end of it**. It was only one house-length, but it involved the house of the high priest.

3:22. The repairs made by the **priests from the surrounding region** were noted in distinction to the priests mentioned in Nehemiah 3:1. The priests mentioned here probably came from priestly towns scattered throughout the Jordan Valley as opposed to the priests who resided in Jerusalem.

3:23–25a. The list next mentions people for whom we have no reference. These seem to be ordinary citizens working on the wall, each pitching in to secure the area around his own home or his neighbor's home. Reference to **the upper palace near the court of the guard** places this section of the wall at Solomon's Palace.

3:25b-27. Pedaiah . . . and the temple servants living on the hill of Ophel made repairs. Historically, the temple servants were foreigners who had come into the service of the Levites and priests after Israelite conquests. This subgroup seems to have lived in a community of their own on the hill of Ophel. *Ophel* literally means "bulge" and thus is descriptive of the geographic feature.

Next to them, **the men of Tekoa** (Neh. 3:5) repaired a section **from the great projecting tower to the wall of Ophel**. The wall of Ophel was a wall protecting the north side of the hill of Ophel. It had previously been the northern wall until, during Solomon's reign, it was extended to include the temple. Nehemiah's new wall probably intersected this older section of the wall.

3:28. Above the Horse Gate, the priests made repairs. The new wall was built further up the slope than the old, and thus the priests worked "above" the Horse Gate (see Jer. 31:40). This area was near the temple, which explains why the priests lived in this area and worked on this section: the priests made repairs, **each in front of his own house**.

3:29–30. Another list of names occurs, each working on different parts of the wall. **Shecaniah . . . the guard at the East Gate**, is so described, probably to distinguish him from another Shecaniah. The East Gate was an entryway into the temple; Shecaniah was probably a Levite. It was probably for this same purpose of identification that **Hanun** was referred to as **the sixth son of Zalaph**. **Meshullam** (Neh. 3:4) **made repairs opposite his living quarters**. These were probably his chambers or rooms in the temple area, rather than an actual house, supporting the notion that Meshullam held an influential post in the priesthood.

3:31–32. Malkijah, one of the goldsmiths, made repairs as far as the house of the temple servants and the merchants. Since a community of temple servants lived on the hill of Ophel, the "house of the temple servants" may have been some rooms reserved for their use when they served in the temple. The same may be true for the merchants who sold sacrificial animals needed for temple worship.

There is little agreement on the identity of the **Inspection Gate**. However, **the room above the corner** probably denoted the place where the northern and eastern walls met. This completed the outline of the wall, returning to the **Sheep Gate**. This area was a commercial center and market, making it reasonable for the **goldsmiths and merchants** to repair this district.

The total perimeter of the wall was about one and one-half miles.

MAIN IDEA REVIEW: *In the work of God, the greatest accomplishments come from a unity of purpose, when people of diverse backgrounds, interests, and abilities join together under a compelling vision. Success is achieved not because we are all the same but because our differences are put aside to work for a greater goal.*

III. CONCLUSION

Where Are the Walls to Build?

Today, the job before us is not to build a wall in Jerusalem but to help build God's eternal kingdom throughout the world. It's not about rebuilding Solomon's temple but about investing in individual lives that can become spiritual temples inhabited by the Spirit of God.

And there is work for all of us.

There is a well-known description of football that states, "It's twenty-two men who desperately need a rest being watched by millions of people who desperately need exercise." Church life can often function the same way. Some people choose to sit and watch others build, just as some refused to participate in Nehemiah's project. They simply watch, and sometimes criticize, those who serve. The story of Nehemiah reminds us to pick up a trowel and join with men, women, boys, and girls from all over the world and from our own community to build Christ's church.

PRINCIPLES

- Each person is important to God.
- Every person has a role to fulfill in God's work.
- A united effort is greater than the sum of its parts.

APPLICATIONS

- Do your work joyfully and with all your strength. Work for the pleasure of God, who notices everything you do.
- Encourage others in their faith and service, since we are all working for the same goal of honoring Christ.
- Do your part in serving in the church. You are needed! When you don't do your share, it places excessive burdens on others.

IV. LIFE APPLICATION

Supermom

Several years ago, as more and more mothers went back to work, there appeared in our vocabulary the term, *supermom*. This was the woman who held down the responsibilities of a full-time job, cooked nutritiously balanced meals from scratch, attended every PTA meeting, cheered at her children's soccer games, washed the clothes and ironed them, did the grocery shopping, developed intimate friendships with her neighbors, maintained a dusted and vacuumed house, kept every item in its place, and still had time for a rewarding and romantic relationship with her husband.

Many women suffered guilt or nervous breakdowns from their inability to manage the fantasy. But the problem was more widespread than that. Quite often everyone else expected the mother to fulfill these unrealistic expectations as well. The realization that others had to help, that some things might not get done, that she had a limit to her strength and abilities was slow to dawn on a great many people. Like the comic book superheroes, supermom simply did not exist.

Sometimes this mentality appears in the church. We expect our pastors or lay leaders to shoulder burdensome schedules and responsibilities. Not only do we assume they will put in a full day at the office; we also anticipate that they will visit the ill in the hospital, take our calls when we phone, attend various and multitudinous meetings throughout the week, teach a class, speak at any club or function that appears on the calendar, pitch in for the annual "clean the church" day, raise perfect children, and in their off hours choose to attend a social at church. And if you're a missionary on furlough, the list is even longer.

Obviously, it can't be done . . . or shouldn't be attempted.

The work of the church, like any of God's purposes, requires the joyful participation of every member. It's not up to the leaders alone. When Nehemiah returned to Jerusalem with a plan and some supplies to rebuild the wall, he couldn't do it by himself. He couldn't even do it with all the assembled leaders in Jerusalem. All families and workers were needed to see the project to completion. Some refused to help. But it was to their loss and shame. Those who did bend their backs to the labor shared in an important work. Each pair of hands lightened the load and made success achievable.

God enables each of us to fulfill a particular role. If we don't join in, we will be the losers because the work of God's kingdom will not fail. But if we delight in the Lord, we will find joy in sharing the task with other believers as we work toward the common goal of glorifying Christ.

There are no "super saints," only the ordinary kind who join with others to do the will of Christ.

V. PRAYER

Father, help your church to work together in the same spirit as demonstrated by these ancient people in repairing the walls of Jerusalem. May we take our different capabilities and, with unity of purpose, work together for the good of your kingdom and your name. Amen.

VI. DEEPER DISCOVERIES

Actions and Reactions

The Bible teaches that a life of love and obedience to God is not passive. It is filled with actions and reactions of grace and love, accompanied by truth.

Reading through the names in Nehemiah 3 reminds us that these people had to work together; they had to get along. Occasionally a negative note surfaces, as in verse 5: "Their nobles would not put their shoulders to the work under their supervisors." But for the most part, everyone pitched in and worked together.

If we survey the Bible's teachings about love and action, we discover clear guidelines for how to get along with one another:

Reactions. When people wrong us, we are to *forgive* (Eph. 4:29–31; Matt. 19:15–19). God wants us to pardon and not hold grudges or harbor bitterness. This benefits everyone.

When people help us, we are to be *grateful* (Eph. 5:20). Christians should cultivate the habit of expressing thanks. The best kind of teamwork in a church happens when we give positive reinforcement to others as they work.

Actions. When we wrong others, we are to *ask for forgiveness* (Matt. 5:23–24). This promotes peace and releases us from the damaging guilt that accompanies hurtful actions. For the most part, the Book of Nehemiah demonstrates teamwork as the people served together toward a common goal. They worked decently and in order so the walls of Jerusalem could be built. For unity among so many people, there had to be times when forgiveness was shown.

We are called to *edify and build others* in their character, faith, and personhood (Rom. 14:19; 15:2; Eph. 4:29). If someone is discouraged or hurting spiritually, we are to restore him (Gal. 6:1–2). We are to do so humbly, never in self-righteous condescension. The goal is to rebuild him into active faith.

Those engaged in good deeds should be *praised* and *thanked* (Prov. 27:2). Rather than being jealous or envious of another's success, we should rejoice.

If someone fails to live a life of goodness and we know that person well, we have a responsibility to stimulate or encourage him to good actions (Heb. 10:24–25).

Following these scriptural imperatives prevents us from adopting a nonchalant or passive attitude toward life or our relationships with others. As the people in Nehemiah's time built the wall, all of these actions and reactions were necessary. Those who chose to live by these standards were helped by the Spirit of God to continue to build not only the wall but also other lives!

VII. TEACHING OUTLINE

A. INTRODUCTION

1. Lead Story: What Would God Say?
2. Context: Nehemiah met with the leaders and the representative citizenry of Jerusalem and secured their support for rebuilding the wall of Jerusalem.
3. Transition: Despite the growing opposition of Sanballat and Tobiah, the people moved ahead with determination to complete the wall. Nehemiah interjected into the developing events a list of those who helped in the wall's reconstruction and the different sections that were completed.

B. COMMENTARY

1. The Northern Wall (3:1–5)
2. The Western Wall (3:6–14)
3. The Eastern Wall (3:15–32)

C. CONCLUSION: WHERE ARE THE WALLS TO BUILD?

VIII. ISSUES FOR DISCUSSION

1. In light of Nehemiah 3, discuss Ephesians 4:3–5,11–13. How can the church achieve unity while encouraging diversity and individual gifts?
2. As a leader, Nehemiah assigned responsibility for the wall's construction to those who did the work. Discuss how this principle of delegated responsibility might apply in business, in the church, and in your home.

Nehemiah 4

Opposition

Any fool can criticize, condemn, and complain—and most fools do.

Dale Carnegie

IN A NUTSHELL

The building of Jerusalem's wall was underway. But the bustle of activity prompted renewed antagonism and threats from Nehemiah's enemies. It began with mocking words and insults and led to serious threats and plans of violence. Through it all, Nehemiah prayed, kept the people focused on the work, and placed armed men along the wall as a defense against attack.

Opposition

I. INTRODUCTION

Stick and Stones

We have all probably heard (and perhaps even invoked) that ageless childhood rhyme, "Sticks and stones may break my bones, but words will never hurt me."

Wrong! It's because words *do* have such profound effect that we devise defenses against them. If words truly did not matter, we wouldn't bother denying their power. But words can carry destruction or security, trust or suspicion. They can exonerate or condemn, bring hope or despair, truth or deceit, hatred or kindness, clarity or confusion. Words can cut into our spirits like no other weapon and leave scars for a lifetime; they can also linger through the years, offering inspiration and confidence.

When Nehemiah and the Jews were working on the wall around Jerusalem, Sanballat and Tobiah launched a war of words. They hurled insults, ridicule, taunts, and threats in the hope that these words would demoralize the people. Rumors of attack were more unsettling to the Jews than the actuality might have been. Guards were posted on the wall, but the gossip and derision assaulted the minds of the people.

Nehemiah, however, kept the people focused on the work before them. More importantly, he encouraged the people by reminding them of God: "Remember the Lord, who is great and awesome" (Neh. 4:14). In that statement he reminded the people that all Tobiah's verbal abuse and haranguing were nothing compared to the power of God.

II. COMMENTARY

Opposition

> **MAIN IDEA:** Prayer does not release a person from responsibility; rather, it inspires creativity while galvanizing resolve.

◼ Derision (4:1–3)

> **SUPPORTING IDEA:** Mockery is a means of masquerading one's insecurity, of feigning confidence, as the suspicion of one's weakness grows more apparent. It is the language of the bully.

4:1–2. With increasing evidence that the Jews intended to restore the walls of Jerusalem, Sanballat's emotions grew more intense, while his expressions of contempt spilled on a wider audience. He moved from being "very much disturbed" or unsettled (Neh. 2:10), to leading a coterie of ridicule (Neh. 2:19), to being **angry** and **greatly incensed**.

Sanballat came to view Nehemiah and the Jews as a growing threat to his power and status. As governor of Samaria, and with marriage ties to the high priest, Sanballat could bask in his own importance. But with the arrival of Nehemiah and the stirring of Jewish opinion favoring the restoration of Jerusalem's prestige, Sanballat saw a crumbling of his own domination in the area. As a consequence, **he ridiculed the Jews**.

His mockery turned from private sniping to public scorn as he voiced his contempt **in the presence of his associates and the army of Samaria**. The men in his company were probably fellow officials, perhaps peers who held political positions in Samaria or the surrounding region. Also present was either a Persian command or local militia; as governor, Sanballat controlled some military power. Before this uncritical audience, he said, **What are those feeble Jews doing?** He not only believed the task was too great but that the Jews were inferior.

The next series of questions swung upon the hinge of Sanballat's contempt. Their rhetorical nature depended on his assumption that the Jews were pitiable and inadequate. **Will they restore their wall?** Actually, the wall is not here specified, making the more literal translation, "Will they restore things?" Some suggest that Sanballat's snide remark referred to the broader issue of reestablishing Jewish identity. His sarcasm was probably directed at the possibilities of restoring Jewish nationalism, honor, and ritual—something more formidable than the wall. This sense is captured by his follow-up comment: **Will they offer sacrifices? Will they finish in a day?**

Sanballat smirked at what he perceived to be the naïveté of the Jewish people—as if, with a sacrifice and a prayer, God would miraculously come to their aid. He considered the Jews foolish: **Can they bring the stones back to life from those heaps of rubble—burned as they are?**

From Sanballat's perspective, all the Jewish people had was a bunch of crumbled rock and stone weakened by fire. These people were working with debris! And yet, if Sanballat was so sure of their foolhardiness, why was he compelled to deride them publicly? If he was certain of their failure, why was he so determined to sabotage their efforts?

4:3. Like a puppet on a string, or a straight man in a dark comedy, **Tobiah the Ammonite** stood beside Sanballat and said, **If even a fox climbed up on it, he would break down their wall of stones!** Tobiah mimicked his superior's disdain. The Jews were building not a stone wall, quarried and fit, but a wall made of stones, piled together and, like their builders, inherently weak.

B Nehemiah's Response (4:4–6)

> **SUPPORTING IDEA:** *Refusing to engage in a war of words or retaliatory actions, Nehemiah prayed, then went to work.*

4:4–5. Nehemiah turned to God: **Hear us, O our God, for we are despised.** From the start he was concerned with the honor of God and his people. It was the shame cast upon the Jews and their God that fired his determination to rebuild Jerusalem. So with news of Sanballat's taunts, Nehemiah understood the situation in terms of God's reputation and that of his people.

Nehemiah was convinced that the restoration work was the will of God. He had seen it evidenced by Artaxerxes's support and good will and by the rousing support of the Jews. In light of this, those who opposed the Jews were viewed as enemies. Sanballat and his cronies were clearly of this camp.

Many interpreters have trouble with Nehemiah's prayer and his request for retribution on his enemies. The modern Christian often views his prayer as unforgiving and harsh, lacking in the love to which Christ calls us. However, Scripture reminds us that vengeance belongs to God (who will exercise it), and judgment belongs to Christ (who will execute it). There are, in fact, enemies of the cross, of God, and of his people.

Nehemiah refrained from personal retribution. He prayed, **Turn their insults back on their own heads.** He asked that God allow the biblical principle—you reap what you sow—to take its course. **Give them over as plunder in a land of captivity.** He asked that they experience what the Jews had during the exile, that they would feel the bitterness of captivity because of their arrogant affront to God. This was no harsher than what God had done to the Jews for their sins.

4:6. After praying to God, Nehemiah left his requests and their outcomes to God. He took up his work and led the people in theirs: **So we rebuilt the wall till all of it reached half its height.** These were the duties and accomplishments of the people because they **worked with all their heart.** This does not diminish God's role in the wall's success because the Jews were able to work only because of God's sovereign grace, but they did have to bend over with their own hands and build the wall stone by stone.

C Obstacles (4:7–23)

> **SUPPORTING IDEA:** *Prayers and hard work do not always make smooth paths or assure us of quick success. With each step forward, Nehemiah was met with another obstacle to finishing the wall.*

1. A plot (4:7–9)

4:7–8. This portion of the record may be a slight step back in time, before the walls were half completed. Sanballat and his associates noticed that the

Jews were serious about the project and **that the repairs to Jerusalem's walls had gone ahead and that the gaps were being closed**. This made them **very angry**. Despite their heckling, the Jews were not frightened; they worked together and progress was made. Sanballat's first tactic had failed. So he gathered his political allies together for a planning session, a round-table on how to stop the Jews.

At the meeting were **Sanballat, Tobiah, the Arabs, the Ammonites and the men of Ashdod**. Sanballat and Tobiah controlled Samaria, the region north of Judah. The Arabs under the leadership of King Geshem (Neh. 2:19) occupied a vast territory to the south. The Ammonites lived in a Persian territory to the east, and the men of Ashdod were to the west of Judah along the Mediterranean Sea. Judah was surrounded by those who wanted to destroy her.

These hostile leaders drew up a war plan; they allied themselves to attack Jerusalem. Apparently, they also devised a propaganda campaign to discredit the Jews and incite violence or anger against them. Whether this took the form of infiltrating the citizenry of Jerusalem, or agitating throughout the surrounding regions, or trying to discredit them at the Persian court, we cannot know.

4:9. In response, Nehemiah took his traditional line of action: **we prayed to our God and posted a guard day and night to meet this threat**. He sought God first, leaving to him what only he could do. Then he prepared and did what he could do. This was Nehemiah's pattern.

2. Discouragement (4:10)

4:10. As if the threat of military intervention was not enough, the people of Judah took up a mournful song: **The strength of the laborers is giving out, and there is so much rubble that we cannot rebuild the wall**. The Jews were feeling stressed—threatened from without, physically tired, and overwhelmed by the enormity of the work.

3. Threats and rumors (4:11–12)

4:11. Sanballat and his allies used intimidation in their effort to stop the Jews from building. Rumors and threats were circulating: **Before they know it or see us, we will be right there among them and will kill them and put an end to the work**. These menacing words played powerfully upon the imagination of the Jews; most of the people remembered that not long before they had experienced violence from these very provinces. Judah's neighbors were capable of brutality. The rumors of stealth and death unsettled the workers.

4:12. The rumors gained more power as the Jews living along the bordering territories repeatedly warned those in Jerusalem (**told us ten times over**), **Wherever you turn, they will attack us**. Their anxiety supported the conviction that Judah was surrounded by enemies. In every direction—north, east, south, and west—hostility awaited them. Even those outside Jerusalem were feeling the tensions. Many of the workers came from outlying towns and villages, and the fears expressed by family and friends threatened Nehemiah with possible desertions.

4. Resolve (4:13–15)

4:13–14. Nehemiah was hit with a problem that he needed to resolve if the work was to end successfully. People were tired and discouraged, nerves were frazzled, and a concerted military threat was rumbling all along Judah's borders. Therefore, Nehemiah **stationed some of the people behind the lowest points of the wall at the exposed places.** He posted them by families, **with their swords, spears and bows.**

Nehemiah actually halted all work and called an assembly of the people. He arranged them by families, the traditional method of organization. They assembled in full battle dress at those places along the wall that allowed a good viewing by their enemies. This was a carefully orchestrated show of strength to those who might try to attack. Their enemies would know that the Jews were prepared.

With the people assembled in their fighting gear, Nehemiah **looked things over.** He reviewed the troops. Then, like a general, and certainly like the governor he was, Nehemiah **stood up** and delivered a war speech. He appealed first to the Jews' religious convictions and their identity as God's people: **Don't be afraid of them. Remember the Lord, who is great and awesome.** Nehemiah pointed the people to God; he tapped into their collective memory and evoked the history of God's protection.

Nehemiah then encouraged them to **fight for your brothers, your sons and your daughters, your wives and your homes.** The battle was not for some abstract notion, or a pile of stones, but for those people who stood next to them. Nehemiah's words fell with a force doubled by the proximity of loved ones.

4:15. The strategy worked. Once their enemies heard that the Jews were **aware of their plot,** the immediate danger subsided and the coalition of hostile forces withdrew their plans. Yet, even in this successful display of strength and resolve, Nehemiah recognized that **God had frustrated** their plans. As a consequence, everyone **returned to the wall, each to his own work.** The crisis had passed, and the people were renewed in their effort.

5. Contingency plans (4:16–23)

4:16–18. The immediate crisis was averted, but the threat of disruption or attack still hung over the city, especially for those working on the wall. In order to guard against hostilities and boost morale, half of Nehemiah's laborers did the work while the other half **were equipped with spears, shields, bows and armor.** These soldiers, positioned by the work crews, not only

Something we are missing ↱

served as a warning to those contemplating attack but also bolstered the courage of those who were working on the wall.

In addition to the trained militia, **those who carried materials did their work with one hand and held a weapon in the other.** These were the men who carried rubble and stone. Some interpreters suggest that their "weapon" was actually one of the stones they collected which they could launch against an attacker. Those involved in the actual building needed both hands for their work, and so each **wore his sword at his side** at the ready.

With everyone assigned a position, **the man who sounded the trumpet stayed with** Nehemiah.

4:19–20. Nehemiah again met with all the people, noting the hierarchy of those involved: **the nobles, the officials and the rest of the people.** He laid out for them the situation they faced: **The work is extensive and spread out, and we are widely separated from each other along the wall.** For the number of people involved, their resources were spread thin. Most of the time the various work groups were out of sight and hearing of one another.

Consequently, Nehemiah established a warning system. **Wherever you hear the sound of the trumpet, join us there.** The trumpeter would sound the alarm, calling everyone to his position. An emergency communication system was established around the wall; this assured that no isolated group would be ambushed. In language suggestive of Israel's past when they warred against great armies, Nehemiah concluded, **Our God will fight for us!**

4:21–23. Not only were the people armed and ready; the work shifts were apparently extended past sundown to when **the stars came out.** These measures were probably implemented in order to hasten the completion of the wall. In addition, Nehemiah told everyone to **stay inside Jerusalem at night.** Most of the workers had been returning to their villages each evening. Nehemiah explained the rationale for having everyone retire to Jerusalem at night: to serve **as guards by night and workmen by day.**

Nehemiah never required more from those under him than he was willing to do. So each night, neither Nehemiah, nor his **brothers**, nor his **men**, nor his **guards** took off their clothes; **each had his weapon, even when he went for water**; they remained always dressed and ready, vigilant toward the cause. These men of position set a high standard and elicited the loyalty of those whom they led.

MAIN IDEA REVIEW: *Prayer does not release a person from responsibility; rather, it inspires creativity while galvanizing resolve.*

III. CONCLUSION

Pressing Toward the Goal

It seems that each chapter finds Nehemiah encountering one new problem after another—taunts, mockery, complaints, plots, disunity. But he kept going.

Obedience is hard work.

If you keep a journal, or even reflect on life, you will notice that there are many days of pain and difficulty. Quite often hardships come from relationships, and these stresses often seem undeserved. Nehemiah released the nettlesome people in his life to God and kept at the work.

Obedience is hard work.

Read through the acts and writings of the apostle Paul and notice all that he accomplished and how, in one sense, he changed the known world. If we aren't careful, we can get the idea that he walked on water—that he was above the emotions and limitations of ordinary human beings.

But listen to what he wrote: "I came to you in weakness and fear, and with much trembling" (1 Cor. 2:3). He struggled, felt intimidated, apprehensive, and nervous. Even after years of preaching the gospel and enduring hardship and opposition, he asked that others would pray "that I may declare it [the gospel] fearlessly, as I should" (Eph. 6:20).

Obedience is hard work.

At the beginning of his public ministry, even Jesus struggled with the temptation to circumvent God's work. Never minimize Christ's struggle in the desert; it was real. And at the end, in the Garden of Gethsemane, he agonized over obedience as he looked toward the torture of being separated from the Father.

Obedience is hard work . . . but it is good.

PRINCIPLES

- There will always be resistance to the work of God.
- Ridicule and violence are often the weapons of opposition to the gospel.
- Faithful prayer allows the exercise of God's strength and creativity through his people.
- Fear can paralyze.

APPLICATIONS

- If you receive laughter, insults, or mockery because of your faith, don't become intimidated or angry. Keep speaking the gospel in love.
- In prayer, give to God those who are enemies of the gospel; only he can turn their hearts.
- Always be ready to explain your faith to others, and live in a way that is above criticism.
- Never let opposition or the opinions of others dissuade you from following and serving Christ.

IV. LIFE APPLICATION

Work on Your Knees

Martin Luther is quoted as saying, "Work as if it all depends on you; pray as if it all depends on God." The life of faith is a cooperative effort, "for we are God's workmanship, created in Christ Jesus to do good works, which God prepared in advance for us to do" (Eph. 2:10).

With the taunts and threats of Sanballat and Tobiah ringing in his ears, Nehemiah prayed to God. He asked for divine retribution, for judgment upon those who dared insult God's people and work. Then he and the people kept building. Later, when it became apparent that there were serious plans to mount an armed attack against Jerusalem, Nehemiah and the workers prayed once again to God "and posted a guard day and night to meet this threat" (Neh. 4:9).

Persistently Nehemiah went to God in prayer. It was his habit because he fully trusted in God. But he didn't sit around waiting for God to do everything. He released to God what only God could do, and then he fortified the city with armed soldiers. But at every point in which he implemented a defense measure, he depended on God as his true defense. He told the people, "Remember the Lord, who is great and awesome . . . and fight for your brothers" (Neh. 4:14); whenever "you hear the sound of the trumpet, join us there. Our God will fight for us!" (Neh. 4:20).

In every situation Nehemiah began on his knees before God, and he ended with bold action. He clearly understood that God was the eternal judge, the universal sovereign, the Holy One. He also understood that God had bestowed upon man certain responsibilities. The proper relationship between God and his creation is a joint interaction, a united purpose in which the Creator and his people work together.

Many times we pray about someone in need and leave it there. We should also do something to help meet the need—perhaps visit or call, cook dinner, or even offer a financial gift. Prayer cannot be neglected in a frenzy of busyness, but the hard work of service cannot be ignored because we are praying.

V. PRAYER

Heavenly Father, help us not only to obey you but also to trust you. We praise you that you are our defense, our shield, and our mighty fortress. Please help us not be afraid when we walk through dark valleys or feel opposition from the enemies of the gospel. Please help us to return good for evil and to show your love. Amen.

VI. DEEPER DISCOVERIES

Hardship

It is one of the clearest messages of the Bible, and it is demonstrated every day in our own time: pain and trouble are part of life, especially for those who follow God. And yet we are always asking, "Why?"

The simple answer is, Because we live in a fallen world. The fall of man reverberated throughout creation and sent shock waves into the future to disrupt continually God's original intent. We do not live in a morally neutral universe but on a planet in upheaval, a place assaulted by sin and the powers of disobedience and rebellion. When we pretend that life should be uninterrupted happiness, we play into Satan's strategy. We begin to think that God has not done a good job.

Rather than asking *Why?*, perhaps we would do better to prepare for *when*. Preparation comes by doing God's will day after day.

We may never have full understanding about the "why" of cetain events or circumstances. But we can grow more confident in God's compassion and care as we loosen our grip on the things of this life and look with anticipation toward the life to come. As we live in the reality of God's eternal promises, we will more readily agree with Paul: "Our present sufferings are not worth comparing with the glory that will be revealed in us" (Rom. 8:18).

VII. TEACHING OUTLINE

A. INTRODUCTION
1. Lead Story: Sticks and Stones
2. Context: When Nehemiah arrived in Jerusalem, he found a weak and demoralized people. Though the Jews had enjoyed a revival of temple worship, the violence they experienced from the Persian government,

by way of the surrounding provinces, left them disheartened and defenseless.

3. Transition: It was to the personal benefit of the surrounding territories to keep Jerusalem and Judah weak. Therefore, when Nehemiah united and inspired the Jews to rebuild Jerusalem's wall, new threats of violence were sounded from their hostile neighbors. Nehemiah was faced with serious challenges as a leader.

B. COMMENTARY

1. Derision (4:1–3)
2. Nehemiah's Response (4:4–6)
3. Obstacles (4:7–23)
   a. A plot (4:7–9)
   b. Discouragement (4:10)
   c. Threats and rumors (4:11–12)
   d. Resolve (4:13–15)
   e. Contingency plans (4:16–23)

C. CONCLUSION: PRESSING TOWARD THE GOAL

VIII. ISSUES FOR DISCUSSION

1. Nehemiah faced multiple challenges as a leader. Discuss at least three qualities of successful leadership. How do these apply to your job, church, and family?
2. Nehemiah and the Jews faced threats and insults from their enemies. How did Nehemiah respond? Does this agree with New Testament teachings? Why or why not?
3. When the people were discouraged and threatened with violence, Nehemiah told them, "Remember the Lord, who is great and awesome" (Neh. 4:14). Share times from your own past when God has guided you. Does this change the way you view your future? Why?

Nehemiah 5

Behind the Walls

I. INTRODUCTION
Facades

II. COMMENTARY
A verse-by-verse explanation of the chapter.

III. CONCLUSION
Please Show Your Credentials

An overview of the principles and applications from the chapter.

IV. LIFE APPLICATION
Let Justice Roll

Melding the chapter to life.

V. PRAYER
Tying the chapter to life with God.

VI. DEEPER DISCOVERIES
Historical, geographical, and grammatical enrichment of the commentary.

VII. TEACHING OUTLINE
Suggested step-by-step group study of the chapter.

VIII. ISSUES FOR DISCUSSION
Zeroing the chapter in on daily life.

Nehemiah 5

I N   A   N U T S H E L L

*O*utside Jerusalem, Tobiah and Sanballat had organized a loose confederacy of malcontents. Inside the Jewish community, unfair practices and mercenary attitudes among the leaders posed a new threat to national reconstruction. Nehemiah next dealt with growing disunity and injustice from within.

Behind the Walls

I. INTRODUCTION

Facades

Throughout the history of architecture, attempts have been made to take an ordinary building and make it extraordinary in some way. These imaginative journeys using stone or wood created different artistic styles from flamboyant to simplistic. Like bakers before an undecorated cake or artists before a blank canvas, architects experimented in an attempt to bring heightened beauty to a building. Essentially faced with a box, the designer tried to improve upon it by adding embellishments and adornments or by minimalizing. It was in reaching for grandeur or in trying to beautify a hopelessly plain structure that facades became so popular.

Whether it was a mercantile in Montana or a posh club in New York, the street-side appearance of buildings received all the attention. Both the designer and the public were concerned only with the front. But if you walked around the corner and took a look at the back, every building looked the same—square boxes set side by side.

Part way through Nehemiah's building project, it became apparent that security against hostile neighbors was not the only issue threatening Jerusalem. Nehemiah was confronted with complaints not against Persia but against fellow Jews. Building a wall would only provide a false front if behind that wall the community was fractured and filled with infighting. Stones and mortar provide little defense against the disintegration of social justice.

II. COMMENTARY

Behind the Walls

> **MAIN IDEA:** *Leadership requires working with different groups and personalities while at the same time supplying a vision to follow. More importantly, however, the leader must demonstrate integrity. The most brilliant plans cannot serve as a substitute for this critical quality.*

A Troubles Within (5:1–13)

> **SUPPORTING IDEA:** *For any organization or nation, internal schisms, inequities, or injustices will bring ruin far quicker than out-side attack. Survival and well-being depend on internal health.*

1. Economic oppression (5:1–5)

5:1. With defensive measures in place, Nehemiah next faced internal ten-sions: **The men and their wives raised a great outcry against their Jewish brothers**. This discontent was represented among a wider population than the wall builders. Quite possibly the people began to see in Nehemiah an advocate; he may have presented the common Jews an opportunity that, before his governorship, was not available—so they voiced their grievances. The specific mentioning of wives among the protestors may indicate how des-perate the situation had become and that economic injustices had penetrated into the fabric of family life.

The hardships had accumulated over time, and the injustices had been felt before Nehemiah's arrival. Consequently, these people raised an emo-tional wail of distress. The object of their indignation was their fellow Jews.

5:2. The first group represented those Jews who owned no land and were dependent on earned wages to survive. **We and our sons and daughters are numerous**, they said. Large families were considered a blessing of God, yet even with many children these families could not survive the inflationary times in which they lived. They asked for government assistance: **In order for us to eat and stay alive, we must get grain**.

5:3. The second group consisted of landowners. Yet even these people faced economic difficulties. **We are mortgaging our fields, our vineyards and our homes to get grain during the famine**, they complained. Crop failure had hit the farmers and the vineyard owners. These people were living through economic upheavals. Many had taken out loans against their crops and prop-erty in order to buy grain to feed their families. The famine threatened to ruin them, making repayment of their loans impossible.

5:4–5. The last group also consisted of landowners. But the cause of their difficulties was taxation: **We have had to borrow money to pay the king's tax on our fields and vineyards.** Like the other landowners, they were also facing ruin through an inability to repay these loans.

The source of their hardship was traced back to their Jewish brethren: **Although we are of the same flesh and blood as our countrymen and though our sons** and daughters **are as good as theirs, yet** . . . The appeal they made before Nehemiah was not based on Levitical law but on the spirit of that law. Special considerations were afforded fellow Jews because they were all partakers in the divine covenant. Jews were supposed to look upon other Jews as "brothers."

Under the economic crisis, however, Jews were taking advantage of their fellow Jews: **We have to subject our sons and daughters to slavery. Some of our daughters have already been enslaved.** The payment of debt through slavery, either of one's children or one's self, was not illegal under the law; however, to prevent abuse, safeguards were built in. The clear implication was that the current hardships were preventable if their Jewish kinsmen had not taken advantage of their hardship.

The parents of these enslaved children were desperate: **We are powerless, because our fields and our vineyards belong to others.** They had no means of buying their children back because the produce from the fields went directly to the creditors.

2. Nehemiah's judgment (5:6–11)

5:6–7a. After listening to **their outcry and . . . charges,** Nehemiah **was very angry.** The oppression of fellow Jews was as shameful as Jerusalem's broken walls. But he refrained from an immediate response. Instead, he **pondered them** in his mind. After careful thought, he rebuked those responsible for unfair lending and economic oppression: **You are exacting usury from your own countrymen!** Nehemiah felt a moral outrage at those who showed no compassion, mercy, or kinship with their fellow Jews. The legalities were secondary to ethical considerations.

5:7b–8. In order to deal with these men and to resolve the issues, he **called together a large meeting.** Nehemiah declared, **As far as possible, we have bought back our Jewish brothers who were sold to the Gentiles.** In other words, the community had spent money to redeem out of slavery those Jews sold to Gentiles. But Jews were enslaving Jews so that other Jews would have to buy them back: **You are selling your brothers, only for them to be sold back to us!**

In Nehemiah's thinking, this was ridiculous. It was a terrible abuse upon brothers and a horrible waste of Jewish money. It demeaned the Jewish kinsmen and depleted the community's resources.

[Handwritten top margin: How do we discredit God in the eyes of the world ~~[struck through]~~]

[Handwritten left margin: How do we do this today! Why did they listen to Nehemiah?]

5:9–11. Nehemiah continued, **What you are doing is not right.** He spoke not to the law but to their values and principles. Ultimately, Nehemiah appealed to that which bound the Jews together—God. **Shouldn't you walk in the fear of our God to avoid the reproach of our Gentile enemies?** he asked the group. An appropriate reverence for God would place personal ambition and greed aside. To behave selfishly at the expense of one's kinsmen was an affront to God, and it discredited him among the pagan nations.

Nehemiah retained the confidence and support of these men by acknowledging, **I and my brothers and my men are also lending the people money and grain.** He was not against lending as such. He, too, had extended credit. The point of contention was the "pledges" taken against the debt that left the people enslaved to the moneylender. Nehemiah's cry was, **Let the exacting of usury stop!**

He demanded that the creditors give back all the property they had seized as payment for debts. He then required them to return the interest payments the people were obliged to pay—**the hundredth part of the money, grain, new wine and oil**—which kept them perpetually indebted, with no hope of release.

[Handwritten: Should we just let people take advantage of us? This was not the situation]

3. The pledge (5:12–13)

5:12–13. After Nehemiah's reproach, there appeared to be unanimous agreement. **"We will give it back," they said.** Not only were the creditors going to return the lands and homes they had seized as security against defaulted loans; it is possible they were also going to stop charging interest: **And we will not demand anything more from them.**

To assure these men complied, Nehemiah **summoned the priests and made the nobles and officials take an oath to do what they had promised.** The promises were attested before God, the religious leaders, and possibly the representative public.

To underscore the severity of the pledge, as well as the seriousness of their offense, Nehemiah **shook out the folds** of his robe. Such gestures were thought to empower a person's words and to assure that God would enforce the pronouncement. Nehemiah followed the symbolic act with these words: **In this way may God shake out of his house and possessions every man who does not keep this promise.** The people voiced agreement for the resolution and viewed it as testimony to God's goodness.

The incident came to conclusion, **and the people did as they had promised.** This probably refers to all involved—the nobles, officials, and the general population, as they forged new, more honorable business methods with one another.

B Leadership by Example (5:14–19)

SUPPORTING IDEA: *The successful and godly leader places the welfare of the group or community above his own. He serves, even if this means forgoing one's "rights and privileges."*

5:14. In context with the financial crisis and state of economics within Judah, Nehemiah interjected an overview of his years as governor. This is, in fact, the first place that Nehemiah mentioned his governorship; he also established his term of service: **From the twentieth year of King Artaxerxes . . . until his thirty-second year—twelve years**. Based upon this entry, it is clear that Nehemiah was either appointed governor before he departed Susa or soon after his arrival in Jerusalem. It was on the strength of this political authority that he was able to organize the building of the wall, establish military protection, and compel economic reforms.

During the twelve years he performed his duties as governor, neither Nehemiah nor his brothers **ate the food allotted to the governor**. The same integrity he had demonstrated in regard to loans (Neh. 5:10), he also confirmed through daily habits. As a political official under authority of Persia, the governor was to levy taxes on the people in order to supply his own wage and satisfy his expenses. Many satraps became wealthy and powerful through this method.

However, despite the legal accommodation to do so, and the political tradition that approved it, Nehemiah refused to participate in a system that placed greater economic strain on the people. While working within the political structure, he stood aloof of its assumptions and responded according to conscience.

5:15. In contrast, the governors who preceded Nehemiah **placed a heavy burden on the people and took forty shekels of silver from them in addition to food and wine**. The forty shekels, about one pound, probably was a daily allowance for the governor, including the purchase of food and wine for his expected hospitality needs. While the excessive spending and entertaining of the governors was burdensome, it was expected and rarely questioned. Those who served these earlier governors **also lorded it over the people**. We may assume this was also economic.

But out of reverence for God, Nehemiah declared, **I did not act like that.** He was motivated by two passions—devotion to God and compassion for his Jewish kinsmen. He exemplified the essence of the law: love for God and love for neighbor.

5:16. Rather than pursue personal wealth, Nehemiah devoted himself **to the work on this wall**. The community's reputation consumed his time and energy. Those who served and worked alongside Nehemiah had caught his passion and assumed his ethics, and they **assembled** at the wall **for the work**; they **did not acquire any land**. Personal ambitions were laid aside.

5:17–18. Not only did Nehemiah forfeit his right to income from taxes; he also provided, at his own expense, the necessities expected of a government official. Each day **a hundred and fifty Jews and officials ate at my table**, he wrote. These were Jewish leaders and Persian officials who, as part of their pay, were entitled to meals from the governor. In addition, he hosted **those who came . . . from the surrounding nations**—probably officials from neighboring satrapies. Nehemiah fulfilled his duties but without adding to the burden of the people. Instead, he supplied from his personal wealth.

5:19. Reflecting on his years as governor, Nehemiah offered this prayer: **Remember me with favor, O my God, for all I have done for these people.** Nehemiah simply wanted God's approval.

> **MAIN IDEA REVIEW**: *Leadership requires working with different interest groups and personalities, while at the same time supplying a vision to follow. More important, however, the leader must demonstrate integrity. The most brilliant plans cannot serve as a substitute for this critical quality.*

III. CONCLUSION

Please Show Your Credentials

There has been an explosion of credential-granting organizations and specialties. It used to be rather easy—MD, PhD, RN, CPA. Now there are numerous letter combinations signifying some expertise. I came across a person's name followed by, C-ACYFSW. I had no clue what this meant. I later learned it identified a "Certified Advanced Children, Youth, and Family Social Worker."

When the new governor entered Jerusalem in 446 B.C., he wrote his name—Nehemiah, CB (cupbearer). Well, probably not. As cupbearer Nehemiah probably received quite an education in government and leadership just by observation at Susa. His most important credential, however, was strength of character. The poor of Judah and Jerusalem came to him to voice their complaints because they noticed a difference in Nehemiah, something that placed him apart from all their former governors and leaders. He displayed a genuine concern for the welfare of the people, and he conducted himself with integrity.

Unbending in his adherence to the laws of God and his moral standards, Nehemiah led not only by an expressed vision but also by example. He brought with him letters from King Artaxerxes, but more importantly he came bearing the favor of God.

[handwritten margin notes:] Does Nehemiah sound like he is boasting?

Everybody wants credentials?

Of course, education and specialized training can be useful in life and in service to Christ. But the more important issue is attitude of heart. Paul wrote:

> Think of what you were when you were called. Not many of you were wise by human standards; not many were influential; not many were of noble birth. But God chose the foolish things of the world to shame the wise . . . the weak things of the world to shame the strong . . . so that no one may boast before him (1 Cor. 1:26–27,29).

Nehemiah had few personal ambitions. He certainly did not follow after the established and presumed methods of leadership. Rather than acquiring lands and privilege, Nehemiah served the people. Rather than seeking advantage, he sought service. Others worked hard for themselves, making business and political alliances and deals and accumulating powerful connections like a string of letters behind their name. Nehemiah was content with one credential—servant of God.

PRINCIPLES

- God is just and is deeply concerned about justice.
- Strength of character and personal integrity matter more to God than talents or skills.
- God cares for the poor.
- Christians should conduct their business with the highest ethics, caring for people above profit.
- To lead is to serve.

APPLICATIONS

- Assess your work and income: do they come at the expense of others? Does your comfort result from someone else's suffering? If so, find ways to change the situation.
- Most of us have leadership positions, either at home, at church, or at work. Rethink your role, and find ways to serve and care for the people in your life.
- How do you spend your money? God cares deeply about how we use the resources he has entrusted to us. Find new ways to exercise the grace of giving.
- In all your affairs, conduct yourself with honesty and integrity.

IV. LIFE APPLICATION

Let Justice Roll

My mother was a single parent because of divorce. Consequently, she had to work hard every week to make a living and help support us. This meant that every Saturday morning when I was young, my older brother and I took turns sweeping and scrubbing the floors of our home and going to the grocery store with our mom. It was part of being family.

Before the Babylonians forced Judah into exile, the prophet Amos pointed to the Jews' injustices as one reason for God's displeasure and their impending captivity. He wrote, "Away with the noise of your songs! I will not listen to the music of your harps. But let justice roll on like a river, righteousness like a never-failing stream!" (Amos 5:23–24).

Seventy years later the Jews began returning to Judah; yet these same issues of fairness and compassion surfaced again. Once more God addressed the people through a prophet. This time Zechariah spoke: "This is what the LORD Almighty says: 'Administer true justice; show mercy and compassion to one another. Do not oppress the widow or the fatherless, the alien or the poor. In your hearts do not think evil of each other'" (Zech. 7:9–10).

Despite previous experience and warnings, Nehemiah heard complaints about injustices within the community. The wealthy were charging such high and burdensome interest rates that the common people were being forced into debt or their children into slavery. The civic and business leaders were advancing their personal interests and accumulating wealth by oppressing their "brothers." Nehemiah confronted the accused: "What you are doing is not right. Shouldn't you walk in the fear of our God?" (Neh. 5:9).

The principle of brotherhood is strong throughout the Bible. The majority of the Ten Commandments center on this concept. Every human being is related to every other, simply by virtue of our creation in God's image. Every human life is to be treated with respect and dignity; each person is to be valued.

Beyond the general principle of human brotherhood, a special relationship exists within a community of believers. Israel represented God's spiritual community. The Jews were to regard one another as inseparably bonded; they were brothers of faith and soul. This concept continues into the New Testament where Christians are instructed to regard other believers as true "brothers and sisters," related more closely because of the blood of Christ. Christians are kinsmen into eternity because we are part of a spiritual family.

While mistreatment of any human being is utterly wrong, neglect or disregard for those with whom we are bound by spirit is reprehensible. Paul wrote, "Therefore, as we have opportunity, let us do good to all people, especially to those who belong to the family of believers" (Gal. 6:10).

Some of our spiritual relatives are surrounded by the terrors and hardships of war, others are sold into slavery, and still more have barely enough to eat. Are we, by our lifestyle, among the oppressors? Are we trying to find ways to relieve our brothers' burdens? Are we more concerned for our profits and comfort than we are for Christ's children?

"Let justice roll on like a river, righteousness like a never-failing stream!" (Amos 5:24).

V. PRAYER

Dear God, we are so busy that it is easy to overlook the poor around us. Help us to share from what you have given. Help us to be good stewards or managers of all that we have, and to know that one of the reasons you have blessed us so much is that you want us to share with others and learn how to give. Amen.

VI. DEEPER DISCOVERIES

Personal Rights (5:14–18)

The idea of personal rights figures prominently in Western cultures. It forms some of the rationale for our democratic political system and our courts.

Throughout the Bible, however, we find a call to submit our rights to a higher good. As governor, Nehemiah had certain rights that came with his leadership position. Rather than insisting on what was his, or even assuming that he should follow tradition, he relinquished his rights for the welfare of the Jewish citizens.

Jesus challenged his followers to release their "rights" and replace them with generosity (Matt. 6). He was not establishing a new law that allowed abuse and timidity; rather, he was calling his followers to love and giving. Personal concerns were to be superseded by interest in others.

Paul followed this up in Romans 12 by instructing Christians to "not think of yourself more highly than you ought" but to "share with God's people who are in need. . . . Live in harmony with one another. . . . Be willing to associate with people of low position. . . . Do not repay anyone evil for evil . . . as far as it depends on you, live at peace with everyone" (Rom. 12:3,13,16–18). These injunctions are impossible if we cling to our rights. In fact, forgiveness, the very cornerstone of our faith, is impossible if we refuse to relinquish our rights for the good of others.

VII. TEACHING OUTLINE

A. INTRODUCTION

1. Lead Story: Facades
2. Context: Before, during, and after Nehemiah's tenure as governor, Jerusalem was a mixture of special interest groups, political competition, economic conflict, and religious confusion. Reforms were introduced, but the propensity to selfish ambition and spiritual waywardness always percolated just below the surface of society.
3. Transition: In contrast to the traditional methods of governance, and the prevailing attitudes of the people, Nehemiah stepped into the cultural milieu with a different approach. As both political and spiritual leader, he determined to serve people. He modeled a life of discipline and compassion.

B. COMMENTARY

1. Troubles Within (5:1–13)
   a. Economic oppression (5:1–5)
   b. Nehemiah's judgment (5:6–11)
   c. The pledge (5:12–13)
2. Leadership by Example (5:14–19)

C. CONCLUSION: PLEASE SHOW YOUR CREDENTIALS

VIII. ISSUES FOR DISCUSSION

1. Compare and contrast Nehemiah 5; 1 Corinthians 9:3–15; and 1 Thessalonians 2:6–9. Are there limits to self-sacrifice? If so, explain.
2. Does Christ place on Christians the social responsibility of caring for the poor? Discuss your position, giving biblical support.
3. Was Nehemiah's advocacy for interest-free loans a temporary measure? Or a permanent policy? What are possible ramifications of either position? Can you come to a biblical consensus about loans, debt, and interest charges?

Nehemiah 6:1–14

Getting Personal

I. INTRODUCTION
Purpose, Purpose, Purpose

II. COMMENTARY
A verse-by-verse explanation of these verses.

III. CONCLUSION
The Lion's Roar

An overview of the principles and applications from these verses.

IV. LIFE APPLICATION
Untoward

Melding these verses to life.

V. PRAYER
Tying these verses to life with God.

VI. DEEPER DISCOVERIES
Historical, geographical, and grammatical enrichment of the commentary.

VII. TEACHING OUTLINE
Suggested step-by-step group study of these verses.

VIII. ISSUES FOR DISCUSSION
Zeroing these verses in on daily life.

Nehemiah 6:1–14

Quote

*C*ourage is fear that has said its prayers.

D o r o t h y   B e r n a r d

I N   A   N U T S H E L L

*S*anballat and Tobiah had opposed the wall's reconstruction from the beginning. They had tried to discourage the workers and had threatened the people. Every attempt was unsuccessful. In one last desperate attempt, they focused on Nehemiah.

Getting Personal

I. INTRODUCTION

Purpose, Purpose, Purpose

A medical doctor at the University of Vienna wrote, "There is nothing in the world which helps a man surmount his difficulties, survive his disasters, and stay healthy and happy, as knowledge of a life task worthy of his devotion."

Place this statements against the backdrop of Nehemiah, and you understand why nothing could turn Nehemiah from his task—neither external threats nor internal challenges.

Having failed to disrupt the wall's reconstruction with threats, Tobiah and Sanballat next used personal attacks against Nehemiah. They understood that this man provided strength for the Jerusalem community through his exceptional leadership. They hoped to destroy the Jews' work by destroying their leader. They began the next phase of attacks by trying to woo Nehemiah away from the project on the pretext of peace talks. But Nehemiah was not distracted. He replied, "I am carrying on a great project and cannot go down." He was involved in a mission that captured his heart; he was working for God, who was worthy of his devotion.

Nehemiah is a good example of focused and unselfish living. Paul demonstrated this as well. Writing to the Philippians, he said, "Forgetting what is behind and straining toward what is ahead, I press on toward the goal to win the prize for which God has called me heavenward in Christ Jesus" (Phil. 3:13–14). The glory of Christ filled his vision, and this kept him from wandering off the path and getting involved in meaningless side issues or selfish pursuits.

What is the motivating force in our lives? What life task is worthy of our devotion? "Let us fix our eyes on Jesus, the author and perfecter of our faith, who for the joy set before him endured the cross . . . consider him who endured such opposition from sinful men, so that you will not grow weary and lose heart" (Heb. 12:2–3).

II. COMMENTARY

Getting Personal

MAIN IDEA: *In the midst of competing interests, leaders often come under personal attack. At such times they must leave their defense to God and hold firmly to his vision and purpose. While remaining peaceable, the leader must not compromise truth and righteousness.*

A The Pretense of Peace (6:1–4)

SUPPORTING IDEA: *The leader's motives and conduct must be blameless. At the same time, he must understand the opposition, dealing shrewdly and wisely with those who seek to compromise God's work.*

6:1–2. Despite the harassment and intimidation they had used, Sanballat, Tobiah, Geshem the Arab, and their allies learned that Nehemiah and the Jews **had rebuilt the wall and not a gap was left in it**. In remarkable time Nehemiah had led the complete restoration of the wall—though up to that time he **had not set the doors in the gates**. With the majority of the work completed, Sanballat, Tobiah, and Geshem realized they could not stop the wall's completion, so they turned their attention to eliminating Nehemiah.

The two leaders, Sanballat and Geshem, sent Nehemiah a message: **Come, let us meet together in one of the villages on the plain of Ono.** The men hoped to lure Nehemiah away from Jerusalem where he had supporters and defense. There is little consensus among scholars about where the "plain of Ono" was, but most believe it was somewhere within the Judean borders, or perhaps in a neutral area. Nothing was mentioned in their message about the purpose of the meeting. Since relations between Judea and its surrounding territories had become tense, perhaps Sanballat offered the meeting as a type of peace conference.

Nehemiah understood that these men were scheming to harm him. While feigning peace, they plotted harm, perhaps assassination.

6:3. Nehemiah understood not only the brutal intent behind the invitation, but the futility that would result if such a meeting took place. These men were antagonistic to everything Nehemiah stood for and worked to accomplish. Therefore, he sent messengers with this reply: **I am carrying on a great project and cannot go down.**

The very thing they wished to destroy, Nehemiah used to circumvent their plans. A conference with these leaders was a small thing compared to the wall. Even the geographical position of Jerusalem above the plain of Ono suggests a metaphorical contrast in which descending to the meeting would

[handwritten margin note: Nehemiah was discerning. I pray for discernment because it is hard to read intentions.]

represent a demotion of purpose. After all, **Why should the work stop while I leave it and go down to you?** he asked.

6:4. Even though the only thing left to do was the hanging of the doors in the gates (for which Nehemiah's presence was probably not required), Nehemiah could assert that the demands of the project took precedence over any other claims on his time. Sanballat and his allies were left with nothing to do except repeat the invitation: **Four times they sent me the same message, and each time I gave them the same answer.** Nehemiah would not become entangled in a conference that would prove harmful to himself or wasteful of his time.

B The Trap of Intimidation (6:5–9)

SUPPORTING IDEA: *The leader must learn to analyze which issues are critical enough to address and which are wasteful distractions.*

6:5–7. Having made no progress with Nehemiah, Sanballat sent his messenger once again, but this time with a thinly veiled threat. Along with the invitation to meet on the plain of Ono, Sanballat included **an unsealed letter.** One may surmise that all communication between the leaders had been conducted privately up to this point. But after four rebuffs Sanballat took his intimidation a step further. The unsealed papyrus was considered an open letter, meaning others could read it.

The letter aired rumors with the intention of having them spread. Sanballat hoped these rumors would either unsettle Nehemiah or create tension among the Jews.

Sanballat wrote to Nehemiah that he had heard disturbing gossip. People in the territories surrounding Judea were talking, and they were worried. Just ask **Geshem,** he said. Even in his widespread province he had heard the same thing—that Nehemiah and the Jews had built the wall because they were **plotting to revolt.** And, according to rumor, Nehemiah was **about to become their king** and had **even appointed prophets** to make this proclamation: There is a king in Judah! *The devil can use bits of truth in his plot*

Sanballat counted on recent history to fuel fear in Nehemiah, and in the population of Jerusalem. Not many years before, these very threats and accusations had succeeded in bringing violence upon the city (Ezra 4). Once before Artaxerxes had been convinced that Jerusalem posed a threat to Persian interests, labeling it "a place of rebellion and sedition" (Ezra 4:19). It was quite possible that the king could again be persuaded of its mutiny. Sanballat hoped that the memory of Jerusalem's violent destruction would weaken the resolve and loyalty of its citizens and that they would see Nehemiah as a liability.

Sanballat also hoped that Nehemiah would follow the logical thread of these rumors, as well as the clear message of his threat: **Now this report will get back to the king**. The king would find out, either by gossip or official report, and Nehemiah would be charged with treason and revolt.

Sanballat probably felt certain that Nehemiah would jump at the chance to go to Ono and **confer together**, though such a secretive meeting would be construed more traitorous than anything Nehemiah had done to that point.

6:8. Nehemiah replied: **Nothing like what you are saying is happening; you are just making it up out of your head**. He dismissed the whole thing as fantasy. Sanballat and his allies assumed that Nehemiah was no different than they—given to ambition, opportunistic maneuvering, and dedicated to self-preservation. They failed to understand his devotion to God and the depth of his sacrificial service.

6:9. Nehemiah's interpretation of the threats reveals a man properly focused and perceptive: **They were all trying to frighten us**. He was not pulled into their assumptions or confused by their arguments. Instead, he ascertained their objective to discourage the people: **Their hands will get too weak for the work, and it will not be completed**. Having determined their tactics, he prayed, **Now strengthen my hands**.

Nehemiah refused to become distracted by the ploy of politics. The schemes of Sanballat only strengthened Nehemiah's resolve.

C The Lure of Safety (6:10–14)

SUPPORTING IDEA: *The leader must remember that the will of God is eternal and has primacy over any individual.*

6:10. Looking back, Nehemiah highlighted particular episodes that exemplified the subversive atmosphere present in Jerusalem at this time. One such incident was a visit he made to **the house of Shemaiah . . . who was shut in at his home**.

Shemaiah appears to have served in some official way within the temple. Though Nehemiah did not reveal his purpose in visiting Shemaiah, we may surmise that Shemaiah requested his visit; he may have indicated to Nehemiah that he had a prophetic word from God. The text does not provide any information or clues about why Shemaiah was confined to his home.

Shemaiah told Nehemiah: **Let us meet in the house of God, inside the temple, and let us close the temple doors, because men are coming to kill you**. This threatening message that had all the marks of authenticity was crafted to elicit fear. Shemaiah advised Nehemiah to hide in the temple—where only priests were allowed—in order to save himself. Nehemiah knew that Sanballat and his cohorts were hoping to destroy him in some way. **By night they are coming to kill you**, Shemaiah intoned, and Nehemiah knew it was highly plausible that murderers were planning to attack.

6:11–13. But Nehemiah did not succumb to panic or self-interest. He measured the message of this "prophet" by the known revelation of God and the law he had entrusted to Israel. **Should a man like me run away?** he asked Shemaiah. He recognized the responsibilities of leadership and the need to remain at one's post despite threats against his safety. As governor, it did not fit his position or duty to run away and hide.

Or should one like me go into the temple to save his life? Nehemiah's second question cast doubt on the veracity of Shemaiah's original message and the integrity of the messenger. Nehemiah knew that Shemaiah proposed a violation of the law because non-priests were not allowed within the sanctuary. **I will not go** was Nehemiah's prompt reply. With the plot exposed, Nehemiah realized that God had not sent Shemaiah, **but that he had prophesied against me because Tobiah and Sanballat had hired him.**

Tobiah, through marriage, had close connections to the priesthood. He also had business connections and a network of loyalists within the ruling hierarchy of Jerusalem. These associations provided Tobiah with leverage among the elite throughout the city. Shemaiah was only one case in point, and he had been hired **to intimidate** Nehemiah so that he **would commit a sin**. Tobiah and Sanballat used this priest to lure Nehemiah, hoping that through fear and the urge for self-protection he would violate the sanctity of the temple.

If Nehemiah had succumbed to their trickery, he would have fallen into disrepute with the priesthood, and then they would have given Nehemiah **a bad name to discredit** him. Sanballat and Tobiah wanted to alienate Nehemiah from those he served and thus destroy his effectiveness to lead within the community.

6:14. Again Nehemiah left his enemies in the hand of God. After exercising wisdom and resolve, he prayed, **Remember Tobiah and Sanballat, O my God, because of what they have done**. He refused to take matters into his own hands. Vengeance belonged to God.

Nehemiah also prayed that God would **remember also the prophetess Noadiah and the rest of the prophets who have been trying to intimidate me**. Outside this text there exists no information about this woman or the other prophets. But it is clear that Shemaiah was only one person in a larger consortium of religious conspirators. Nehemiah worked in a hostile environment even within Jerusalem.

MAIN IDEA REVIEW: *In the midst of competing interests, leaders often come under personal attack. At such times they must leave their defense to God and hold firmly to his vision and purpose. While remaining peaceable, the leader must not compromise truth and righteousness.*

III. CONCLUSION

The Lion's Roar

Winston Churchill seemed to be the man least likely to lead Great Britain successfully through the traumas and challenges of World War II. Before Hitler's invasion of Poland, Churchill's political career had been marked by failures and a growing coalition of enemies. His childhood was characterized by unloving parents, illness, fears, and a speech impediment. Yet Churchill emerged as one of the great leaders of the twentieth century.

There may be many explanations for his extraordinary ability to lead the nation during crisis. Certainly, neither he nor the people were distracted by petty politics or competing interests. Everyone was focused on winning the war, and every decision was passed through this one obsession. But circumstances don't create the man; they only reveal his character. One of the qualities that Churchill possessed was a ferocious courage. This was not to say he lacked fear but rather that he did not submit to it.

"Never give in, never give in, never, never, never, never—in nothing, great or small, large or petty—never give in except to convictions of honor and good sense." It was this "never give in" approach that stayed the British people through the sacrifices of war and allowed Churchill to face his critics and keep to the task.

Nehemiah was also such a man.

In Nehemiah's time Jerusalem was a mixture of self-interest, conspiracy, spiritual devotion, feigned religiosity, faith, and parochialism. Devoted workers as well as unprincipled people surrounded Nehemiah. With the realization that the wall was nearing completion despite the many attempts to halt the work, the focus of intimidation moved from the populace to their leader. They tried to lure Nehemiah away from Jerusalem in order to murder him or to charge him with sedition; they hired prophets to trap and discredit him. Yet Nehemiah held to his task. He never gave in. His courage was founded on trust in the God who had called him.

PRINCIPLES

- Courage is fear under control.
- Trust in God brings great confidence.
- God is our defense.
- Personal integrity should never be compromised.
- Purpose cultivates endurance and perseverance.

APPLICATIONS

- If you are afraid of something, write down the reasons for your fear. Then release these to God and refuse to be controlled by them.

- Set aside some time to consider your purpose in life. Think through God's goals for the world and the way he created you. Set your course to follow Christ.

- Listen carefully to what people suggest, weigh options, and think through proposals. God never accomplishes his purposes through dishonest or unrighteous means.

- Do what is right, and then commit your reputation into God's hands. He is your safeguard.

IV. LIFE APPLICATION

Untoward

In a beautiful sermon at Pentecost delivered by Peter through the inspiration of the Holy Spirit, he concluded by urging the people to repent and submit their lives to Jesus, who had been made Messiah and Lord. The acceptance of Christ's sacrifice was demonstrated by his resurrection from the dead. Then Peter told the crowd, "Save yourselves from this untoward generation" (Acts 2:40 KJV).

Untoward. We don't use that old English word any more. But it's a good one. That little prefix "un-" creates a complete reversal of the word to which it is attached. *Untoward* describes people who are not going toward anything. This was the appellation Peter attached to an entire generation—wandering aimlessly, chasing one new idea after another, confused.

It could well describe our own generation. So many just wake up, go to work, come home, watch TV, go to bed, wake up, go to work, come home, watch TV: *untoward.* Others rush around, frantically chasing the next fad, the next pop theology, or the next theory: *untoward.* For too many people their days either fade away in a haze of sameness or scream for meaning.

If Nehemiah's life demonstrates anything, it is purpose. He was focused. His heart was gripped by the desire to serve and honor God. His adoration and reverence of God propelled him through the challenges, dangers, and threats that each new day brought. Worship characterized his decisions and his actions. He was not distracted by empty arguments and endless discussions. He was not restrained by intimidation or stopped by fear. He was a man who knew where he was going because he was following God.

V. PRAYER

Lord, it is so easy to become distracted by our circumstances, to plot our responses based on what is happening around us. Help us to hold steadily to your Word and plans. Give us discernment and purify our hearts so we may join with those who labor for your glory. Amen.

VI. DEEPER DISCOVERIES

Pain and Trouble (6:1–14)

Many people blame Satan for all the pain in their lives. Sometimes he may interfere in our lives, disrupt them, and cause problems. It is well to know his strategies and objectives. But it is equally important to know that the Bible reveals many other sources for pain.

- *A fallen world.* Romans 8 teaches that all creation groans and waits for the day when Christ will redeem the whole world and restore it to its original intent. This includes everything from disease to dandelions to tornados. The world is in a state of disruption and degeneration brought about by the fall of mankind into sin. These shock waves through the physical order affect our lives.

- *Evil people.* All of us have enough depravity and sinfulness to harm others. It includes caustic words, sarcasm, gossip, murder, abuse, and terror. From within the human heart comes the destructive energy of selfishness.

- *God's discipline.* Hebrews 12 illustrates love as a father disciplining a child. God disciplines his children by allowing pain in their lives in order to train or correct them. It hurts, but love cannot neglect the object of its affection; to withhold discipline would be to deny the opportunity for growth and change.

- *Self-inflicted wounds.* Sometimes we hurt ourselves and bring grief into our life through our own poor choices. Our foolish decisions produce painful results. While we should show sympathy and compassion for the agonies and problems in our world, it should be evident that much trouble comes because we refuse to follow God's clear commands.

VII. TEACHING OUTLINE

A. INTRODUCTION

1. Lead Story: Purpose, Purpose, Purpose
2. Context: Nehemiah's tenure as governor disrupted the status quo in Jerusalem, Judah, and the surrounding territories. His dedication to the law, national pride, and social justice unsettled an established economic and political system among the Jewish nobility and the neighboring territories.
3. Transition: Before the arrival of Nehemiah, those who profited most from the region's economic disparity also wielded the most political power. When Nehemiah's policies threatened these strongholds, the leaders and their cohorts devised ways to discredit Nehemiah.

B. COMMENTARY

1. The Pretense of Peace (6:1–4)
2. The Trap of Intimidation (6:5–9)
3. The Lure of Safety (6:10–14)

C. CONCLUSION: THE LION'S ROAR

VIII. ISSUES FOR DISCUSSION

1. Discuss what issues or attitudes within our culture distract Christians from serving Christ.
2. How would you respond to a person who accused you of being intolerant because you didn't agree with his religious views?
3. When people discredit or misrepresent you, how should you respond? What course of action should you take, if any?
4. Jesus said, "In this world you will have trouble" (John 16:33). How should a Christian regard difficulties and danger?

Nehemiah 6:15–7:73

❦❧

Now What?

I. INTRODUCTION
Down on the Farm

II. COMMENTARY
A verse-by-verse explanation of these verses.

III. CONCLUSION
Ratios

An overview of the principles and applications from these verses.

IV. LIFE APPLICATION
The Shrewd Manager

Melding these verses to life.

V. PRAYER
Tying these verses to life with God.

VI. DEEPER DISCOVERIES
Historical, geographical, and grammatical enrichment of the commentary.

VII. TEACHING OUTLINE
Suggested step-by-step group study of these verses.
Issues for Discussion

VIII. ISSUES FOR DISCUSSION
Zeroing these verses in on daily life.

---

*𝒥*have no fear of the future. Let us go forward into its

mysteries, let us tear aside the veils that hide it from our

eyes and let us move onward with confidence and courage.

W i n s t o n   C h u r c h i l l

Nehemiah 6:15–7:73

I N   A   N U T S H E L L

*𝒜*t last the wall was completed; but the hostilities continued.
Nehemiah instigated emergency measures to protect Jerusalem. He
then consulted the genealogical records from Zerubbabel's time to establish the criteria for repopulating Jerusalem.

Now What?

I. INTRODUCTION

Down on the Farm

Jesus once told a parable about a farmer who plowed his soil and then planted some wheat. It was high quality seed so there was expectation of a good harvest. That night as he and his farmhands were sleeping, a rival neighbor sneaked onto his land and scattered different seeds over the tilled ground. Days and weeks passed, and the plants grew.

When the wheat finally sprouted and formed heads, the workers rushed to the farmer and reported that weeds were growing among the grain. "Where did the weeds come from?" they asked.

The farmer replied, "An enemy did this."

The workers asked if they should yank the weeds out. "'No,' he answered, 'because while you are pulling the weeds, you may root up the wheat with them. Let both grow together until the harvest'" (Matt. 13:29–30).

The work Nehemiah had begun was finally complete. The wall was finished. Yet within the Jewish community, people still tried to destabilize Nehemiah's efforts and rule. Placing the last stone into the wall did not end the opposition. Most disturbing was the compromise and damage caused by Jewish leaders in Jerusalem. Their self-interests took precedence over the community and God. As many of the Jews returned to faithful obedience and worship of the Lord, others held tenaciously to alliances and business deals that could damage Nehemiah's reformation efforts.

II. COMMENTARY

Now What?

MAIN IDEA: *The establishment of fortifications does not, in itself, bring security. Opposition and dangers always threaten the community of faith; a people's godly character is its greatest defense.*

Continued Resistance (6:15–19)

SUPPORTING IDEA: *The completion of a task or mission does not always result in the cessation of hostilities.*

6:15–16. After repeated opposition, intrigue, and difficulties, Nehemiah noted that the wall was finished—completed **on the twenty-fifth of Elul.** This placed the project's conclusion some time in early fall, possibly September. From start to finish, the rebuilding project took only **fifty-two days**. This attested to God's favor and protection and Nehemiah's ability to inspire and lead the people.

The reports of the completion of the wall, as well the realization of the speed at which it was accomplished, created quite a stir among the enemies of the Jews throughout the region. Their dismay and discouragement in the face of the Jews' stunning success most likely filtered down through the populace of those regions over which they governed. Those provinces and peoples surrounding Judah and Jerusalem were demoralized **because they realized that this work had been done with the help of our God**. Those in ancient Mesopotamia and adjoining regions connected a nation's status with divine favor or judgment.

6:17–19. Against the backdrop of the wall's completion and God's favor, Nehemiah returned to the intrigue and politicking that characterized the times in which he served as governor: **the nobles of Judah were sending many letters to Tobiah, and replies from Tobiah kept coming to them**.

Despite Nehemiah's inspirational leadership, his exemplary service, and his godly vision, the wealthy Jews throughout Judah continued an alliance with Tobiah. In fact, **many in Judah were under oath to him**, though the nature of this allegiance is not specified. Perhaps these nobles had formed a financial partnership with Tobiah that was mutually beneficial.

But Tobiah's connections to Jewish interests were founded on more than economics. He had married the daughter of **Shecaniah son of Arah**, and Tobiah's son had **married the daughter of Meshullam son of Berekiah**. These Jewish connections indicate that Tobiah may have lived in Jerusalem at one time, enjoying a great deal of influence among its leaders and wealthy residents. Unlike Sanballat, Tobiah was not an outsider.

Additionally, these nobles carried on a public relations campaign on behalf of Tobiah, reporting to Nehemiah **his good deeds** and then reporting Nehemiah's response back to Tobiah. Quite likely these men were not enthusiastic supporters of Nehemiah's policies; they probably wanted to continue a more relaxed economic posture toward the surrounding territories. Undoubtedly this was to their advantage. So while some of these men may have supported the rebuilding of the wall, they did not agree with Nehemiah's political plans.

But Nehemiah's position seems validated since the result of all the reporting and talk was that **Tobiah sent letters to intimidate me**. Tobiah appears to have changed tactics. Rather than trying to dislodge Nehemiah through assassination, legal charges, or disgrace, he turned his energy toward securing his influence in Jewish affairs, particularly Jewish commerce. To that end, he followed his tendency to threaten and coerce.

The wall was completed, but the corruption and oppression throughout Judah and Jerusalem continued. Clearly, the wall was not an end in itself but a first step toward further reform.

B Next Steps (7:1–73)

SUPPORTING IDEA: *The wall around Jerusalem was not an end in itself but a necessary defense and dynamic symbol of Israel's distinctiveness among the nations.*

1. Vigilance (7:1–3)

7:1. Having described the subversive atmosphere and attitudes still prevalent in and around Jerusalem, Nehemiah backtracked slightly. He stated again that the wall was completed, establishing its finality by setting **the doors in place.** In addition, everything was done orderly and properly: **the gatekeepers and the singers and the Levites were appointed.** Nehemiah was attentive to every detail.

7:2. As provincial governor, Nehemiah appointed two key leaders. He put in charge of Jerusalem his **brother Hanani, along with Hananiah the commander of the citadel.** Nehemiah's brother had demonstrated his faithfulness and integrity from the beginning. It was Hanani who first reported to Nehemiah the conditions in Judah (Neh. 1:2–3). We may also suppose that he was among those who diligently guarded the wall and the workers against attack (Neh. 4:23) and served the people by refusing to indulge in a lavish lifestyle (Neh. 5:14–15). Hananiah was commended **because he was a man of integrity and feared God more than most men do.**

7:3. The wording of this verse has left many scholars confused about the actual instructions Nehemiah gave. The Hebrew construction is convoluted. It is unclear whether the gates were opened early and closed when the sun was hot, during the drowsy time of early afternoon. Or whether the gates were left shut during the morning. The first explanation seems most probable since early afternoon, after the midday meal, was the quietest and most relaxed time of the day, leaving the city more vulnerable.

Whatever the precise arrangements, we may rest assured that the leaders and gatekeepers understood the instructions. The system had been devised to protect the city and its inhabitants at those points of greatest weakness. In addition to the official guards and gatekeepers, **residents of Jerusalem** were appointed **as guards, some at their posts and some near their own houses.** These citizens were placed in strategic locations to offer defense from attack. Some residents, whose homes were on or near the wall, used their houses as protective posts.

2. The census (7:4–73)

7:4–5. The defensive measures that Nehemiah, Hanani, and Hananiah implemented were probably short-term. The greater goal was to reestablish Jerusalem as a vibrant center of Jewish culture and religious purity. The completion of the wall was only the first phase in this process.

Nehemiah turned his attention from walls and physical defenses to the people and their spiritual integrity and development. He noted that Jerusalem **was large and spacious, but there were few people in it, and the houses had not yet been rebuilt.** Jerusalem was still a desolate place with the scars of its destruction evident. Its sparse population left it open to foreign hostilities and internal coups and rebellion.

Nehemiah wrote, **So my God put it into my heart to assemble the nobles, the officials and the common people for registration by families.** The type of repopulation that Nehemiah had in mind was not particularly Jewish in origin. In fact, it seemed more akin to the imperial practices of pagan nations who used forced relocation to populate cities and regions. Consequently, Nehemiah made clear that this idea came from God.

Additionally, Nehemiah did not want just anybody to transfer residence to Jerusalem. He was looking for Jews of verifiable Hebrew heritage. This prompted the gathering of the people for registration so each family could prove their lineage. To aid him in the process, Nehemiah **found the genealogical record of those who had been the first to return.** Rather than starting his census from scratch, Nehemiah was helped by this original listing that specified clan origins.

7:6–73. The list used by Nehemiah is an almost exact replication of the list found in Ezra 2. There are only slight variations, probably because of the transcribing and transmission of such records over time. For an explanation of these verses, see the discussion on Ezra 2.

> **MAIN IDEA REVIEW:** *The establishment of fortifications does not, in itself, bring security. Opposition and dangers always threaten the community of faith; a people's godly character is its greatest defense.*

III. CONCLUSION

Ratios

If you've ever watched a movie and hung around for the credits, you may have been amazed at the many people required for transforming a story into a film. After the names of the major and supporting actors and actress scroll by, you notice costume designers, choreographers, stuntmen, A cameraman, B cameraman, script supervisor, special effects, construction, lighting, payroll, travel coordinator, publicist, set directors, lamp operators . . . on and on it rolls—and the credits don't cover half of those involved. Behind the recognizable faces of those who played roles in the movie, thousands assure that the film moves from concept to product. Without ordinary workers, movies would remain only dreams.

The same could be said for many different endeavors. An enormous support team is required for each fighter pilot in the U.S. Air Force; for every CEO, an army of support staff, managers, and laborers work to produce success; for every missionary on the field, a network of secretaries, advisers, directors, givers, and prayer partners commit themselves.

When Nehemiah decided to repopulate Jerusalem, he went not to the nobles but to a list of names representing ordinary Jews. The long genealogical tables and numbers symbolize for us the significance of individuals in the work of God. Though we may not recognize any of the names that guided Nehemiah's selection process, we can see the method God uses to bring about his will: ordinary people living out their lives for his glory.

The lists are the only surviving record of these people's existence—at least for us. But their personalities, circumstances, value, and labor did not escape the watchful eye of God. It was everyday people who piled the stones that formed the wall, or who volunteered to resettle Jerusalem and defend the city against violence and corruption, or who listened with reverence to the Word of God and responded with repentance, turning the community back to faithfulness. Average citizens under able leadership can bring about extraordinary change.

PRINCIPLES

- Success requires endurance.
- Good work done in the name of Christ brings glory to God.
- Success sometimes leads to vulnerability and the need for continued vigilance against opposition.
- The people of God must carry out the work of God.

APPLICATIONS

- Be careful after a time of special spiritual growth or after a goal has been accomplished. Such times can bring a susceptibility to failure or sin.
- Whatever your role in the effort to extend God's kingdom, do it with all your heart and to the best of your ability.
- Remember that everyone is necessary to God's kingdom; and every act done for Christ is seen and rewarded by God.

IV. LIFE APPLICATION

The Shrewd Manager

Luke 16 tells the story of a supervisor who was found guilty of misman-agement. His boss gave him notice that the following day he would have to find a new job. Dismayed by the realization that he would have to join the ranks of the unemployed, he devised a plan. He began calling up those people who were indebted to his employer. Without the knowledge of his boss, he started bargaining and reducing the debts owed by other businessmen. If someone owed his employer eight hundred gallons of oil, he told him to reduce the bill to four hundred. As manager, he still had the authority to deal and oversee resources.

Eventually his boss found out what he was doing. Though he never expressed approval of his method, the employer did commend the manager for having foresight. He praised him for being shrewd. By reducing the bills of various people, he had gained friends who would welcome him into their homes and offer him meals once he had lost his job. The wealthy owner approved of the supervisor's wisdom that compelled him to look ahead and prepare for the future.

Jesus wanted his disciples to adopt that same shrewdness; he wanted his followers to use their earthly wealth and possessions for eternal purposes. He desired that they adopt the wisdom that looks to the future.

After the completion of the wall, Nehemiah used good judgment by implementing a plan that would repopulate Jerusalem with ethnic Jews. The reason for his approach was not racial but spiritual. By moving to Jerusalem those Jews who could trace their ancestry to the time of Zerubbabel, who in turn could trace their ancestry to the preexilic kingdom, he put in place a process that would secure for the future a people dedicated to God and Judah.

Nehemiah was shrewd enough to look beyond the wall, and even beyond his own leadership, to a time when the people must work and worship on their own. He prepared for that time by investing in people. Every leader needs to exercise the same shrewdness that Nehemiah had. By applying insight and sound judgment, those who lead should prepare others to assume leadership.

V. PRAYER

Lord, as people of this earth, it is so easy to place our hope and security in physical things—institutions, buildings, bank accounts, and our own plans. Help us remember that you alone are our defense, our hope, and our security. Help us sharpen our character as we rely on you. Amen.

VI. DEEPER DISCOVERIES

Lists (7:8–73)

In this chapter of Nehemiah, we come across another list of people. A previous list detailed some of the workers on the wall and the various sections they repaired. This list in chapter 7 actually comes from a genealogical list of the names of those who returned in the first caravan out of Persia. Other lists will follow in chapters 10, 11, and 12 of the Book of Nehemiah.

Many people start reading the Bible, but then stop when they come upon similar records of names or family descendants. They seem boring. We often want to skip ahead to the action. But these lists are important. They demonstrate that God not only watches history but that he guards his people and protects his community. Through these ancient people the Savior eventually came into the world. Through these individuals we have received the Word of God, the examples of grace, and perpetuation of hope.

The lists give evidence of God's care and intimate concern for every individual. He knows what we do, even "in secret," out of the spotlight of world attention, away from the crowd. He notices the work, the attitude, and the time we give in submission to his goals and love. The implication is that we can be faithful with the responsibilities we have, no matter what they are.

Thank God for the lists!

VII. TEACHING OUTLINE

A. INTRODUCTION

1. Lead Story: Down on the Farm

2. Context: From the time of his arrival in Jerusalem until the wall's completion, Nehemiah faced opposition from territorial leaders. But the political and social conditions within Judah and Jerusalem also presented challenges. Oppression and elitist economics drew a group of Jewish leaders into conflict with Nehemiah.

3. Transition: Once the wall was completed, these competing forces continued to test Nehemiah's leadership and policies. He turned his attention to repopulating Jerusalem in order to assure social, economic, and religious reforms.

B. COMMENTARY

1. Continued Resistance (6:15–19)
2. Next Steps (7:1–73)
   a. Vigilance (7:1–3)
   b. The census (7:4–73)

C. CONCLUSION: RATIOS

VIII. ISSUES FOR DISCUSSION

1. Why do you think finances and economics often create divisiveness, even in the church? What can we do to prevent this?
2. It was said of Hananiah that he "feared God more than most men." What does it mean to "fear God"? What are some practical implications for those who desire this characteristic?
3. What helped Nehemiah not succumb to the intimidation of Tobiah or the politics of the Jerusalem nobles? What can you learn from this for your own life and for your church?

Nehemiah 8

Spiritual Renewal

I. **INTRODUCTION**
Breath of God

II. **COMMENTARY**
A verse-by-verse explanation of the chapter.

III. **CONCLUSION**
The Heart of the Matter

An overview of the principles and applications from the chapter.

IV. **LIFE APPLICATION**
Reinventing Truth

Melding the chapter to life.

V. **PRAYER**
Tying the chapter to life with God.

VI. **DEEPER DISCOVERIES**
Historical, geographical, and grammatical enrichment of the commentary.

VII. **TEACHING OUTLINE**
Suggested step-by-step group study of the chapter.

VIII. **ISSUES FOR DISCUSSION**
Zeroing the chapter in on daily life.

Man is what he believes.

Anton   Chekhov

Nehemiah 8

IN A NUTSHELL

After Nehemiah opened the genealogical records dating from the time of Zerubbabel, the compiler of the text took the opportunity to describe the development of the faith community. He takes the reader back to Ezra's reading of the law and the effect God's Word had upon the people.

Spiritual Renewal

I. INTRODUCTION

Breath of God

*W*here would we be if God had not spoken? Where would you be if God had kept silent?

It's hard to imagine such a universal condition; it's difficult to conceive of such darkness, where even a glimmer of hope does not exist—to be conscious of a longing that cannot find relief; to be aware of an incompleteness for which there is no remedy. In such a place we could ask no questions, because there would be no answers.

But from the opening page of creation to the concluding promise of Christ's return, the Bible and Christian faith conclude that God has indeed spoken . . . and continues to speak. He alone is complete and undiminished; he alone is total beauty and terror; he alone determines reality. Who can contradict him?

When Jesus stood before Pilate he said, "For this reason I was born, and for this I came into the world, to testify to the truth. Everyone on the side of truth listens to me" (John 18:37).

The veracity of God's Word is the center around which life arranges itself. Read it with awe; listen to its words; stake your life on it.

II. COMMENTARY

Spiritual Renewal

> **MAIN IDEA:** *Spiritual renewal and vitality do not occur apart from God's Word. It convicts of sin, affirms grace, instructs in righteousness, and reveals the will of God.*

Ezra Reads the Law (8:1–12)

> **SUPPORTING IDEA:** *Ezra's commission was to restructure the Jewish community under the laws of God. The people gathered to hear Ezra read and instruct them in the commands and intentions of God's revelation.*

1. Historical context (8:1–2)

Various views are held about the historical context of Nehemiah 8–10. The data available does not conclusively decide the issue, though it favors placing the events of these chapters in the time period between Ezra 8 and 9, shortly after Ezra's arrival in Jerusalem. The events of Nehemiah 8 are described in the third person, a departure from Nehemiah's first-person journal. In addition, the Hebrew construction of Nehemiah 8:9–10 make it highly doubtful that Nehemiah's name occurred in the original manuscripts. The construction and focus of these chapters support the view that they were inserted later, with the action begun in Nehemiah 7 picked up again in Nehemiah 11.

As was noted in the Book of Ezra, these books were concerned with more than simply recording the chronological march of history. While everything within these books remains truthful and factual, the compilers sometimes broke out of their current setting or story to relate incidents from another time (see Ezra 4), thereby emphasizing a particular point. In this instance, the placement of these three chapters at this juncture emphasizes the purity of the community of faith from which Nehemiah would select people to live in Jerusalem. Holiness and religious propriety were vital to the reestablishment of an acceptable society.

8:1. Ezra and his caravan arrived in Jerusalem on the first day of the fifth month (Ezra 7:8–9). In the following two months, the people settled in their tribal towns throughout Judea. Ezra probably used that time to become acquainted with the Jerusalem leadership and to instruct the Levites in the meaning of the law. Since Ezra was commissioned by King Artaxerxes to structure the Jewish community around God's law, the support of the existing Jewish leaders and the training of the Levites were critical to his mission.

Then, in the seventh month, **all the people assembled as one man in the square before the Water Gate**. Many believe the Water Gate was located outside the city walls. **They told Ezra the scribe to bring out the Book of the Law of Moses, which the LORD had commanded for Israel**. Whoever "they" are is not specified, but they spoke as representatives of the assembled people. Ezra allowed decisions and actions to initiate from the people or their leaders. They requested that Ezra bring the Pentateuch to the gathering.

8:2. So on the first day of the seventh month Ezra the priest brought the Law before the assembly. At first it seems like a spontaneous gathering, but this assembly was well planned and strategically arranged. The seventh month was probably the most religiously important time of the year for the Jews. During this month they celebrated the Feast of Trumpets, the Day of Atonement, and the Feast of Tabernacles. In addition, Deuteronomy 31:10–12 commanded the Israelites to gather once every seven years for the reading of the law "so they can listen and learn to fear the LORD your God and follow carefully all the words of this law" (v. 12).

Ezra may have had this in mind when he arranged for the people to assemble. In keeping with the Deuteronomic injunction, the assembly was comprised of **men and women and all who were able to understand**, including children.

2. The setting (8:3–5)

The form of Nehemiah 8:2–11 creates a slowly emerging picture of a historical event. The writer of Nehemiah gives a little information, reviews it, adds another detail, and reviews again, each time refining the image and information.

8:3. Ezra read the law aloud **from daybreak till noon as he faced the square before the Water Gate**. Ezra's decision to read the law at this location implied that the law was greater than the temple, that the Word of God was more authoritative than the altar or its sacrifices. The time involved was from five to seven hours, depending on when daybreak occurred. It is clear that the people listened to portions of the law for an extensive period and that they **listened attentively.**

8:4. We are next given a glimpse of the preparations that attended this gathering: **Ezra the scribe stood on a high wooden platform built for the occasion.** A raised platform allowed the people to see and hear Ezra better. Also, having the law read from above, the people reinforced its authority and importance.

The writer of Nehemiah follows with a list of men who stood on the platform with Ezra. No titles or identifying markers are provided, so these men may have been lay leaders within the community. Their presence next to Ezra seems to have been supportive, giving the weight of their position and influence to all that followed.

8:5. Ezra unrolled the scroll, or **opened the book**. Once again the writer of Nehemiah underscores the fact that **all the people could see him because he was standing above them.** In a demonstration of respect for the reading of God's Word, **the people all stood up.**

3. The people respond to the law (8:6–9)

8:6. Traditionally, a benediction or blessing preceded the reading of Scripture. So before Ezra presented the law, he **praised the LORD, the great God.** In response to Ezra's declaration, **the people lifted their hands and responded,** "Amen! Amen!" The raising of hands signified worship and dependence on God. The double "Amen," "it is so," reinforced the people's concurrence with the adoration Ezra offered. **Then they bowed down and worshiped the LORD with their faces to the ground.** Prostration represented humility before a sovereign and expressed once again the people's devotion and respect.

8:7–8. While the dignitaries stood on the platform, the text names thirteen Levites who **instructed the people in the Law while the people were standing there.** These same Levites would have served at the time of Ezra as well as at the time of Nehemiah since only thirteen years had elapsed between their service. It seems the Levites circulated among the people explaining the meaning of what was being read. Teaching was the traditional function of the Levites.

Looking back at Ezra 8:15–20, we note that Ezra made a special search for Levites to accompany him to Jerusalem, perhaps with a view toward this particular event. At that time Sherebiah was considered a great addition to the caravan (Ezra 8:18), and he is listed here among those who instructed the people.

Since the reading continued for several hours, it is possible that Ezra read at first but was later assisted by the Levites: **They read from the Book of the Law of God.** This sentence also supports the notion that preselected portions of the law were read and not the entire Pentateuch. After each portion was concluded, it seems the Levites then moved from group to group, **making it clear and giving the meaning so that the people could understand what was being read.**

8:9. Ezra the priest and scribe, and the Levites who were instructing the people said to them all, "This day is sacred to the LORD your God. Do not mourn or weep." As the writer of Hebrews reminds us:

> The word of God is living and active. Sharper than any double-edged sword, it penetrates even to dividing soul and spirit, joints and marrow; it judges the thoughts and attitudes of the heart. Nothing in all creation is hidden from God's sight. Everything is uncovered and laid bare before the eyes of him to whom we must give account (Heb. 4:12–13).

This same piercing of the heart occurred as the law was read. Though the people were not ignorant of the law, they had been neglectful.

Consequently, **all the people had been weeping as they listened to the words of the Law.** Even so, public repentance was inappropriate at this time, and their leaders reminded them to stop mourning because the day was sacred to God. Throughout the Old Testament, days set aside to commemorate God's grace and kindness were intended as joyful celebrations. It was a day for rejoicing in God's mercy and goodness, not for weeping.

4. Celebration (8:10–12)

8:10–11. The people were told, **Go and enjoy choice food and sweet drinks, and send some to those who have nothing prepared. This day is sacred to our Lord.** While the reading of the law produced genuine remorse, sacred days were meant as celebrations of God's benevolence. Ezra instructed the people to enjoy a feast and to eat the best they had. In addition, they were to share with others. Both of these instructions come from the Deuteronomic writings (see Deut. 26).

The commemoration of God's goodness was to result in joyous festivities, and no sacred food was to be eaten while in mourning. It was a day to delight in being part of God's covenantal people. Once again we see that this assembly was not a spontaneous get-together but a planned event since the people had already prepared their foods. The instruction to share with those who had nothing prepared probably refers to the poor and the foreigners among them.

Ezra concluded, **Do not grieve, for the joy of the LORD is your strength.** The emphasis was on God's grace. Although they had sinned and had not fulfilled the law, God was celebrated as the gracious Sovereign who "does not treat us as our sins deserve or repay us according to our iniquities. For as high as the heavens are above the earth, so great is his love for those who fear him" (Ps. 103:10–11). Their protection came from God's grace.

Like backup singers for a soloist, the Levites moved throughout the crowd and **calmed all the people, saying "Be still, for this is a sacred day. Do not grieve."**

8:12. The people left the square and **went away to eat and drink, to send portions of food and to celebrate with great joy.** However, they obeyed not just because Ezra said so but **because they now understood the words that had been made known to them.** True understanding, when it penetrates to the heart, produces genuine joy.

🅱 The Feast of Tabernacles (8:13–18)

> **SUPPORTING IDEA:** *Ezra focused on the requirements of the law that were founded on God's grace. The Festival of Booths commemorated God's miraculous deliverance of his people.*

8:13. Quite likely the crowds had gone home. **On the second day of the month,** a smaller group assembled: **the heads of all the families, along with the priests and the Levites.** This was probably still a sizable number of people, but the general populace had departed. Since the second day of the month had no requisite festivities, these leaders were free to gather **around Ezra the scribe to give attention to the words of the Law.** It was another Bible study but of a more intimate and intensive sort than the previous day.

8:14–15. As Ezra taught the clans and religious leaders, he drew their attention to a portion of the law they had not been aware of: **They found written in the Law . . . that the Israelites were to live in booths during the feast of the seventh month.** It was no news that they should celebrate the Feast of Tabernacles; they had been doing this at least since the first exiles returned to Jerusalem (Ezra 3:4). What was novel to them was the construction of booths. Leviticus 23:33–43 is the only text within the Pentateuch that stipulates the building of booths. This demonstrates Ezra's penchant for comparing Scripture with Scripture, for accumulating the various pieces in order to construct a cohesive theology and practice.

The Feast of Tabernacles began on the fifteenth day of the seventh month. Before that was the Day of Atonement on the tenth day. It was already the second day, and this new information had to be spread throughout Judah quickly, giving the people time to prepare and travel to Jerusalem. The proclamation instructed the Jews to **go out into the hill country and bring back branches . . . to make booths.**

8:16. The people responded to the proclamation by gathering branches and building **themselves booths on their own roofs, in their courtyards, in the courts of the house of God and in the square by the Water Gate and the one by the Gate of Ephraim.** The description symbolizes an encampment, which was, indeed, the point. Ezra intended to bring the festivals back to their original intent and to give back to the people the law and its celebrations. He worked to free the law from its priestly domination and seclusion, releasing it to the people for whom it was given. From the public reading of the law to acts of worship, Ezra stands at the head of a line of reformers who envisioned God's Word among the people.

8:17. **The whole company that had returned from exile built booths and lived in them.** To the writer of Nehemiah, all Jews who observe the law were "returned exiles." These words emphasize again the connection Ezra saw between their current celebration and the original instructions to those who had come out of Egypt with Moses. **From the days of Joshua son of Nun until that day, the Israelites had not celebrated it like this.** The Israelites had, in fact, celebrated the Feast of Tabernacles throughout their history. But the festival had evolved into a harvest celebration. Ezra introduced a new, yet old, idea—the festival was to commemorate God's grace "so your descendants will know that I had the Israelites live in booths when I brought them out of Egypt. I am the LORD your God" (Lev. 23:43). As a consequence, the people's **joy was very great.**

8:18. The people of Israel **celebrated the feast for seven days**, as was commanded. Then, **on the eighth day, in accordance with the regulation, there was an assembly.** This, too, was in keeping with Leviticus 23.

> **MAIN IDEA REVIEW:** *Spiritual renewal and vitality do not occur apart from God's Word. It convicts of sin, affirms grace, instructs in righteousness, and reveals the will of God.*

III. CONCLUSION

The Heart of the Matter

John Piper has written, "Warning has value in stirring us up to take the glories of holiness and heaven seriously so that we come to see them for what they are and delight in them. But it is the delight in them that causes the true grief when we fall short. *No one cries over missing what they don't want to have*" (emphasis added) (Piper, p. 124).

Indeed, the things that raise our passions indicate what has captured our heart. What we view as loss reveals our values. Does it bother us when we can't spend time alone with God, not from guilt, but because a longing has gone unfulfilled? Does sin create deep repentance because we feel the pain caused by the loss of fellowship?

Israel repeatedly had prophets calling them back to repentance and back to obedience of God. These prophets predicted punishment, but the people usually responded halfheartedly. They were enticed by the practices of other religions; they demonstrated a shallow understanding of their relationship with God. Quite often they simply did not care.

When Ezra stood before the people and opened the law, they listened for hours. The text implies that they paid careful attention and wanted to know God's revelation and will. The Levites, as they moved from group to group explaining the meaning of each scriptural selection, helped convey to the people the implications that came with hearing God's voice.

The Jews were struck to the heart by what they heard. The grace that God had extended to them in giving them his law ignited in their souls a yearning for holiness. While they grieved over the disparity between what was offered through the law and what they had settled for in practice, they experienced great joy "because they now understood the words that had been made known to them" (Neh. 8:12).

PRINCIPLES

- The Bible is God's holy Word, inspired by him and without error.
- From the beginning, God has spoken, desiring that all people should know him and do his will.
- God's Word deserves honor and obedience.
- Spiritual leaders should explain and clarify the Scriptures.
- Great joy comes from obedience to God.

APPLICATIONS

- Take time each day to read the Bible. You cannot know God's will and character without reading his revelation.
- Devote time to explaining the texts of Scripture carefully and thoroughly. Go deeply into their meaning so those who listen will be challenged by its beauty and truth.
- Dedicate yourself to obeying whatever you learn through Bible reading, study, or listening.

IV. LIFE APPLICATION

Reinventing Truth

In 1859, Charles Darwin, in order to explain occurrences in the natural world, published the theory known to us today as "Evolution" (with a capital E). His naturalist philosophy somehow mutated into "indisputable" scientific fact over time. The basic theory has become so attractive to modern relativists that it has served as the model for explaining everything from economics to history to religion.

Those who advocate understanding Christianity through the lens of evolution are not just secularists, however. More and more seminaries and departments of theological study are adopting the notion that Christianity, like other religious faiths, is a fluid set of beliefs devised to bring meaning to the world yet constantly under revision by cultural pressures and necessities.

In explaining the "rise of Christianity," Dr. Gregory J. Riley of Claremont School of Theology believes that Christianity is just another phase in mankind's attempt to explain the world. He understands it as part of the flux and flow of human invention. Consequently, in order to legitimize their new religion, the early Christians cleverly used Jewish texts to meld the new with the old. In addition, they had to explain Jesus' ignominious death. So they turned, Riley believes, to the earlier Greek heroic tradition; this "helped Christians understand the cross" (Riley, p. 226). For Riley, heresy "was simply a perfectly workable and defensible viewpoint that did not get enough votes in the councils to carry the day" (Riley, p. 237). For such "theologians," there is no room for divine revelation and truth.

This one opinion among a throng of such voices underscores the necessity of believers to dig deeply into the texts of Scripture. Do not neglect its study. Meditate on what it says. We must listen intently, depending on God's Holy Spirit to enlighten and reveal his truth. We must approach the Scriptures with the expectation of discovery and the intent of obedience. Like those who gathered to hear Ezra read the law, we must permit God's truth to penetrate to the heart so that "the joy of the LORD" (Neh. 8:10) is our strength.

V. PRAYER

Lord, may we not be content to just hear your words. May we have a thirst to learn, to be taught by your Spirit, to examine and understand what you have written in the Bible. But more than this, may we take what you reveal and live it. Amen.

VI. DEEPER DISCOVERIES

A. Foundations; Inspiration

The words of the Bible were "out breathed" by God: "All Scripture is God-breathed and is useful for teaching, rebuking, correcting and training in righteousness" (2 Tim. 3:16). Second Peter 1:20–21 reminds us that God's heralds did not invent their messages; they were "carried along," or inspired, by the Holy Spirit. Inspiration means that God directed the writers so that there was no error. In order to communicate with humankind, God's ideas had to be translated into words. While the various writers show distinctive styles and approaches in their writing, the author is God.

B. Revelation

God has shown the truth. We could not have come up with this on our own. The nature of man leads him to suppress the truth (Rom. 1:18) that "in the beginning God created the heavens and the earth" (Gen. 1:1). We could not have fitted together the prophecies or designed something so wondrous as grace. It takes revelation.

Christianity and Judaism are based on revelation: God meets Moses and bestows the law. God comes down in the person of Christ and reveals salvation and hope.

Revelation is the unveiling of that which is hidden. It is God pulling aside the curtain, sweeping away the clutter, opening the door of understanding and truth. His clearest revelations are in creation, Scripture, and Christ.

C. Authority

The result of inspiration and revelation is that the Bible has authority for all of life. As one famous confession puts it, "It is the only rule of faith and practice." Unfortunately, many people, while finding it an interesting book, will not accept its authority. Jesus was thoroughly committed to the authority of Scripture. He obeyed it in his every move. And he is our example.

VII. TEACHING OUTLINE

A. INTRODUCTION

1. Lead Story: Breath of God
2. Context: Nehemiah looked back into the historical records to find genealogical listings of those who had come out of exile to live in Judea. Also of historical significance were the reforms Ezra had instigated thirteen years before Nehemiah's arrival.

3. Transition: Ezra initiated a reformation within Judaism. He took the law, its ceremonies, and its requirements and handed them to the people. He was concerned that the average citizen should know and understand God's revelation. He was compelled to purify the community and regulate its life under God's Word. This account of Ezra reading the law affirms the holy character that characterizes a community of faith.

B. COMMENTARY

1. Ezra Reads the Law (8:1–12)
   a. Historical context (8:1–2)
   b. The setting (8:3–5)
   c. The people respond to the law (8:6–9)
   d. Celebration (8:10–12)
2. The Feast of Tabernacles (8:13–18)

C. CONCLUSION: THE HEART OF THE MATTER

VIII. ISSUES FOR DISCUSSION

1. Psalm 19:7–13 describes the power of God's revelation. Discuss the implication of each phrase and whether these verses are true in your life.
2. Historically, Israel vacillated between repentance, obedience, and empty ritual. Is it possible to escape this cycle? If so, what can you do as an individual, and what can the church do, to avoid shallow conformity to ritual and tradition?
3. Communion is often a solemn time for reflecting on sin's high cost to God and Jesus Christ. Can we introduce to our communion services Ezra's attitude of joy for God's grace? Can the church capture a sense of celebration? Is this appropriate? If so, how could it be expressed?

Nehemiah 9:1–37

Remembrance

I. INTRODUCTION
P·R·A·Y

II. COMMENTARY
A verse-by-verse explanation of these verses.

III. CONCLUSION
The Hound of Heaven

An overview of the principles and applications from these verses.

IV. LIFE APPLICATION
Lengthening Shadows

Melding these verses to life.

V. PRAYER
Tying these verses to life with God.

VI. DEEPER DISCOVERIES
Historical, geographical, and grammatical enrichment of the commentary.

VII. TEACHING OUTLINE
Suggested step-by-step group study of these verses.

VIII. ISSUES FOR DISCUSSION
Zeroing these verses in on daily life.

*T*hose who cannot remember the past

are condemned to repeat it.

George Santayana

Nehemiah 9:1–37

IN A NUTSHELL

*T*he Jews gathered for an assembly of confession and mourning over their sins. Led by the Levites, the people recounted their history and God's enduring love.

Remembrance

I. INTRODUCTION

P-R-A-Y

*B*ooks have been written about prayer, yet it remains one of the more difficult aspects of Christian living. People feel that prayer is necessary, yet they often find their minds wandering and their resolve waning.

Prayer can be fluid conversation, formalized recitation, or congregational confession, but the most critical issue we bring to any time of prayer is the attitude of the heart. When we cut through our requests, anxieties, frustrations, or joy—what do we desire? Is prayer self-serving or God glorifying? If the chief end of man is to glorify God, then prayer must move us toward that end.

This is not to suggest that we coat our words in religious jargon or never truly struggle before God. It does mean that, as we grapple with issues, voice our fears, and ask for his help, we must pursue God's glory and honor. It may take time and many conversations before the throne of God before we attain that place of soul that honestly exalts God above all else, but this should be our goal.

Many people use the acrostic P-R-A-Y to guide them through their praying and keep them focused.

P = Praise. We turn our eyes and thoughts away from ourselves to God and honor him for who he is and what he has done. In this chapter the Levites stood before the assembly and, addressing God, said, "Blessed be your glorious name, and may it be exalted above all blessing and praise. You alone are the LORD" (Neh. 9:5–6). They then proceed to acknowledge God's greatness and goodness in very specific ways.

R = Repentance. This becomes a natural response when we see the greatness of God and his holiness. The classic illustration of this comes from Isaiah's encounter with God as he heard the seraphs calling, "Holy, holy, holy is the LORD Almighty; the whole earth is full of his glory" (Isa. 6:3). In response, Isaiah cried, "Woe to me! . . . I am ruined! For I am a man of unclean lips" (Isa. 6:5). At the sight of God and his holiness, Isaiah was stricken by his own sinfulness. In the same way, the Levites of Nehemiah 9 confessed Israel's tendency to become "arrogant and stiff-necked" (Neh. 9:16).

A = Ask. Asking acknowledges our dependence on God. We cannot live life on our own. Throughout Scripture we are encouraged to ask because God the Father delights in giving. But it is well to remember the words of James:

"You do not have, because you do not ask God. When you ask, you do not receive, because you ask with wrong motives, that you may spend what you get on your pleasures" (Jas. 4:2b–3). As the Levites stood before the congregation recounting Israel's sins and God's faithfulness, they asked only, "Do not let all this hardship seem trifling in your eyes" (Neh. 9:32).

Y = Yield. In the end we yield everything to God, who is all wise and who loves us with an enduring love. He desires our best and understands our weakness. We rest.

As the Israelites assembled for congregational confession and worship, they moved through each of these aspects of prayer. They did not progress through them in order, but they praised God, repented of their sins, asked God's favor, and yielded to his wisdom and goodness.

II. COMMENTARY

Remembrance

MAIN IDEA: *Times occur in the life of the faith community when public sorrow and confession of sin are appropriate. These occasions bind together believers and reinforce their humble state before God; they also result in praise for God's great mercy and grace.*

A A Time of Mourning (9:1–5a)

SUPPORTING IDEA: *The Jews gathered in a demonstration of mourning, confession, and praise to God.*

1. The people (9:1–3)

9:1. The historical context for this chapter cannot be definitively set, and arguments exist for various views. Whether one places it between verses 15 and 16 of Ezra 10 (after the general assembly called by Ezra yet before the legalized divorces) or in sequence with Nehemiah 8, the inclusion of these events demonstrates the Jews' determination to follow God and become a separate and holy people.

It was either the ninth month when the great assembly was called about marriages to foreign women (Ezra 10) or the seventh month of Nehemiah 8, just two days after the joyful celebration of the Feast of Tabernacles. **On the twenty-fourth day of the same month, the Israelites gathered together.** This was not a fixed, annual event dictated by the law, and no information exists to help us discover who called this great get-together. It appears to be a grassroots gathering, but the Levites directed each phase of the occasion. It must have been well organized.

The people came **fasting and wearing sackcloth and having dust on their heads**. These were methods for demonstrating grief. Fasting, or going without food, placed a person in dependence on God, signifying penitence and deep remorse. Sackcloth was a dark, coarse material associated with sorrow and repentance. Throwing dust, or putting it on one's head, symbolized humiliation. All these were signs of sorrow for wrongs committed.

9:2. Those of Israelite descent had separated themselves from all foreigners. Some believe this refers to those who divorced their foreign wives. Just as reasonable, however, it may refer to a purely Jewish assembly in distinction to the Feast of Tabernacles where non-Jews were included. It was quite appropriate to exclude those who had no part in the former sins of Israel. These people **stood in their places and confessed their sins and the wickedness of their fathers**.

9:3. They stood where they were and read from the Book of the Law of the LORD their God for a quarter of the day. The Levites probably took turns reading from the scrolls while the people listened. Reminiscent of Ezra's reading, they proclaimed God's Word for about six hours. Another six hours were spent **in confession and in worshiping the LORD their God**. This is probably a summary statement of what happened over the remainder of the chapter.

2. The Levites (9:4–5a)

9:4. Standing on the stairs were the Levites. Though we can't be certain, the Levites may have stood on some stairs in the temple area. Because of the religious nature of the occasion and the fact that non-Jews were not involved, the temple area seems probable for such a congregation. The text lists eight Levites who **called with loud voices to the LORD their God**. This was a cry for help, a plea for God to hear his people.

9:5a. A second list of Levites follows, but five of the names are repeated from the first list. This suggests that these particular Levites were leaders. These men led the first group in calling out to God. They next led a similar group that instructed the assembled Jews to **stand up and praise the LORD your God, who is from everlasting to everlasting**. In a demonstration of respect, the people rose from their stooped position to praise the eternal God.

B The Prayer (9:5b–37)

> **SUPPORTING IDEA:** *On behalf of the gathered Jews, the Levites offered a prayer of praise and petition, appealing to God's grace and character.*

3. The sovereign Lord (9:5b–6)

9:5b. Although the Levites expressed the prayer, the standing congregation was understood to agree to all they had said. They began with praise, confessing God's worthiness: **Blessed be your glorious name**. A blessing sets someone apart as deserving special attention. The people acknowledged God's magnificent name. They agreed that God's character sets him apart from everything within the created order. Mortal man cannot do him justice, even in his best attempts to worship and exalt him.

9:6. God deserved exaltation not because man decided so but because **You alone are the LORD**. He is not one among many, or best among the candidates, but he is sovereign—the one and only. Despite what people may say and the claims of other religions, only God truly exists. All other claimants are illusions, phantoms of rebellious imaginations.

The declarative statements offered by the Levites left no room for usurpers: **You made the heavens, even the highest heavens, and all their starry host**. The Jews believed in a tiered universe. Man lives in the first "heaven" or the atmosphere and air of earth; this is where Satan has some limited influence as the "prince of the power of the air" (Eph. 2:2 KJV). The second heaven belongs to the visible universe, the stars and planets. The third heaven is the dwelling place of God, referred to by Paul in 2 Corinthians 12. God made everything, even those regions beyond our imagination.

He also made **the earth and all that is on it, the seas and all that is in them**. Beneath the canopy of heaven is the earth, and all its features and inhabitants were created by the will of God. This affirmation dismissed the religionists around them who worshipped animals or rivers, or the astrologists who venerated the stars. The surrounding nations worshipped nongods. **You give life to everything**. Nothing exists outside the expressed desire of God, and nothing can continue without his provision.

The Levites next looked beyond the small scope of human understanding and experience. God is perpetually and eternally worshipped by **the multitudes of heaven**. His kingdom and sovereign rule extend into realms of which we know very little. He deserves our praise.

4. God: righteous and true (9:7–8)

9:7–8. God exhibits his magnificence not only in the wonder of his creation and in the power of his rule but in his condescension to form a relationship with humankind: **You are the LORD God, who chose Abram**. God initiated the relationship; he chose a man from whom a people for his glory would come. This was God's doing, and he **brought him out of Ur of the Chaldeans and named him Abraham**. The Jews' roots were traced to the divine will of God and his inexplicable grace.

The Levites' prayer, begun with this example of Abraham, follows a cyclic path that leads back to the faithfulness of God, his dependable character, and the hope that issues from this.

In contrast to the future waywardness among the Jews, God found Abraham's **heart faithful**. God shook hands with a nomad and **made a covenant with him to give to his descendants the land of the Canaanites**. It was from this covenant, or agreement, that all of God's blessings and commands flowed. It became the basis for God's dealings with the nation of Israel and formed the core of God's revelation and Israel's hope. The promised land, first mentioned here but appealed to repeatedly throughout the prayer, was evidence of God's goodness and blessing.

You have kept your promise because you are righteous. The focus was placed on God's character. The Jews inherited the land not because of anything they had done but because God is righteous. Because he is dependable, his followers dare to seek him, appealing to his faithfulness.

5. God: Savior and Deliverer (9:9–12)

9:9–10. The prayer moves next to God's incomparable salvation as experienced in the great exodus from Egypt. **You saw the suffering of our forefathers in Egypt**, the Levite declared. God is not aloof from his creation, but he observes and watches. He responded to the Jews' Egyptian slavery and abuse with compassion by sending **miraculous signs and wonders against Pharaoh, against all his officials and all the people of his land**. This statement encompasses all the plagues God unleashed against Pharaoh and the Egyptians through Moses and Aaron. He acted not only out of kindness for his people but in judgment on the Egyptians' arrogance—a judgment that would later fall upon his own people, the Jews (Neh. 9:29).

Set among the great historical recollections, the Levite made this pivotal statement around which all the parts of the prayer depend: **You made a name for yourself, which remains to this day**. The reputation and character of God was revealed and established in space and time as he acted in history. His nature was indisputably demonstrated, and it had remained constant until the present time.

9:11. God acted in response to the plight of the people. He **divided the sea before them, so that they passed though it on dry ground**. Once again Israel's deliverance was marked by judgment upon others. As the Jews passed safely to the other side of the sea, God **hurled their pursuers into the depths, like a stone into mighty waters**.

9:12. God remained faithful to his people throughout the wilderness wanderings. During the day he **led them with a pillar of cloud, and by night with a pillar of fire to give them light on the way they were to take**. The people praised God for his abundant goodness as their savior.

6. God: provider (9:13–21)

9:13–14. God's condescension provided the setting: **You came down on Mount Sinai**. God always approaches mankind; he is the initiator. **You spoke**

to them from heaven. Heaven and earth met not by human will but by divine decision.

The prayer recalls the wilderness events out of sequence from their actual occurrence. The giving of the law takes the prominent position since this was the singular gift God entrusted to the Israelites, distinguishing them from other nations: **You gave them regulations and laws that are just and right, and decrees and commands that are good**. These regulations were positive parameters that created a well-run and blessed society.

God had allowed the Israelites entrance into the divine order. He had chosen them to receive instructions on holy living—decrees that would safeguard them from disaster and protect them from the ravages of sin.

9:15. Not only did God provide for their spiritual, social, and political welfare, but he also provided for their physical needs: **In their hunger you gave them bread from heaven**. He fed them spiritually from heaven in the giving of the law, and he fed them physically from heaven in sending manna.

In this context of God's generosity, he **told them to go in and take possession of the land**. This was the objective of the exodus journey and the point of their desert travels. This also brought them full circle to the opening strains of the prayer when God called Abraham and made a covenant with him, granting his descendants the land of Canaan (Neh. 9:8).

9:16. The prayer returns to its former themes and subjects. This time, God's amazing character and grace are displayed by the Israelites' contrasting attitudes and actions. Though God had repeatedly demonstrated generosity, faithfulness, and compassion, our forefathers **became arrogant and stiff-necked, and did not obey your commands**. This willful stubbornness became the defining characteristic of the Israelites.

9:17. Whereas God heard their cries and delivered them, the Jews **refused to listen and failed to remember the miracles you performed among them**. They lost sight of what God had done among them. The refrain throughout this portion of the prayer is Israel's disobedience and obstinacy, and it acts as a foil for God's greatness and constancy.

9:18. God's patience and compassion could not be thwarted even by the most wicked behavior of his chosen people, **even when they cast for themselves an image of a calf and said, "This is your god, who brought you up out of Egypt."** As the people ascribed to a metal calf the role of savior, God did not abandon them. Israel's faithlessness could not destroy or diminish his committed devotion and determined love.

9:19–21. In this section the Israelites recalled that God gave them his **good Spirit to instruct them**. The events of Mount Sinai were not repeated, but the gift of the Holy Spirit was renewed as he taught them wisdom and understanding. Once again God was praised for giving them manna and water. The hand of God provided everything they desired or needed. He is trustworthy and faithful.

7. *The inheritance (9:22–25)*

9:22. As the Israelites entered the land that God had pledged to them, each victory was because of God. In summary they offered praise: **You gave them kingdoms and nations, allotting to them even the remotest frontiers.** The prayer then follows the Jews as they near the realization of God's promises. The defeat of **Sihon king of Heshbon** and **Og king of Bashan** refer to battles waged and won before they crossed the Jordan River and entered Canaan. Both encounters are described in Numbers 21.

9:23. Throughout the forty years of desert wandering, God **made their sons as numerous as the stars in the sky.** God brought these sons **into the land that you told their fathers to enter and possess.** This reference acknowledges Israel's earlier sin of distrust and faithlessness when they stood on the edge of Canaan and refused to enter the land.

9:24. Where the fathers had proved faithless, **their sons went in and took possession of the land.** But this was not because of their exceptional strength or their cunning. God **subdued before them the Canaanites, who lived in the land.** However it may have appeared from a human perspective, it was God who **handed the Canaanites over to them.**

9:25. The closing words of this section set up the action to follow. As Israel conquered Canaan and its **fortified cities and fertile land,** they inherited many benefits: **houses filled with all kinds of good things, wells already dug, vineyards, olive groves and fruit trees in abundance.** Behind the recitation of these words were the warnings given to Israel before they entered the land. Moses spoke to the nation:

> When the LORD your God brings you into the land . . . a land with large, flourishing cities you did not build, houses filled with all kinds of good things you did not provide, wells you did not dig, and vineyards and olive groves you did not plant—then when you eat and are satisfied, be careful that you do not forget the LORD (Deut. 6:10–12).

8. *Cycles of history (9:26–31)*

9:26. In the space of a breath, the prayer moves from the abundant generosity of God and his faithful fulfillment of his promises, to **they were disobedient and rebelled against you.** The prayer reviews the pattern that emerged in Israel's national life: **They killed your prophets, who had admonished them . . . they committed awful blasphemies.** This is the first part of what becomes an ongoing and predictable cycle of sin, distress, and rescue.

9:27. So you handed them over to their enemies, who oppressed them. The sins of Israel led them to divine judgment. Just as God had used Israel to punish the wicked practices and violent behavior of those living in Canaan, so he used the pagan nations around Israel to inflict judgment on Israel's waywardness. But even when they behaved like the ungodly, as God's chosen people they retained an advocate in heaven. God never deserted them, though he let them go for a while in order to awaken them and draw them back into relationship with him.

9:28–30. In the prayer each new phase of rebellion seems worse than what has preceded it, and each judgment of God grows in intensity. In Nehemiah 9:27 God "handed them over to their enemies," but now he **abandoned them to the hand of their enemies so that they ruled over them.** Again the Jews cried for help, and again God's compassion rescued them.

God's grace becomes all the more amazing as the repetition of sin and deliverance continues. **You warned them to return to your law, but they became arrogant and disobeyed your commands.** As persistent as God was in pursuing the Jews, they were just as persistent in rejecting him.

9:31. Even though the spiral of rebellion and punishment continued, yet there was a place for hope: **But in your great mercy you did not put an end to them or abandon them.** Here was hope for the Jews' present situation. Even when Israel was at its worse, God did not desert them—not because of their merit or potential but because he is **a gracious and merciful God.**

9. The present plea (9:32–37)

9:32. The prayer turns more personal. If the Israelites had come to realize and confess anything from their review of history, it was that their God is the **great, mighty and awesome God, who keeps his covenant of love.** In view of Israel's persistence in sin and rebellion, they could only appeal to God's compassion. The nation had broken the covenant over and over again, so they had only one hope—God's love.

9:33. While the prayer allowed for Israel's plight, it was not presumptuous. The people were distressed and living under foreign domination, but they admitted that **in all that has happened to us, you have been just; you have acted faithfully, while we did wrong.** The people dared place their hope in God, who had demonstrated love and faithfulness throughout the generations. They embraced their heritage as they stood humbly before God.

9:34–35. As if to assure themselves and fix in their own thinking the righteousness of God's act, they again recalled Israel's sins. **Our kings, our leaders, our priests and our fathers did not follow your law.** Except for the exclusion of prophets, this is the same list of people who, in Nehemiah 9:32, were seen as suffering under the hardship of God's justice. No doubt the prophets were viewed as righteous and innocent of the rebellion that sent Israel into captivity.

9:36–37. Again they asked only that God look and see their situation. They appealed for nothing more: **see, we are slaves today, slaves in the land you gave our forefathers so they could eat its fruit and the other good things it produces**. The return from exile, the resettlement of Judea and Jerusalem were wonderful blessings but with a bittersweet result. They had come home, back to the land promised long ago to Abraham. They had rebuilt their homes and established their vineyards and farms, but because of their sins, the land's **abundant harvest goes to the kings you have placed over us**.

The Israelites had returned to the land, but they were still under the oppressive rule of a pagan empire. Artaxerxes and the Persian officials and satraps could do as they wished, it seemed. The prayer concluded with a confession: **We are in great distress**.

MAIN IDEA REVIEW: *Times occur in the life of the faith community when public sorrow and confession of sin are appropriate. These occasions bind together believers and reinforce their humble state before God; they also result in praise for God's great mercy and grace.*

III. CONCLUSION

The Hound of Heaven

In the autobiographical poem *The Hound of Heaven,* Francis Thompson began:

> I fled Him, down the nights and down the days;
> I fled Him, down the arches of the years;
> I fled Him, down the labyrinthiane ways
> Of my own mind; and in the mist of tears
> I hid from Him.

The recurring theme of flight from God could be written across the entire history of humankind. None understood this better than God's own people, Israel.

As they stood together in worship, they recalled their history—God's covenant with Abraham, their deliverance from Egypt, God's bestowal of the law at Sinai, his provision in the desert. But in response, they confessed that their ancestors had "refused to listen and failed to remember the miracles. . . . They became stiff-necked" and rebellious (Neh. 9:17). The human pattern of running from God—of disobedience and spiritual wandering—became more and more evident as they progressed through their history. Like Francis Thompson, they fled him "down the nights and down the days."

But Thompson wrote that he became aware of something in his life beside the persistence of his own waywardness. From behind he heard the rhythm of chasing feet:

. . . those strong Feet that followed, followed after.

But with unhurrying chase,

And unperturbéd pace,

Deliberate speed, majestic instancy,

They beat—and a Voice beat

More instant than the Feet—

"All things betray thee, who betrayest Me" (Buckley, p. 856).

Israel also testified to the pursuing Hound of Heaven, to the God who chased and remained faithful. After each confession of sin, they remembered, "You did not desert them . . . because of your great compassion you did not abandon them" (Neh. 9:17,19).

Look back on your own life, and you will detect the relentless pursuit of God's grace.

PRINCIPLES

- Confession is necessary for fellowship.
- God is worthy of all honor; he will not share his glory with another.
- God is faithful.
- People are born with a sinful nature and, by disposition, disobey God.
- God's grace exceeds our sins.

APPLICATIONS

- Find ways to tell the story of God's grace and faithfulness in your life. Write these in a journal or tell them verbally. Pass them on to your family and children.
- Take time each day to praise God, confess sin, ask for his favor, and yield to his sovereignty in your life.

IV. LIFE APPLICATION

Lengthening Shadows

C. S. Lewis, after the death of his wife, Joy, wrote of the despair and spiritual twilight he experienced. Part of the agony Lewis felt was the fading from his memory of her appearance. He began to forget what she looked like. He couldn't quite recall, and it filled him with a sense of betrayal and a deep anguish of soul.

When we forget, we live as strangers.

The Old Testament is filled with recollections. The Psalms often recount Israel's history and how God delivered them. Hebrew prayers often center on retelling the goodness of God in history. In this chapter the Levites led the people in looking back, reminding them of what God looked like—to marvel at his faithful love, his compassion and generosity. It was also a chance for them to look in the mirror.

It is a valuable practice to keep a journal, writing down decisions, prayers, and events so that you recognize the presence of God. Such remembrances keep life and our relationship with Christ accurate and alive.

V. PRAYER

Gracious God, how we see ourselves in the lives of these ancient people. How often we have wandered from your commands, refused to listen to your Spirit, and indulged in what was wrong. Yet you have always dealt with us in love and patience. Truly you are compassionate, merciful, and breathtaking in your greatness. Amen.

VI. DEEPER DISCOVERIES

The law (9:13–14,29,34)

For the Jew the law was not viewed as a set of restrictive commands and regulations. Instead, they saw the law as God's benevolent gift that set them apart from other nations and gave them life. Psalm 19:7–8 states, "The law of the LORD is perfect, reviving the soul. The statutes of the LORD are trustworthy, making wise the simple. The precepts of the LORD are right, giving joy to the heart. The commands of the LORD are radiant, giving light to the eyes." The Mosaic commands, blessings, and curses flowed out of God's faithful mercy. "In keeping them there is great reward" (Ps. 19:11).

The Ezra era marked some of the first interpretative approaches to the law. From this time forward the scribes and Levites began comparing Scripture with Scripture and reinterpreting the text's meaning for a current situation. From these explanations new traditions and understanding of orthodoxy developed. Eventually new "laws" were instituted. These were not part of the original law of God but were put in place by rabbis to establish a protective "fence" around the Torah.

These laws were meant to prevent people from breaking the Law of Moses. While the law prohibited work on the Sabbath, the protective laws prohibited handling a tool (a hammer, pencil, or money) without good reason, lest one forget that it was the Sabbath and perform some forbidden work. These rabbinic laws eventually became voluminous, far outweighing God's original commands.

VII. TEACHING OUTLINE

A. INTRODUCTION

1. Lead Story: P-R-A-Y
2. Context: The historical context of this congregational prayer of confession and praise is not known. Even so, it is apparent that the prayer was offered at an assembly of ethnic Jews in the postexilic period during the reign of King Artaxerxes of Persia.
3. Transition: The purpose of this prayer was more than ritual confession. These people were examining their hearts as well as reflecting on their relationship with God. They were looking at the tension that can develop between God's law and justice and his mercy and grace.

B. COMMENTARY

1. A Time of Mourning (9:1–5a)
   a. The people (9:1–3)
   b. The Levites (9:4–5a)
2. The Prayer (9:5b–37)
   a. The sovereign Lord (9:5b–6)
   b. God: righteous and true (9:7–8)
   c. God: Savior and Deliverer (9:9–12)
   d. God: Provider (9:13–21)
   e. The inheritance (9:22–25)
   f. Cycles of history (9:26–31)
   g. The present plea (9:32–37)

C. CONCLUSION: THE HOUND OF HEAVEN

VIII. ISSUES FOR DISCUSSION

1. Looking back on your own life, discuss which aspects of God's character seem most significant. Share specific ways God has been faithful and compassionate to you.
2. The Israelites constantly reviewed God's promises to them given through Abraham. Make a list of the promises God has given us through Jesus Christ.
3. Is there any relationship between the Jews' distress under a foreign power and the Christian's relationship to society? If so, explain.

Nehemiah 9:38–10:39

Commitment

I. INTRODUCTION
At the Front

II. COMMENTARY
A verse-by-verse explanation of these verses.

III. CONCLUSION
Promises

An overview of the principles and applications from these verses.

IV. LIFE APPLICATION
I Do, We Will . . . Maybe

Melding these verses to life.

V. PRAYER
Tying these verses to life with God.

VI. DEEPER DISCOVERIES
Historical, geographical, and grammatical enrichment of the commentary.

VII. TEACHING OUTLINE
Suggested step-by-step group study of these verses.

VIII. ISSUES FOR DISCUSSION
Zeroing these verses in on daily life.

Nehemiah 9:38–10:39

IN A NUTSHELL

*N*ehemiah, in response to particular negligences of the law, led the community in a public commitment to obeying the law of God.

Commitment

I. INTRODUCTION

At the Front

In 1914, Ernest Shackleton placed an ad in a London newspaper requesting men for a hazardous journey. The jobs guaranteed minimal pay, bitter cold, months without sunlight, constant danger, and a return that was highly doubtful. Over five thousand men applied for the twenty positions available.

Shackleton had previously established himself as a respected explorer of the South Pole region. Those who volunteered to return with him to the frozen Arctic signed up for the sheer adventure of it—and because they had confidence in his leadership.

The adventure turned out to be more than anyone could have imagined. After a short time in the Arctic, their ship was crushed by the shifting ice pack, stranding the crew in a desolate and harsh environment. In 1914, there was no way to signal London for rescue. So Shackleton and his officers eventually decided their only recourse was to take a smaller boat and attempt an ocean journey to find help. Leaving most of the crew behind, Shackleton and a few of his men set out on a one-thousand-mile voyage in some of the roughest and most unforgiving seas of the world.

Shackleton's leadership met the challenge. He proved to be a man of sound decision, careful strategy, unwavering courage, and commitment. He never required of anyone something he was not willing to do. When ice built up on their little ship, it was Shackleton who hammered the ice away while under the deluge of bitter-cold waves. When rotations for night watch were instituted, he took the first. When they finally beached their craft and had to make their way overland, Shackleton was always in the lead.

They finally reached a small settlement and secured a ship to rescue the rest of the crew they had left behind. It was Shackleton's voice that called out toward shore, "Are you all right?"

When the people of Israel faced themselves, they saw their neglect of God's law. In response they committed themselves to obedience; they renewed their pledge to follow God's commands. Together they signed an oath. The first signature on the oath was Nehemiah's.

II. COMMENTARY

Commitment

> **MAIN IDEA:** *It often helps to put commitments and pledges in writing, to affix one's name to an agreement, to declare one's intent publicly. In this way we hold ourselves accountable and fasten in our own hearts and minds the promises we have made.*

A The People Make a Pledge (9:38–10:29)

> **SUPPORTING IDEA:** *The religious, political, and social leaders of Israel, along with the laity, pledged themselves publicly to follow God's law.*

1. The leaders sign the pledge (9:38–10:27)

9:38. Debate exists over whether the wording of this verse connects the material of chapter 10 to chapter 9, or whether it stands independent of the preceding prayer.

In view of all this, we are making a binding agreement. This could refer back to the prayer where Israel's waywardness emerged as the predominant behavior, marking the people's resolve to act differently by entering into a pledge. However, the historical placement of this verse and the following chapter depend, to some extent, on the placement of chapters 8 and 9.

It seems probable that Nehemiah 9:38 and following actually occurred after Nehemiah 13 when Nehemiah returned to Jerusalem and enforced some reforms. Each vow within the binding agreement was an issue that Nehemiah confronted when he came back to Judea. It was probably in view of all these failures and abuses of the law that they decided to pledge themselves to abide by the law's commands. It was also in keeping with Nehemiah's style to place people under oath to ensure that they would follow through on their word (Neh. 5:12).

Our leaders, our Levites and our priests are affixing their seals to it. By fixing their seals, or names, to the document, they pledged themselves to uphold all that was written. This was appropriate because the political and religious leaders were responsible for much of what was contained in the document. Not only did the leaders affix their seal to the document; they led by example.

10:1. Those who sealed it were: Nehemiah the governor, the son of Hacaliah. Heading the list was Nehemiah. He may have placed his seal first in order to lead the way, making a firm pledge to the reforms he was seeking to enforce.

10:2–27. From this point on, a long list of names is presented: **Zedekiah . . . Seraiah . . . Azariah . . . Jeremiah . . . Pashhur.** The list was representative of important groups in Hebrew society: **the priests . . . the Levites . . . the leaders of the people**. Most of the names occur in other compilations throughout the books of Ezra and Nehemiah, from the earliest return with Zerubbabel to the time of Nehemiah's governorship. It seems reasonable that the names are ancestral, family names and do not refer to individuals. This was a common method of identification in Jewish society. Clans were the means of verifying a person's Jewish heritage.

2. The community makes a commitment (10:28–29)

10:28. In order to emphasize the support and depth of communal commitment, the writer of Nehemiah reviewed **the rest of the people** who, along with the leaders, pledged themselves: **priests, Levites, gatekeepers, singers, temple servants**. This may underscore the breadth of those attending to the vow, emphasizing that it involved more than the leadership.

In addition, it included **all who separated themselves from the neighboring peoples for the sake of the Law of God**. Some interpret this phrase as referring to those who had divorced their foreign wives, or Jews who had withdrawn from the surrounding people. More likely, this specified non-Jews who had converted to Judaism and taken upon themselves the full implications and demands of the law, including circumcision. These were Jews in every practice but not by birth. They had voluntarily separated themselves from the neighboring peoples.

10:29. Whereas the leaders had publicly and officially pledged themselves to follow the reforms by signing their names to a document, the greater community assented verbally, binding themselves **with a curse and an oath to follow the Law of God given through Moses**. Using a curse and an oath to seal an agreement can be traced back to the time when Moses gave Israel the law, and again as they entered the promised land under Joshua (Deut. 28; Josh. 8:34–35). The people accepted the curses, or disasters, that would occur if they should break their vow.

B The Promise (10:30–39)

SUPPORTING IDEA: *A commitment to any good goal succeeds only by dedicating oneself to specific actions. Without a purposeful plan, good intentions give way to established habits.*

3. Marriages (10:30)

10:30. This was a promise for the future: **We promise not to give our daughters in marriage to the peoples around us or take their daughters for our sons**. Ezra had dealt with this issue of marriage before, and Nehemiah encountered it years later on his second trip to Jerusalem (Neh. 13:23–28). During the intervening years of Nehemiah's governorship and his later return, Jews had married pagan women. While some interpreters regard this prohibition as a desire to purify the Jewish race, it served primarily to keep the Jews spiritually pure. Throughout their history, it was the allure of foreign practices that continually got them into trouble. Separation was seen as a safeguard for the distinctive life to which God had called them.

4. Sabbath (10:31)

10:31a. It was well established that God's people should not work on the Sabbath. This grew out of the creation record when, on the seventh day, God "rested from all his work" (Gen. 2:2). This divine resting served as an example, and by it God "blessed the seventh day and made it holy" (Gen. 2:3). Sabbath rest was later codified under the law: "Six days do your work, but on the seventh day do not work, so that your ox and your donkey may rest and the slave born in your household, and the alien as well, may be refreshed" (Exod. 23:12).

Underlying this command was God's wisdom. He knew that refreshment was needed by all the created order. Sabbath observance also distinguished the Jews from surrounding cultures as a means of declaring dependence on God's provision. The people pledged anew to honor the Sabbath.

10:31b. The word *Sabbath* literally means "cessation." While the name has become identified with the seventh day of the week, it actually denoted any rest. The same work/rest cycle of the week was also applied to the sequence of seven years. Exodus 23:10–11 states: "For six years you are to sow your fields and harvest the crops, but during the seventh year let the land lie unplowed and unused. Then the poor among your people may get food from it, and the wild animals may eat." In a renewal of this ancient command, the people pledged, **every seventh year we will forgo working the land**.

A similar law was also given in Exodus 21:2: "If you buy a Hebrew servant, he is to serve you for six years. But in the seventh year, he shall go free, without paying anything." While these laws about the seventh year were previously handled as separate commands, at this point in Israel's history they were combined as a single act to be enforced in the same year: **we will forgo working the land and will cancel all debts**. The Lord also commanded a Jubilee year, the seventh cycle of seven years or a nationwide celebration of rest every fifty years.

5. The temple tax (10:32–33)

10:32. The temple tax was not a command found within the law. Instead, it was a tax derived from some historical occurrences and implemented by current necessity. **We assume the responsibility . . . to give a third of a shekel each year**, the people declared. Historically, the half shekel was temporarily used at the time of Moses to support the tent of meeting (Exod. 30:11–16). It was again used for temple repairs during the reign of King Joash

(2 Kgs. 12:4–5). By agreeing to this tax, the people assumed responsibility for the care and **service of the house of our God**.

10:33. Specifically they promised to use the collected money for the prescribed offerings and celebrations. **The bread** was twelve loaves representing the twelve tribes and signified a thank offering; **grain offerings and burnt offerings** were daily sacrifices and offerings; **offerings on the Sabbaths, New Moon festivals and appointed feasts** were special celebrations throughout the year. The temple tax would go toward building upkeep and repair.

6. Contributions of wood (10:34)

10:34. Leviticus 6:13 states: "The fire must be kept burning on the altar continuously; it must not go out." To adhere to this requirement of the law, a great amount of wood was needed. Acknowledging this, the priests, the Levites, and the people **cast lots**. This "dice throwing" was an acceptable means in Middle Eastern culture, even into the times of the apostles (Acts 1:21–26), for making decisions when all options were acceptable, or when human knowledge could not determine an answer. In this way the people determined when each family was **to bring to the house of our God at set times each year a contribution of wood to burn on the altar.**

7. Personal Contributions (10:35–39)

10:35. Before the Israelites settled in Canaan, God gave commands and ordinances to guide the people. Through Moses they were told, "Bring the best of the firstfruits of your soil to the house of the LORD your God" (Exod. 23:19). In compliance with this command, the people and leaders assumed responsibility for **bringing to the house of the LORD each year the firstfruits of our crops and every fruit tree**. These offerings were symbols of God's ownership of everything the Hebrews cultivated and cared for.

10:36. The people also agreed to **bring the firstborn of our sons and of our cattle, of our herds and of our flocks to the house of our God.** God deserved the first portion of everything they had, including their sons and animals. Numbers 18 specifies that firstborn sons were not to be sacrificed but redeemed by the payment of five shekels of silver (Num. 18:16). This redemption money was given to the priests. The firstborn among unclean animals was also to be redeemed by money paid to the priests. However, the firstborn among the clean animals (ox, sheep, or goats) were to be burned by fire as a holy sacrifice to God. The priests were then given these portions to eat. That was why the people vowed to bring the firstborn of all they possessed to the priests who ministered in the house of God.

10:37a. The people also promised to **bring to the storerooms of the house of our God, to the priests, the first of our ground meal, of our grain offerings, of the fruit of all our trees and of our new wine and oil.** This encompassed everything else specified before, yet more. It included those items made by man—ground meal, wine, and oil—things that had to be processed and refined. These were not the first of the harvest but the best. These, too, were given to the priests since they had no landed inheritance and were dedicated to the service of God on behalf of the people.

10:37b. The tithes, or tenths, were the Levites' "inheritance" (Num. 18:26). According to the instructions in Numbers 18, the Levites also offered a tenth from the tithes they received. This was to be the best of the best so they would "not defile the holy offerings of the Israelites" (Num. 18:32b). So the people pledged to continue to bring **a tithe of our crops to the Levites** for their welfare and provision, and as an offering to God.

10:38. A priest descended from Aaron is to accompany the Levites when they receive the tithes. Perhaps this was to keep everyone honest since the priests had a vested interest in what was collected. The specification that the priest be a descendant of Aaron may suggest that the high priest was to accompany the Levites in their collection, though this would seem burdensome. More likely, the qualification was meant to underscore the holy function of the priests in receiving the Levitical tithe.

After the collection of the tithes at the various depositories through Judea, the Levites were **to bring a tenth of the tithes up to the house of our God, to the storerooms of the treasury.** Upon receipt of the tenth offered by the people, the Levites then gave a tenth to the priests. This was their rightful portion. The priests placed the produce in storerooms within the temple for later use.

10:39. The chapter concludes with a summary statement of what the people, including the Levites, had bound themselves to do: **to bring their contributions of grain, new wine and oil to the storerooms where the articles for the sanctuary are kept and where the ministering priests, the gatekeepers and the singers stay.** The collected produce and supplies were stored in rooms designated for this purpose. It was used to support the priests, gatekeepers, and singers during their work at the temple. The people concluded their pledge with the declaration, **We will not neglect the house of our God.**

> **MAIN IDEA REVIEW:** *It often helps to put commitments and pledges in writing, to affix one's name to an agreement, to declare publicly one's intent. In this way we hold ourselves accountable and fasten in our hearts and minds the promises we have made.*

III. CONCLUSION

Promises

This chapter is a string of promises made to God, first by Judah's leadership and then by the community. It is an affirmation of God's unchanging law and a confession of man's tendencies to stray from the Lord.

In a public confession, the people went back to the original intention of belonging to God, of being his people and reflecting his character. The moral laws would guide their lives; the cultural laws would distinguish them as God's special people; and the religious laws would create a holy community, pointing ahead to the cross of Christ.

Dedication was more than a new spirit; it was renewed action. When the church at Ephesus was warned to return to its first love, the people were told to "repent and do the things you did at first" (Rev. 2:5). The stirring of emotion was not the issue; it was devotion demonstrated in actions of obedience. Christ said, "If you love me, you will obey what I command" (John 14:15).

Promises are easy to make, but they become hollow and even offensive when not coupled with action. Nehemiah and the people of Judah gave verbal assent to obey—and they followed through with action.

We know what we should do; we just need to put it into practice!

PRINCIPLES

- Leaders should always be first in honoring and obeying God.
- Obedience involves every facet of life.
- Public affirmation and confession help establish obedience and accountability.
- The people of God should support the ministers of God.

APPLICATIONS

- Be public and open in your allegiance to the Lord and commitment to the church.
- When you teach God's Word, call for personal application of obedience. The Bible is for living, not just for extra knowledge.
- Look over your finances and evaluate where your heart and money belong. Giving indicates devotion to the Lord.

IV. LIFE APPLICATION

I Do, We Will . . . Maybe

Community life depends on covenants—some written, some spoken, some assumed. But no group can function without agreement among its members about specific behaviors, values, and objectives.

Marriage is a covenant between two people, and witnessed and supported by friends; it is a pledge of honor and faithfulness, an agreement to live in exclusive love for each other. Companies write mission statements that become the goals of the business and its employees; they are values that everyone agrees to follow.

In many ways church membership is a covenant. The members commit to one another and to the group to work responsibly in carrying out the goals and purposes of the church.

A family performs best when its members promise to act for the welfare of each individual as well as the entire family unit. Some families even write out specific goals and agreements in order to live purposefully and responsibly, holding one another accountable for their commitments. But promises, pledges, and documents are only as good as the integrity and commitment of the people involved. Our courts are clogged with individuals and groups who treat their commitments lightly.

The people gathered with Nehemiah and pledged themselves to specific instructions within the law; they committed themselves to action. Let us commit ourselves first to Jesus Christ and then to one another—not just with words but with love and obedience.

V. PRAYER

Lord, may we not consider the truths and commands of your Word as burdensome. We join the psalmist in declaring: "The law of the LORD is perfect, reviving the soul. The statutes of the LORD are trustworthy, making wise the simple. The precepts of the LORD are right, giving joy to the heart. The commands of the LORD are radiant, giving light to the eyes" (Ps. 19:7). Amen.

VI. DEEPER DISCOVERIES

A. Intermarriage (10:30)

The promise of the Israelites not to marry from among the neighboring peoples was a spiritual commitment between them and God. The Jews were separated to God (sanctified) for his purposes; they were holy to God. Because of this, they were to remain independent from pagan cultures. It was about this same time that the prophet Malachi spoke to Judah, saying, "Judah has desecrated the sanctuary the LORD loves, by marrying the daughter of a foreign god" (Mal. 2:11). God looks on people with other beliefs as children of another god. The Hebrew people were first of all united to God through the covenant. Because of this, they profaned the holy pledge when they joined themselves to pagan peoples.

The same principle is applied by Paul in 1 Corinthians 6 about sexual immorality when he states:

> He who unites himself with a prostitute is one with her in body. . . . But he who unites himself with the Lord is one with him in spirit. . . . Do you not know that your body is a temple of the Holy

Spirit, who is in you, whom you have received from God? You are not your own; you were bought at a price" (1 Cor. 6:16–17,19–20).

Paul also wrote, "Do not be yoked together with unbelievers. For what do righteousness and wickedness have in common? . . . What does a believer have in common with an unbeliever? What agreement is there between the temple of God and idols? For we are the temple of the living God" (2 Cor. 6:14–16).

The issue has never been racial but spiritual—and it is a principle that should guide us today.

B. Offerings (10:32–33)

In the Old Testament there were two different types of offerings: those for atonement (sin offerings) and those that celebrated God's goodness (thank offerings). Nehemiah and all the people promised to continue or renew all of these.

The sin offering required the shedding of blood, the sacrifice of an animal on the altar. It was a judicial act to cover the offense made before God. Forgiveness was not found in the blood of an animal but in the act of obedience and the faith exercised, and in recognition that sin deserved death. The animal substituted for the person, symbolically taking his sins and suffering his death.

These sin offerings pointed to the Lamb of God, Jesus Christ, who took upon himself the sins of humankind; he suffered our death; his blood covered all sin for all time. As the perfect and acceptable sin offering, Jesus demolished the system of animal sacrifice. After Jesus "offered for all time one sacrifice for sins, he sat down at the right hand of God . . . because by one sacrifice he has made perfect forever those who are being made holy" (Heb. 10:12,14).

Nothing more can be added to the sacrifice Christ has made for us. But we can celebrate and offer "sacrifices" of praise, doing good deeds and honoring God with our lives for his glory.

VII. TEACHING OUTLINE

A. INTRODUCTION

1. Lead Story: At the Front
2. Context: After twelve years as governor, Nehemiah went back into the service of King Artaxerxes. He returned to Jerusalem to find a general neglect of God's law and various abuses of God's commands. Indignant, Nehemiah issued reforms and vigorously enforced them.
3. Transition: As a result of Nehemiah's strong actions in punishing those who violated the law, the people gathered in a public demonstration of

mourning. They pledged to separate themselves from all pagan practices and committed themselves to upholding the law.

B. COMMENTARY
1. The People Make a Pledge (9:38–10:29)
   a. The leaders sign the pledge (9:38–10:27)
   b. The community makes a commitment (10:28–29)
2. The Promise (10:30–39)
   a. Marriages (10:30)
   b. Sabbath (10:31)
   c. The temple tax (10:32–33)
   d. Contributions of wood (10:34)
   e. Personal contributions (10:35–39)

C. CONCLUSION: PROMISES

VIII. ISSUES FOR DISCUSSION

1. Is "Sabbath rest" appropriate for today, even though we are no longer regulated by the law's stipulations? If not, defend your position biblically. If so, list some practical ways in which it can be observed.
2. The law required giving God the "firstfruits" of one's labor. Since we no longer live in an agricultural economy, what are some modern "firstfruits" that Christians can give?
3. Can you think of any situations within the church when a public commitment might be appropriate? Why?

Nehemiah 11:1–12:43

Toward the Future

I. INTRODUCTION
What's in a Name?

II. COMMENTARY
A verse-by-verse explanation of these verses.

III. CONCLUSION
Beyond Imagination

An overview of the principles and applications from these verses.

IV. LIFE APPLICATION
Praise 24–7

Melding these verses to life.

V. PRAYER
Tying the chapter to life with God.

VI. DEEPER DISCOVERIES
Historical, geographical, and grammatical enrichment of the commentary.

VII. TEACHING OUTLINE
Suggested step-by-step group study of these verses.

VIII. ISSUES FOR DISCUSSION
Zeroing these verses in on daily life.

| Quote |

What would life be if we had no courage

to attempt anything?

V i n c e n t   V a n   G o g h

Nehemiah 11:1–12:43

IN A NUTSHELL

The process of selecting people to repopulate Jerusalem began, and names of the people were entered into the record. In addition, a genealogical listing of priests and Levites was recorded in preparation for the dedication of the wall. Then the people gathered to celebrate.

Toward the Future

I. INTRODUCTION

What's in a Name?

*T*his chapter would make boring reading unless your name was there. It's one thing to read about Athaiah or Amariah, but if your name is Alan, you just might want to skip over it all and move on to something more action packed.

But these names, unfamiliar and foreign to our ears, represent real people. God, through the writer of Nehemiah, was recognizing their significance. He loves people.

Eugene Peterson has written:

> Any time that we move from personal names to abstract labels or graphs or statistics, we are less in touch with reality and diminished in our capacity to deal with what is best and at the center of life. . . . Every time that we go along with this movement from the personal to the impersonal, from the immediate to the remote, from the concrete to the abstract, we are diminished, we are less (Peterson, p. 26).

Jesus expressed a parallel thought when he taught that God knows the number of hairs on our head, and he knows when a sparrow falls to the ground. We have greater value than a flock of birds. God cares for each individual. He knows each of us by name, and in him we find our fullness.

II. COMMENTARY

Toward the Future

MAIN IDEA: *History not only teaches lessons to embrace and mistakes to avoid; it can affirm our purpose and distinctive place in the world. When history connects to the present and is understood through the lens of God's grace, it can instill endurance and inspire hope.*

A Repopulation of Jerusalem (11:1–24)

SUPPORTING IDEA: *For an organization to remain viable, it needs the vibrancy of a diverse population.*

1. The method of repopulation (11:1–2)

11:1. Jerusalem needed an influx of new citizens. Evidently, an adequate number among the ruling class already lived in Jerusalem: **the leaders of the**

people settled in Jerusalem. As the provincial capital, Jerusalem would have drawn those in leadership positions, as demonstrated by the 150 officials who dined with Nehemiah (Neh. 5:17).

But Jerusalem needed to grow its general population. So **the rest of the people cast lots to bring one out of every ten to live in Jerusalem, the holy city**. Since God's will decided all of life and there was no such thing as luck or chance, casting lots was an accepted way by which to determine the divine will. The people were gathered in groups of ten. These were family representatives, since no families were split in the process. Those on whom the lot fell had to relocate from their hometown or ancestral village to Jerusalem. **The remaining nine were to stay in their own towns**.

11:2. As a result, **the people commended all the men who volunteered to live in Jerusalem**. Though they were drafted, those who moved to Jerusalem were considered volunteers since they submitted to the providence of God.

2. The Jerusalem List (11:3–24)

11:3–4a. Having described how people were selected to live in Jerusalem, a list followed. Categorized by families, this list did not indicate individuals. The writer of Nehemiah drew attention to the fact that **some Israelites, priests, Levites . . . lived in the towns of Judah, each on his own property in the various towns, while other people from both Judah and Benjamin lived in Jerusalem**. Perhaps he wanted to demonstrate how representative the group living in Jerusalem was, since each group mentioned as living outside the city also lived within its walls.

11:4b–19. A great list of clan and tribal names was entered into the text. We will not look at each individual name since little is known about most of them. Many of the names appearing in these verses are found in other lists in 1 Chronicles and Ezra. They demonstrate a cohesive, core population that was considered ethnically and religiously pure.

The major portion of the list falls into five major groupings: **the descendants of Judah . . . the descendants of Benjamin . . . the priests . . . the Levites . . . the gatekeepers**. The descendants of Judah and Benjamin were the lay citizens who constituted the majority of the population of the city. The priests, Levites, and gatekeepers served as religious leaders and workers. After each category a total of men within the group is given.

11:20. This verse interrupts the list, repeating the essence of Nehemiah 11:3: **The rest of the Israelites, with the priests and Levites, were in all the towns of Judah, each on his ancestral property**. The purpose for this interjection cannot be adequately determined unless it was meant to conclude the list by coming full circle to its beginnings. But there are a few additions to the residents of Jerusalem that occur after this point, making its insertion bewildering.

11:21. The writer added that **the temple servants lived on the hill of Ophel**. This hill was located in the northern section of the city, as noted in Nehemiah 3:26.

11:22–23. Since no particular leader was listed among the Levites in Nehemiah 11:15–18, the author of Nehemiah added that **the chief officer of the Levites in Jerusalem was Uzzi son of Bani**. Uzzi's ancestry was then traced to Asaph, a clan responsible for temple music, especially as **singers responsible for the service of the house of God**. Some of Asaph's hymns are included in the Book of Psalms (81–83, for example).

The singers were under the king's orders, which regulated their daily activity. Apparently King Artaxerxes, through a court-appointed official, supported and maintained the music of the temple. In what way the Persian government regulated their daily work is unknown.

11:24. Pethahiah son of Meshezabel concluded the list of those residing in Jerusalem. He was evidently a prominent figure in Jerusalem society and came from the clan of **Judah**. Like Nehemiah and Ezra, he was an official of the Persian government, serving as **the king's agent in all affairs relating to the people**. This suggests he had a broad range of authority in Jerusalem.

B Outside Jerusalem (11:25–36)

SUPPORTING IDEA: *The writer turned from Jerusalem to envision the entire nation, with enclaves and settlements throughout the Judean countryside.*

3. The towns of Judah (11:25–30)

11:25–30. The writer scanned the horizon, noting the breadth and width of Jewish habitation. **As for the villages with their fields, some of the people of Judah lived in Kiriath Arba and its surrouding settlements.** Though Judah was still under the domination of Persia, this survey of outlying villages appears to represent the tantalizing possibility of nationhood and repossession of the land in accordance with God's promise. The list of towns is extracted primarily from Joshua 15, which records the inheritance of the tribes after the conquest of the promised land. The towns of Judah were dotted across the land south of Jerusalem. They extended into the Negev, with **Beersheba** as the southernmost town, and into the western foothills. **Zorah**, Samson's hometown, was located in this region.

The intent of this list was to remind the Jews of their inheritance and to suggest that the time of God's favor might be approaching. It was the Jewish hope to reestablish their nation. The temple was restored, the walls of Jerusalem were rebuilt, the law was affirmed, and the people were settled in their ancestral towns and villages **all the way from Beersheba to the Valley of Hinnom**—from the north to the south.

4. The towns of Benjamin (11:31–35)

11:31–35. The writer next turned to **the descendants of the Benjamites**. As far as the people of this era were concerned, true Israelites were those of the two southern tribes and not their northern brothers. The towns mentioned in this section were located primarily north of Jerusalem and west along the coastal plain. Some of these towns were outside the Judean province at the time of Nehemiah. Again the choice of towns to include in this overview seems determined by links to Israel's divine inheritance and former days when the Jews conquered the land.

5. The Levites (11:36)

11:36. In context with the vision of a renewed Israel, with Jerusalem at its center, the description of the settlements ends by noting that **some of the divisions of the Levites of Judah settled in Benjamin**. Since the writer was careful to describe the resettlement of ancestral tribal lands, it was fitting to conclude with the tribe of Levi. More correctly, some of the divisions of the Levites settled in Judah and Benjamin.

The Levites had no landed inheritance. Their portion was the Lord and the honor of his service. Consequently, they were given specific towns among the various tribes (Josh. 21).

Priests and Levites (12:1–26)

SUPPORTING IDEA: *Legitimacy was important in establishing the postexilic community. Because of this, the chronicler inserted various lists of priests and Levites to document the genuineness of the faith community and its religious authority.*

6. During Zerubbabel (12:1–9)

12:1–7. The chronicler next assembled several lists from various time periods in order to validate the religious authority of the priesthood in Jerusalem. He began with those who returned in the first postexilic wave at the time of the Persian king, Cyrus: **These were the priests and Levites who returned with Zerubbabel son of Shealtiel and with Jeshua.**

The list of priests provided in Ezra 2 at the time of Zerubbabel's return appears quite different from this list. Scholars offer various explanations, but no single explanation has been persuasive to all. It seems most logical, however, that this list included subgroups within the priesthood that became well established over the postexilic time period. In Ezra 2, only four priestly family heads were mentioned, yet from these four came over one thousand priests. So it seems plausible that this large number of priests came from the subgrouping mentioned here since it included not only the major family heads but **the leaders of the priests and their associates** as well.

12:8–9. The Levitical list provides some problems, since only **Jeshua** and **Kadmiel** were mentioned in Ezra 2 where the number of Levites returning with Zerubbabel was relatively small (only 74). The only **Sherebiah** we know served during the time of Ezra. **Mattaniah**, the choir leader **in charge of the songs of thanksgiving**, and his associate **Bakbukiah**, served during the time of Nehemiah (Neh. 12:25). Both Bakbukiah and Unni were listed among the Levites rather than singers. That they **stood opposite** the Levites **in the services** denotes antiphonal singing.

7. High priests (12:10–11)

12:10–11. The last high priest at the time of the exile was Jozadak, father of **Jeshua**. Jeshua was high priest at the time of the first return and served during the time of the temple's reconstruction; his son **Joiakim** succeeded him. Afterwards, **Eliashib** assumed the high priestly office and was contemporary with Nehemiah (Neh. 3:1). **Joiada** and **Jonathan** remain relatively unknown. However, most scholars believe **Jaddua** was high priest during the time of Alexander the Great.

8. During Ezra (12:12–21)

12:12–21. **Joiakim** was believed to serve as high priest up to and around the time of Ezra. After Zerubbabel, Ezra's work was considered the next high point in the reestablishment of the postexilic community. Consequently, the compiler of Nehemiah next listed **the heads of the priestly families** during Joiakim's tenure. This list establishes continuity and legitimacy of the priestly lines. Each major family name from Nehemiah 12:1–7 is repeated with personal family leaders. There are a few variations between the lists that may be explained as variations in spellings over time (Rehum in v. 3 is replaced by Harim in v. 15). **Zechariah** we know as the prophet whose book bears his name and who prophesied around the time of Ezra.

9. Sources (12:22–23)

12:22–23. The chronicler was careful to cite his sources. The previous lists were well documented in other compilations provided throughout the books of Ezra and Nehemiah. These later lists, **in the days of Eliashib, Joiada, Johanan and Jaddua . . . were recorded in the reign of Darius the Persian**. There are varying opinions about which Darius this refers to, but it was probably Darius II. The record that the writer used was **the book of the annals**, or the Book of the Chronicles—not the same canonical book we know.

10. Levites (12:24–26)

12:24. The writer next provided an overview of the leading Levitical clans that claimed lineage to a common ancestor. These associations became more firmly established in the postexilic era as the organizational elements of Judaism evolved. There was great concern to establish the line of descent among the Jewish faithful so that God's originally established mandates and blessings could be linked to current events and peoples.

The compiler listed the leaders of the Levites as **Hashabiah, Sherebiah, Jeshua son of Kadmiel, and their associates**. These names have appeared in several other lists throughout the books of Ezra and Nehemiah. They represent the leading ancestral clans after the exile.

As in Nehemiah 12:8–9, the writer provided the setting for these Levitical leaders. They stood in the temple with the singers **opposite them to give praise and thanksgiving, one section responding to the other, as prescribed by David the man of God**. Just as the clans were traced in their lineage, so their functions were linked to the past. David, because of his ordering of psalms and singing, was considered God's messenger; he had established the religious songs in the temple service.

12:25. Mattaniah and **Bakbukiah** were previously listed among the singers (Neh. 12:8–9) and so probably belong to the preceding verse. The name **Meshullam** has occurred in several instances—at the time of Ezra's departure from Persia (Ezra 8:16) and in the rebuilding of the wall (Neh. 3). **Talmon** and **Akkub** were already identified as gatekeepers in Nehemiah 11:19. These gatekeepers **guarded the storerooms at the gates** where the tithes and offerings of the people were collected and warehoused.

12:26. In conclusion, the compiler noted that they **served in the days of Joiakim son of Jeshua, the son of Jozadak, and in the days of Nehemiah the governor and of Ezra the priest and scribe**. These people had served during each of the major returns to Judea—Zerubbabel's, Ezra's, and Nehemiah's. In addition, they were all linked to the preexilic nation as represented by the last high priest of that time, Jozadak.

D Dedication of the Wall (12:27–43)

SUPPORTING IDEA: *The climax of Nehemiah's efforts was reached in the dedication of Jerusalem's wall. It symbolized the people's protection both physically and spiritually.*

11. Preparation (12:27–30)

12:27. The repopulation of Jerusalem, along with the establishment of the priests' and Levites' ancestry, provided the backdrop for the dedication of Jerusalem's wall. By itself the wall was nothing more than stone, but in conjunction with the orthodoxy of the religious leaders and the renewed city life, it symbolized Israel's purpose and distinction. For such a meaningful event, **the Levites were sought out from where they lived and were brought to Jerusalem.**

Many Levites had settled in towns and villages around Jerusalem. They came into the city only when it was their turn for temple duties. But for such a grand and significant occasion, as many Levites as possible were recruited to **celebrate joyfully the dedication.**

12:28–29. In addition, **the singers also were brought together from the region around Jerusalem.** The Levitical clans had no land inheritance. Even in their allotted cities they possessed no land beyond their homes and some grazing land. Consequently, **the singers had built villages for themselves around Jerusalem.** These were in the area **of the Netophathites . . . Beth Gilgal . . . Geba and Azmaveth**—all unfortified villages in about an eight-mile radius from Jerusalem.

12:30. Before the wall's dedication ceremony, **the priests and Levites had purified themselves ceremonially.** This is a common theme in Judaism, symbolizing cleansing from sin and separation for holy use. Sexual abstinence, washings of clothes, and bathing were often involved in the purification rituals. The religious leaders also **purified the people, the gates and the wall.** This may have involved sprinkling of water to symbolize the sanctification of the people and their city.

12. The procession (12:31–39)

12:31. Nehemiah **had the leaders of Judah go up on top of the wall.** He also assigned **two large choirs to give thanks.** For the celebration Nehemiah used historical models of choirs and singers, but he gave the dedication a distinctive twist by dividing those assembled into two groups. Rather than one group following the path of the wall, he had two groups circle the city in opposite directions.

The first group **was to proceed on top of the wall to the right, toward the Dung Gate.** Most believe the two groups departed from the Valley Gate, since it provided a median point on the wall.

12:32–36. Behind the choir, **Hoshaiah and half the leaders of Judah followed.** Hoshaiah is unknown except in this setting. He was probably a prominent lay leader who led his peers in this specific group. The leaders were family heads, nobles, and princes.

Next came seven leading priests—**Azariah, Ezra, Meshullam, Judah, Benjamin, Shemaiah, Jeremiah.** The Ezra mentioned here was not the scribe, nor was this Jeremiah the prophet; these were common names of the time. Along with them came **some priests with trumpets.** Levite musicians usually used stringed instruments, and priests played trumpets.

After the priests were nine Levitical musicians, their leader being traced through the generations to **Asaph**. These Levites played **musical instruments prescribed by David the man of God**. In the chronicler's mind, this reference to David helped establish the authority of the Levitical structure and function.

The first group concluded by noting that **Ezra the scribe led the procession**. Scholars disagree on whether Ezra and Nehemiah were in Jerusalem at the same time or their ministries overlapped. However, each had a distinctive function in the life and reform of the nation. While the two men arrived at different times and for different reasons, there is no reason they could not have been together at the time of the dedication of the wall.

12:37. While the intent was to walk along the top of the wall, there were sections that did not allow this. At those points the procession left the wall and then returned to it where they could continue to walk. This was probably the situation at the **Fountain Gate** where they left the wall and walked **directly up the steps of the City of David**. However, they were able to get back on top of the wall and proceed along it **above the house of David to the Water Gate**.

12:38–39. The second choir proceeded in the opposite direction. Having left at the same point, these two choirs and those that went with them were to meet together at the temple court. Behind the choir Nehemiah led this particular group. The same structure applied to this processional assembly—choir, followed by lay leaders, then priests and Levites. The landmarks provide the path this group followed. The **Gate of the Guard**, where they stopped, was a temple gate. Both companies met so the entire assembly could celebrate together within the temple courts.

13. The Dedication Service (12:40–43)

12:40–42. The two choirs that gave thanks then took their places in the house of God. Having departed in opposite directions, the two groups circled the city and reunited at the house of God. Nehemiah joined the choir, along with those officials who had accompanied him around the city. He then named those priests and Levites who were in his company.

12:43. The dedicatory service was marked by unrestrained joy: **On that day they offered great sacrifices, rejoicing because God had given them great joy**. Many thank offerings were given in recognition of God's provision and goodness. God was the provider of all things—both the wall and the resultant joy. This was an entire community in loud and happy merriment: **the women and children also rejoiced**. This was not a quiet and solemn church service but a noisy celebration, for **the sound of rejoicing in Jerusalem could be heard far away.**

> **MAIN IDEA REVIEW:** *History not only teaches lessons to embrace and mistakes to avoid; it can affirm our purpose and distinctive place in the world. When history connects to the present and is understood through the lens of God's grace, it can instill endurance and inspire hope.*

III. CONCLUSION

Beyond Imagination

Why are there so many stars in the sky? Wouldn't a few do? Why all the varieties of flowers? Why not just daisies? Why the vast array of colors and shapes found in the fish under the sea—and some of them three miles deep? What's the point of that? Why the giraffe or the hippopotamus? Why cats?

Creation is, in many respects, a perpetual celebration of God's wonder and magnificence. In all its variety and strangeness, beauty and extravagance, the created order worships God by exhibiting something of his nature. People, too, are meant for this purpose.

While worship encompasses all of life, there are times when we should gather with just one objective—to celebrate God and his goodness. We may not bring people in from all the villages, but family reunions, meals, holidays, and special days at church should be marked by this festive enjoyment of God.

There is variety in creation, and there is variety in worship; no particular style is required to honor Christ. He loves differences and joy. The celebration at the completion of Jerusalem's wall was tied to history, but it was also uniquely arranged for that specific event. Trumpets were blown, choirs sang, and the people rejoiced.

Does your heart rejoice in worship? Do you delight in God?

PRINCIPLES

- Each person is valuable to God.
- Everything done for God's kingdom is remembered; God never forgets.
- Spiritual growth and development require periods of reform, evaluation, and renewal.
- God should be praised.

APPLICATIONS

- Read Christian biographies or church history. These accounts will inspire you in your walk with Christ.
- Respect and honor all people, even those who disagree with you. Christ died for all and desires to bring them into his family.
- Be strong in your work for Christ and his kingdom. God remembers everything done for him—even the hidden things.
- Plan a celebration with family and friends to praise God for his goodness. Make birthdays a time of thanksgiving; use dinnertime to review God's goodness during the day.

IV. LIFE APPLICATION

Praise 24–7

We often talk about "songs of praise," or "times of praise," or even "praise services." But God desires that our lives progress into continual praise—that life now will reflect the life to come. Paul, in writing to the Ephesians, emphasized that every aspect of our life in Christ has as its fundamental purpose, the "praise of his glory" (Eph. 1:12). We have been granted salvation and given the Holy Spirit for this purpose. How do we exhibit this praise?

1. *Giving our bodies as living sacrifices* (Rom. 12:1–2). Paul urges us to "offer your bodies as living sacrifices, holy and pleasing to God." Literally, the word *present* means to "stand beside." In other words, whatever we do in our body—all the activities, habits, and choices in which the body participates—should stand beside Christ. This means obedience, but it stretches us to consider absolutely everything in relation to his presence. Rather than viewing obedience as something we do for someone, this pictures us working alongside Jesus Christ in solidarity with him.

2. *Affirming Christ as Lord* (Heb. 13:15). We have heard that "actions speak louder than words." Certainly if there is conflict between what we say and what we do, our actions are the more believable since actions spring from our beliefs. But silence never convinced anyone to trust in Christ or follow him. At some point words become necessary to explain the hope that drives our lives. "Always be prepared to give an answer to everyone who asks you to give the reason for the hope that you have. But do this with gentleness and respect" (1 Pet. 3:15).

3. *Doing good* (Heb. 13:16). It hardly needs explanation; it's not a difficult concept. We are to do good to all people. "For we are God's workmanship, created in Christ Jesus to do good works, which God prepared in advance for us to do" (Eph. 2:10).

4. *Giving money* (1 Tim. 6:17–18). Warnings against greed and the entrapment of riches occur throughout the New Testament. Paul wrote to Timothy to "command those who are rich in this present world not to be arrogant nor to put their hope in wealth. . . . Command them to do good, to be rich in good deeds, and to be generous and willing to share." God blesses us not so we can keep accumulating but so we can share with those in need and partake in the privilege of sending the gospel throughout the world. This increases praise for his glory.

V. PRAYER

Lord, renew in us an appreciation for our heritage in the faith. May we embrace and identify with those Christians who lived in previous times. Enable us, like them, to defend the truth, proclaim your Word, and live your love. May their example provide us with a sense of family, tradition, and personal legacy. Amen.

VI. DEEPER DISCOVERIES

Casting lots (11:1)

It was common in Israel to cast lots, or throw a type of dice, in order to discern God's will. So strongly did they believe in God's sovereignty over the affairs of humankind that they believed it extended to the "chancy" and small issue of rolling dice. Joshua used lots to determine that Achan had sinned by taking plunder from Ai (Josh. 7:16–18). Lots were cast to decide the division of land when Israel entered Canaan. Samuel used lots in narrowing down the selection process for choosing Saul as Israel's first king (1 Sam. 10).

Nehemiah and the Jews of his time were also confident that God dominated and ruled even the smallest actions of life. Based on this conviction, thousands of families uprooted themselves from their homes to relocate to Jerusalem through a system of casting lots. Proverbs 16:33 states: "The lot is cast into the lap, but its every decision is from the LORD." Hundreds of years later, the disciples of Jesus determined Judas's replacement by casting lots (Acts 1:26).

VII. TEACHING OUTLINE

A. INTRODUCTION
1. Lead Story: What's in a Name?
2. Context: Into Nehemiah's memoirs a later writer inserted some overview materials to validate and confirm Judah's place as the community

of faith. He pulled events from Ezra's ministry to establish the people's genuine repentance and understanding of God's law. He interjected material from Nehemiah's second visit to substantiate the Jew's resolve to follow God's commands.

3. Transition: As readers we rejoin the story where it left off in chapter 7. Jerusalem needed to be repopulated. So Nehemiah and others established a lottery system for relocating people from the country to the city. A list was made of those families that had moved from ancestral lands. Following this was a compilation of priestly and Levitical clans that showed the emerging priestly organization and its link to Israel's heritage. Crowning all of this was the dedication of Jerusalem's rebuilt wall.

B. COMMENTARY

1. Repopulation of Jerusalem (11:1–24)
   a. The method of repopulation (11:1–2)
   b. The Jerusalem list (11:3–24)
2. Outside Jerusalem (11:25–36)
   a. The towns of Judah (11:25–30)
   b. The towns of Benjamin (11:31–35)
   c. The Levites (11:36)
3. Priests and Levites (12:1–26)
   a. During Zerubbabel (12:1–9)
   b. High Priests (12:10–11)
   c. During Ezra (12:12–21)
   d. Sources (12:22–23)
   e. Levites (12:24–26)
4. Dedication of the Wall (12:27–43)
   a. Preparation (12:27–30)
   b. The procession (12:31–39)
   c. The dedication service (12:40–43)

C. CONCLUSION: BEYOND IMAGINATION

VIII. ISSUES FOR DISCUSSION

1. Why do you suppose it was important to catalog the generational lists of the priests and Levites?
2. Some of the Jews were chosen to move from their country towns to Jerusalem in order to safeguard the city and the nation. Can you think of any circumstances when, as Christians, we should move or give up personal possessions for the welfare of the church? Explain.

3. Discuss why our names are important to us. What is conveyed by a person's name?

4. Are there benefits to all-church celebrations and special services? If so, describe.

Nehemiah 12:44–13:31

Reform

Quote

*S*ometimes I wonder who is going to win the battle first,

the barbarians beating at our gates from without, or the ter-

mites of immorality from within.

B i l l y   G r a h a m

Nehemiah 12:44-13:31

I N   A   N U T S H E L L

*N*ehemiah fulfilled his term as governor and was recalled to serve King Artaxerxes. While he was gone, the Jerusalem community ignored many of the law's requirements and, even among the priesthood, abuses occurred. Nehemiah returned to Jerusalem and quickly set about instituting reforms.

Reform

I. INTRODUCTION

Ants

A young couple bought a house, moved in, and began some remodeling projects. In the course of their work, they spotted a couple of ants in their basement. A few days later they found one in their bedroom. It didn't seem like much of a problem, so they set out some "ant hotels" to trap them. But they never could totally eradicate the ants. Then one day as they were installing new windows, they noticed some sawdust on a windowsill. With a sense of dread, they wondered if perhaps they had termites.

They arranged for a pest inspection. They did not have termites, but they did have carpenter ants. These pests can be more destructive than termites. They destroy anything wooden in order to keep the queen alive. Find the queen, and you destroy the colony. In the meantime, if you have no idea where that queen resides, your house is slowly eaten out from under you. Quite literally, it could collapse from the inside.

Under Nehemiah's leadership, the people of Judah had rebuilt Jerusalem's wall; they had reestablished the city's defenses and reaffirmed the people's sense of identity. The work done, Nehemiah returned to his position in the court of King Artaxerxes. However, whether because of unsettling reports or personal curiosity, Nehemiah returned to Jerusalem.

Upon his arrival he found neglect of the law and abuses among the priests and Levites. The wall surrounding Jerusalem still stood, but within its protection destructive behaviors and attitudes were spreading. These may have appeared small on the surface and rather nonthreatening, but Nehemiah perceived the implications of compromise. In an effort to eradicate spiritual sloth and negligence, he instituted specific reforms.

II. COMMENTARY

Reform

> **MAIN IDEA:** *Renewal and reform are constants in the life of faith. Since the human condition tends toward compromise, failure, and disobedience, it is imperative to keep vigilant watch over one's heart, actions, and habits.*

Ⓐ An Overview of Judah (12:44–13:3)

> **SUPPORTING IDEA:** *The compiler of the Book of Nehemiah concluded the wall's dedication by describing the community's faithful adherence to the law's requirements, particularly as it related to Levitical procedures.*

1. Levitical protocol (12:44–47)

12:44. After the dedication of the wall, the chronicler summarized the postexilic community. He wrote, **at that time men were appointed**. The phrase, "at that time," refers not to the immediate occasion of the wall's dedication but to the general time period of Nehemiah. Men were selected **to be in charge of the storerooms for the contributions, firstfruits and tithes**. The "contributions" were prime produce given to the priests while the "tithes" were intended for the Levites.

These were stored for their use throughout the year and brought **from the fields around the towns . . . into the storerooms**. The storerooms were chambers attached to the temple area for this purpose. According to the chronicler, the people gladly brought their tithes and contributions into the storerooms.

12:45–46. There was a sense of community-wide dedication and commitment on the part of the laity as well as the professional clergy. Everything was done according to the law and its prescriptions, **according to the commands of David and his son Solomon**. With David the permanence of God's dwelling and site of community worship was established in Jerusalem.

12:47. The writer of Nehemiah summarized the postexilic community, stating that **in the days of Zerubbabel and of Nehemiah, all Israel contributed the daily portions for the singers and gatekeepers**. While it becomes apparent in Nehemiah 13 that this process was not as flawless as might appear here, there probably was a systematic collection for the temple servants from the first return under Zerubbabel until the time of Nehemiah. In accordance with the community's obedience, the Levites obeyed, too, as they **set aside the portion for the other Levites, and the Levites set aside the portion for the descendants of Aaron**.

2. Purification (13:1–3)

13:1–2. On that day the Book of Moses was read aloud in the hearing of the people. Again, no particular time or specific assembly is intended by these remarks. The "day" was simply the Nehemiah era. The context does not clarify whether the people heard the law at a specific assembly or in the course of Sabbath observance.

13:3. The people in Nehemiah's day **excluded from Israel all who were of foreign descent**. We know that converts to Judaism have always been allowed. In fact, Ruth was a Moabite. So to what extent this exclusion occurred cannot be determined from the text.

🅱 Nehemiah's Final Corrections (13:4–31)

SUPPORTING IDEA: *While the general atmosphere throughout Judah may have been one of obedience to the law, there were lapses and abuses. These required Nehemiah's strong hand of discipline.*

3. The temple chambers (13:4–14)

13:4–5. Eliashib the priest had been put in charge of the storerooms of the house of our God. This man was administrator of the temple chambers where the people's contributions were brought. The text also tells us that Eliashib **was closely associated with Tobiah**. In what way these two men were associated is unclear. They probably had political or economic ties of some sort. Eliashib allowed Tobiah, an Ammonite, to use one of the temple storerooms for some other purpose. That Eliashib had taken one of these sacred rooms and turned it over to someone for nonsacral use was a grave violation.

13:6a. How this entire blasphemous arrangement came about was because of Nehemiah's absence. He explained in his memoirs: **While all this was going on, I was not in Jerusalem, for in the thirty-second year of Artaxerxes king of Babylon I had returned to the king**. After twelve years as governor, Nehemiah was recalled to the Persian capital. For what reason we do not know.

13:6b–7. Neither do we know how much time elapsed between Nehemiah's return to Artaxerxes and his revisit to Jerusalem. However, **some time later** he asked the king's **permission and came back to Jerusalem**. More than likely, Nehemiah received reports of what was happening in Jerusalem and some of the religious lapses and abuses that were taking place.

Once in Jerusalem he learned firsthand about **the evil thing Eliashib had done in providing Tobiah a room in the courts of the house of God**. Once again Nehemiah was faced with his enemy Tobiah. This time Tobiah had taken advantage of the leadership vacuum left by Nehemiah's departure, and he seized the opportunity to plant himself at the center of Jewish life.

(margin note, handwritten, vertical): One wrong act in the leadership trickled down to workers

13:8. Tobiah's smug positioning was cut short by Nehemiah's return. Nehemiah was **greatly displeased and threw all Tobiah's household goods out of the room**. Nehemiah felt the strong offense against God that such an arrangement conveyed. He displayed a zeal similar to that exhibited by Christ when he cleansed the temple (Matt. 21:12–13).

13:9. Nehemiah then **gave orders to purify the rooms**. Tobiah's use of the chamber had desecrated it. However, it seems the purification went beyond the particular room allotted to Tobiah. Nehemiah may have had the entire chamber area cleansed and ritually purified. He then put back into the rooms **the equipment of the house of God, with the grain offerings and the incense**.

13:10. After throwing Tobiah's possessions out and resettling the storeroom with its proper goods, Nehemiah realized that the tithes and contributions for the priests and Levites were missing. The incident revealed **that the portions assigned to the Levites had not been given to them**. These tithes, or portions, belonged to the Levites by command of the law. This was their means of support, enabling them to carry out their duties in the temple. When this source dried up, **all the Levites and singers responsible for the service had gone back to their own fields**. The Levites had moved out of Jerusalem and gone home.

13:11–12. Nehemiah responded by rubuking the officials. He was not a suave diplomat or practiced politician. When he saw an abuse or violation, he confronted those involved. He pointedly asked them, **Why is the house of God neglected?** He viewed the problem not as an offense to the Levites but to God. They had neglected his commands and dismissed the services of worship.

Nehemiah called everyone together and laid out a plan. Collection stations were set up throughout Judah so the people could bring in their tithes more easily and efficiently. Nehemiah also stationed the officials **at their posts**. As a result, **all Judah brought the tithes of grain, new wine and oil into the storerooms**.

13:13. Nehemiah then reorganized the care and maintenance of the temple storerooms. He put **Shelemiah the priest, Zadok the scribe, and a Levite named Pedaiah in charge . . . and made Hanan son of Zaccur . . . their assistant**. To assure that no further lapses and abuses would occur, Nehemiah placed not one man but a committee in charge of the storerooms and their distributions. Each man represents those who benefited from the tithe system—a priest, a Levite, and a singer. In addition, a scribe, or government official, was added to the group, perhaps as a disinterested member who would ensure justice and diligence. These men were responsible **for distributing the supplies**.

13:14. At the conclusion of each reform instituted by Nehemiah, he offered a prayer asking that God remember what he had done. In this case, Nehemiah asked that God **not blot out what I have so faithfully done for the house of my God and its services.** He envisioned the books of heaven in which deeds of righteousness are recorded. He prayed that God would enter into these books all that he had done because of his devotion to God and his covenant.

4. The Sabbath (13:15–22)

13:15. In those days, or during the time of his second tenure in Jerusalem, Nehemiah **saw men in Judah treading winepresses on the Sabbath.** Work on the Sabbath was forbidden by the Mosaic Law. He also saw Jews **bringing in grain and loading it on donkeys, together with wine, grapes, figs and all other kinds of loads.** Nehemiah warned them against selling food on that day.

13:16. In addition, **men from Tyre who lived in Jerusalem were bringing in fish and all kinds of merchandise.** These were aliens who lived among the Jews. Tyre was a city on the Mediterranean coast in the country of Phoenicia. Phoenicians were well-known seafarers who had established commerce and trade in far-off regions of the civilized world. These businessmen probably lived in a Jerusalem district where they had created a brisk trade among the Jewish residents.

13:17. Nehemiah confronted those he felt responsible for the violation of the Sabbath. This time he rebuked the nobles of Judah: **What is this wicked thing you are doing—desecrating the Sabbath day?** It was immaterial whether the nobles were personally involved in marketing on the Sabbath or loading their donkeys. As family heads and city leaders, these men were responsible for civic attitudes and regulations. That they ignored these commercial exchanges demonstrated a breach of responsibility. Their neglect was an affront to God.

13:18. Nehemiah pointed the attention of these leaders to the not-so-distant past: **Didn't your forefathers do the same things, so that our God brought all this calamity upon us and upon this city?** Nehemiah understood history, and he understood God's zeal for all that was holy. They were repeating the failures and sins of their ancestors. They were not immune from God's judgment just because the wall around Jerusalem had been rebuilt and the people had returned to reclaim their ancestral lands.

13:19. Nehemiah formulated plans to ensure that circumstances or situations would change. In this case, in the evening just before sunset and the beginning of Sabbath, he **ordered the doors to be shut and not opened until the Sabbath was over.** This ensured that no one could bring merchandise into the city to sell on the Sabbath.

13:20–21. Finding their entrance into the city blocked, **once or twice the merchants and sellers of all kinds of goods spent the night outside Jerusalem.** This was probably meant to mock Nehemiah's efforts. If they couldn't sell within the city, they would lure the people outside. But Nehemiah warned the salesmen that if they continued to camp outside the city with the intent to sell, he would have them removed by force.

13:22. Nehemiah concluded his reform by a purification. This time he **commanded the Levites to purify themselves.** Because the issue was a sacred and religious one, he felt it required the participation of the religious leaders. Therefore, he had the Levites **guard the gates in order to keep the Sabbath day holy.**

5. Foreign influence (13:23–31)

13:23. One of the final issues to which Nehemiah turned was the allurement of foreign influences, especially as related to marriage. It was a temptation to which Israel succumbed over and over throughout its history. Despite all the efforts to reestablish the law as the standard for life within the Jewish community, Nehemiah **saw men of Judah who had married women from Ashdod, Ammon and Moab.** These groups were enemies of Israel and opponents of Judah's revitalization.

13:24. Not only were these marriages contracted with Israel's enemies, but they were producing children who **spoke the language of Ashdod or the language of one of the other peoples, and did not know how to speak the language of Judah.** The inability to understand or speak Hebrew would distance succeeding generations from the nation of Israel and its covenantal history and their religious distinctions.

13:25. Nehemiah **beat some of the men and pulled out their hair.** Pulling or plucking hair was intended to humiliate the guilty person. In the Middle Eastern culture in which this occurred, such aggressive behavior toward those deemed guilty was not uncommon. Add to this the temperament of Nehemiah, and we see a spontaneous reaction against what he viewed as a deplorable offense and threat to the nation and God's law.

Nehemiah demanded, **You are not to give your daughters in marriage to their sons, nor are you to take their daughters in marriage for your sons or for yourselves.** Initially, men from Judah were marrying foreign women. Nehemiah moved beyond that and had them pledge that Jewish girls would not be married outside the Jewish faith.

13:26. Nehemiah asked the people, **Was it not because of marriages like these that Solomon king of Israel sinned?** Solomon was one of Israel's greatest and wisest kings. But in spite of all his insight and intelligence, **even he was led into sin by foreign women.**

13:27. Nehemiah was angered and bewildered that these men on the outskirts of Judah could have thought themselves immune to the thing that led to the downfall of one of the greatest kings of Israel. They would not survive the influence of these women in their homes.

13:28. But Nehemiah discovered something far more severe. One of the grandsons of **Eliashib the high priest was son-in-law to Sanballat the Horonite**. In line to the high priestly office, this nameless person had snubbed God's command that the woman a priest marries must be "a virgin from his own people, so he will not defile his offspring among his people" (Lev. 21:14–15). As the son-in-law of Sanballat, he had not only defiled himself and his heirs, but he had allied himself with one of Israel's strongest enemies. Nehemiah **drove him away**, exiling him from Israel.

13:29. Nehemiah ended the confrontation on mixed marriages by again asking that God **remember**. This time, however, he wanted the Lord to remember those in the high priestly family who had spurned God's command and **defiled the priestly office and the covenant of the priesthood and of the Levites**. By allowing such disobedience within their ranks, they had brought into question the authority and teaching of the Levites.

13:30. Nehemiah **purified the priests and the Levites of everything foreign, and assigned them duties, each to his own task**. What the specifics of these actions were cannot be determined from this text. The force of Nehemiah's reforms was to bring the entire community under the rule of God's covenant.

13:31. Nehemiah also **made provision for contributions of wood at designated times, and for the firstfruits**. These were issues addressed in the oath of Nehemiah 10. Nehemiah laid everything before God. In all his work, he only asked, **Remember me with favor, O my God**.

> **MAIN IDEA REVIEW:** *Renewal and reform are constants in the life of faith. Since the human condition tends toward compromise, failure, and disobedience, it is imperative to keep vigilant watch over one's heart, actions, and habits.*

III. CONCLUSION

Are You Serious?

A national hotel chain once ran a television ad that stated: "Eternal damnation is for pansies. . . . Try a family vacation if you really want the worst."

They expected people to smile and recall some disastrous family excursion; but the comparison is not funny. Eternal judgment is not the territory for humor or flippant remarks. It's a reality that people do not take seriously in our modern world. God's judgment is either discounted and minimized, rejected as being harsh, or ignored because "God just wouldn't do that."

But if the Bible says anything, it warns of judgment.

The reason Israel defeated the people of Canaan was in order to exact God's judgment against their sin and disobedience. Nehemiah judged the waywardness of Judah by punishing their defiance.

In a culture where moral standards have become unpopular, and right and wrong depend on consensus, the idea of justice has been diluted to monetary settlements and plea bargaining. Society shrugs and wonders, "What's the big deal?" But try cutting in front of someone in traffic, and suddenly justice becomes an issue; the driver literally screams for retribution. Evidently, an insult matters only if it is against us.

But our offenses before God are cosmic. We have assaulted his throne and glory. Yet, for some reason, we think God should get over it. But what confidence can you have in a God who ignores injustice? What hope is there in a God who trivializes crime? We have lost sight of God's holiness and our depravity; we have defaced the concept of justice and exalted our paltry opinions.

It isn't difficult to reconcile judgment and wrath with a God who is holy and sovereign. What is far more incomprehensible is that this God has condescended to extend mercy to those who despise him, to those who trample on his goodness. This he has done through the sacrifice of his Son, Jesus Christ.

PRINCIPLES

- God is both judge and redeemer; he is holy and merciful.
- The Lord will accomplish his purposes on the earth regardless of human opinions.
- God expects and deserves obedience.

APPLICATIONS

- Never let your busy schedule crowd out time with God. Work hard to be in a perpetual state of worship by giving every moment and decision to the will of Christ.
- Honor Sunday by getting together with other Christians to celebrate the resurrection of Christ.
- Evaluate your life occasionally not for selfish introspection but in order to assess your spiritual growth and needs. Then make specific goals for following Christ.

IV. LIFE APPLICATION

Let's Get Specific

Some of us grew up in a church environment where decisions of "rededication" were common. In many traditions summer camp or weekend retreats for teenagers were times to surrender again your life to Christ. It involved confessing sins from last school year; symbolically, a twig was thrown on the fire to represent that you were going to yield to Christ and consecrate your life anew for the year to come.

There is some good in such reevaluation. The Scriptures encourage us to consider our lives and, when needed, restore our commitment to our Savior. But we must also know that reforms in our life are most effective when they are most specific.

People who develop general goals rarely achieve them, while those who create specific objectives usually accomplish them. Those who say, "I want to lose some weight," have no measurable goal or any plan to succeed. But the person who says, "I want to lose ten pounds by June so I am going to walk three miles each day, drink six glasses of water, and eliminate desserts" has specific steps to keep him on course toward his goal.

In the same way, those who want to grow spiritually cannot simply "wish" for it to happen. Sentiments such as "I want to share my faith more" or "I want to love Christ more," while commendable, are rarely enough to carry us to our desire. If you want to share your faith more, then you need to set down a specific plan that involves memorizing Scripture, scheduling more interaction with neighbors, or rethinking your use of time.

Let's get specific, by the power of God's indwelling Spirit.

V. PRAYER

Compromise is such an easy path, Lord. It pulls on every side; it appeals to our selfish nature. Help us cling to you, to value your Word above all else, to follow your instructions wholeheartedly, and to remain faithful. Amen.

VI. DEEPER DISCOVERIES

The Sabbath (13:15–22)

Special regard for the seventh day of the week was established at the time of creation. God acted in works of creative energy for six days, then sanctified the seventh day as a time of rest. The word *Sabbath* literally means, "cessation," and it was meant as a time to cease from labor. It had the dual purposes of restoration (physical and spiritual) and worship.

Exodus 20:8–11 provides a clear rationale for the observance of Sabbath rest. Moses specified that no one was to work on that day, not even servants, foreigners, or animals. The reason extended back to God's creative acts and his blessing of the Sabbath. These made the day holy.

VII. TEACHING OUTLINE

A. INTRODUCTION

1. Lead Story: Ants
2. Context: The wall around Jerusalem was completed and its dedication was celebrated. The people had come together to renew their commitment to follow after God and worship him according to the law.
3. Transition: Nehemiah was recalled to the Persian capital after an absence of twelve years. But after a time, King Artaxerxes allowed Nehemiah a return trip to Jerusalem. He discovered that after his departure, spiritual and religious conditions in Jerusalem and Judah had deteriorated. Abuses of the law had crept into daily life, and blatant disobedience had worked its way into the priesthood. With a sense of outrage, Nehemiah confronted each problem.

B. COMMENTARY

1. An Overview of Judah (12:44–13:3)
   a. Levitical protocol (12:44–47)
   b. Purification (13:1–3)
2. Nehemiah's Final Corrections (13:4–31)
   a. The temple chambers (13:4–14)
   b. The Sabbath (13:15–22)
   c. Foreign influence (13:23–31)

C. CONCLUSION: ARE YOU SERIOUS?

VIII. ISSUES FOR DISCUSSION

1. In 2 Corinthians 6:14, Paul writes that Christians should not marry unbelievers. Discuss some problems that occur when people marry outside the faith. Why is God so passionate about this issue?

2. After Nehemiah purified the temple chambers, he put men who were considered trustworthy in charge. Read 1 Timothy 3 and compile a list of qualifications for leaders in the church.
3. The Sabbath was a day of rest, set aside as holy to God. Does this apply to the church? Should Sunday be different in any way?
4. Nehemiah strictly enforced the law and its requirements. Discuss the difference between enforcement of standards and legalism.

Introduction to

Esther

AUTHORSHIP

- The author of the Book of Esther is unknown, though most believe he was Jewish.
- The author had either personal knowledge of Persian court intrigues and life or access to detailed information.

READERS

- Postexilic Jews; particularly those dispersed throughout foreign lands.

DATE

- Covers events during the reign of Xerxes I, who ruled Persia from 486 to 465 B.C.
- Was probably written a few decades after Xerxes's reign, around 400 B.C.

CHARACTERISTICS

- Though God is never mentioned in the Book of Esther, this is a story about him and his sovereignty, faithfulness, and activity in the world.
- The story contrasts two opposing worldviews—impersonal fate and divine purpose and sovereignty.
- The book also encourages Jewish ethnicity and proclaims the endurance of the Jewish people as God's chosen.
- The story of Esther illustrates the difficult though attainable balance between loyalty to God and life within a pagan culture.
- The book proclaims the surety of justice. In an ironic twist, evil becomes the victim of its own devices.

Esther 1

Questions of Power

The proud and arrogant man—"Mocker" is his name; he behaves with overweening pride.

Proverbs 21:24

Esther 1

IN A NUTSHELL

The book opens by plunging the reader into the lavish and petty world of the Persian court. Many of the themes and contrasts throughout the book are introduced in this first chapter; here, too, we discover the background explanation for Esther's eventual rise to queen of Persia.

Questions of Power

I. INTRODUCTION

Curtain, Please

*I*f you've ever attended a play or opera, you know that there comes that moment when the lights dim, the chatter dies, and the curtain opens. A world that once was hidden is carefully revealed. Each prop has its place and purpose; each light focuses upon a determined point; the colors and shadows interplay with designed calculation. Everything converges so that the audience understands the mood, setting, characters, and plot.

In the same way, the Book of Esther begins with the drawing of a curtain. Each detail rendered and each omission allowed by the writer serves a purpose and drives the plot.

The reader enters the world of Persian opulence and excess. Certain characters appear only briefly; others strut on the stage from the start and remain to the conclusion. We begin to measure the king's character from his actions and reactions, as well as from the men he gathers around him for advice and counsel. We get a glimpse of unrestrained egoism, personality cult politics, and the vicissitudes of human wisdom.

In addition, the opening of the book sets in motion an ongoing series of contrasts—Xerxes's ostentatious displays and the moderate behavior of women; the babbling overreaction of the wise men and the simple cunning of Esther; Vashti's defiance and Esther's apparent submission; Xerxes's drunkenness and Vashti's sobriety; male pride and female service.

Primarily, however, the first chapter explains in human terms the subsequent rise of an unknown Jewish girl to the throne of Persia.

II. COMMENTARY

Questions of Power

> **MAIN IDEA:** *Despite the Persian Empire's wealth and Xerxes's unquestioned control over numerous peoples, the king and his advisors—ruled by arrogance, anger, petty grievances, and insecurity—illustrate that man's wisdom often springs from foolish hearts.*

A The Setting (1:1–9)

> **SUPPORTING IDEA:** *King Xerxes, in a display of pomp and wealth, holds two extravagant feasts.*

1. Feast one (1:1–4)

1:1–2. The writer's purpose in the book's opening section is twofold: to set the stage for the following events and to develop a series of contrasts between the extravagant wealth, power, and material splendor of the Persian monarchy and the humble wisdom of the Jews.

The story unfolds **during the time of Xerxes . . . who ruled over 127 provinces stretching from India to Cush**. Xerxes I ruled the Persian Empire from 486 to 465 B.C. The specification of 127 provinces has confused some scholars since Persia seems never to have had more than thirty-one satrapies, or regional political seats. However, the term *provinces* most likely included subregional divisions within the satrapies, such as Judea. By including these subdivisions, the writer emphasized the vast expanse of Xerxes's empire, which stretched from modern Pakistan to Northern Sudan.

Xerxes ruled this enormous region **from his royal throne in the citadel of Susa**. This was an old Elamite city destroyed by the Assyrians in 640 B.C. However, Darius I, Xerxes's father, rebuilt Susa. Within the city was a fortified palace complex, or citadel, where the king and his retinue lived. Xerxes made Susa his springtime residence.

The author of Esther portrays Xerxes as supreme authority sitting elevated on his throne above all the people, living in a citadel above the city, ruling over a sprawling domain. These descriptions heighten the contrast and irony of the following events.

1:3–4. Three years into his reign, Xerxes **gave a banquet**, or reception. **For a full 180 days** (six months) the king entertained **his nobles and officials**, as well as **the military leaders of Persia and Media**. Government functions were probably not postponed for a full six months. The king displayed **the vast wealth of his kingdom and the splendor and glory of his majesty** while receiving various groups throughout the period.

2. Feast two (1:5–8)

1:5–6. At the end of the six-month spectacle, Xerxes gave a second banquet—**lasting seven days**—for the citizens of the citadel **from the least to the greatest**. Having dazzled the imperial officials, Xerxes threw a party for the ordinary male populace of the palatial complex. These were not the citizens of the city proper but those who resided within the royal fortress.

1:7–8. Though exotic foods were served, these banquets were distinguished for their drinking. In fact, the Hebrew term for these feasts can be translated "drinking bouts." The wine was so abundant that a vast array of drinking and serving vessels was required. The **wine was served in goblets of gold, each one different from the other**, indicating the excess that occurred. All this, however, was **in keeping with the king's liberality**, or as befits a king's generosity and plenty. One can imagine the debauchery that occurred with such royally sanctioned license.

3. Feast three (1:9)

1:9. The writer of Esther tells us that **Queen Vashti also gave a banquet for the women in the royal palace of King Xerxes**. Aristocratic Persian women were known to keep pace with their male counterparts in exhibitions of wealth, pomp, and drinking. The omission of a counterbalancing report demonstrates the writer's favorable view of women and portrays the queen as having a more noble and modest nature than her husband.

B Domestic Discord and National Crisis (1:10–22)

> **SUPPORTING IDEA:** Anger and folly usually keep company with each other. Feeling wounded and humiliated, King Xerxes initiated a series of decisions based on pride, anger, and drunkenness.

4. The king's request (1:10–12)

1:10–11. On the **seventh** and final day of the banquet **King Xerxes was in high spirits from wine**. In other words, the king was drunk. In this state he commanded **the seven eunuchs who served him . . . to bring . . . Queen Vashti . . . in order to display her beauty to the people and nobles**. For over six months Xerxes had placed all his wealth and prestige on display, and in the final day of his extravagance he decided to show off his most treasured trophy—his queen.

1:12. But **Queen Vashti refused to come**. One can almost hear the gasps of alarm or imagine the furtive glances. The ruler of the known world, rebuffed before the partying public, **became furious and burned with anger**.

5. The king's response (1:13–15)

1:13–14. The irony of the story builds. Xerxes, whose power extended from Pakistan to North Africa, could not make a decision about his own household without consulting the **experts in matters of law and justice . . . the wise men who understood the times and were closest to the king.** These men were considered perceptive, savvy about culture, and wise about imperial interests. The king required the sharpest minds of Persia to decide a domestic problem; he was a conqueror who could not devise a rejoinder to his own wife.

1:15. In an authoritarian regime, rulers rarely asked for personal advice, so Xerxes presented his dilemma in terms of legalities. He asked, **According to law, what must be done to Queen Vashti? . . . She has not obeyed the command of King Xerxes.**

6. A plan devised (1:16–20)

1:16–17. There was no edict that addressed the queen's refusal. Technically, this was not a matter of enforcing a law but of placating the king. So one of the king's advisors, Memucan, offered not legal advice but personal opinion. He exaggerated beyond all bounds the offense and its implications: **Vashti has done wrong, not only against the king but also against all the nobles and the peoples of all the provinces of King Xerxes.**

Memucan continued, **The queen's conduct will become known to all the women, and so they will despise their husbands.** How Xerxes's entire kingdom would hear of Vashti's disobedience is hard to imagine. Even so, it was preposterous to think that all the women in the kingdom were obeying their husbands under duress, simply waiting for one brave soul to lead the way in rebellion.

1:18. Not only would the rumor of Xerxes's humiliation spread throughout the land, Memucan also predicted that within twenty-four hours **the Persian and Median women of the nobility . . . will respond to all the king's nobles in the same way.** Perhaps this was Memucan's greatest fear—he might lose control over his own wife!

This "wise" counselor of Persia looked upon the situation and responded with a kind of personal hysteria in which all the wives of nobility would react like Vashti, and all the husbands would, like the king, be usurped. Every home would eventually be filled with **disrespect and discord,** according to Memucan. He offered the king a solution.

1:19–20. Memucan advised that the king issue an edict which would **be written in the laws of Persia and Media, which cannot be repealed.** He also suggested that the king give Vashti's royal position **to someone else who is better than she.** Each day Vashti would live among the women of the king's harem—never called, never acknowledged—living out her quiet tragedy with no hope for children, husband, or a future. With the instigation of his brilliant plan, **all the women**, according to Memucan, would **respect their husbands**.

7. *An edict declared (1:21–22)*

1:21–22. All the men agreed: **The king and his nobles were pleased with this advice**. Evidently, Memucan constructed the proposal spontaneously without consultation with the other nobles. But with the king expressing pleasure in his ideas, everyone else naturally applauded the plan.

Xerxes **sent dispatches to all parts of the kingdom, to each province in its own script and to each people in its own language**. Persia's postal system and road network were renowned and efficient, and messengers were sent into the far-flung corners of Xerxes's domain broadcasting the news of Vashti's indiscretion and declaring **that every man should be ruler over his own household**.

> **MAIN IDEA REVIEW:** *Despite the Persian Empire's wealth, and Xerxes's unquestioned control over numerous peoples, the king and his advisors—ruled by arrogance, anger, petty grievances, and insecurity—illustrate that man's wisdom often springs from foolish hearts.*

III. CONCLUSION

The Battle of the Sexes

He began playing tennis seriously at the age of twelve. By the time he was twenty-one, he was ranked number one in the world and considered a rising star. In 1946, 1947, and 1949 he won the U.S. national professional singles championships. Many thought he was the best tennis player ever and admired his grace and athleticism on the court. But it was his derision and eventual humiliation that firmly fixed Bobby Riggs's fame.

In 1973, within the milieu of the women's liberation movement, Riggs proclaimed, "Any half-decent male player could defeat even the best female player." In a media extravaganza, Bobby Riggs, age fifty-five, came out of retirement to play against the top female of the day, Billie Jean King. The match was dubbed the "Battle of the Sexes," and 30,472 spectators crammed into the Houston Astrodome while an estimated fifty million people watched on television.

It didn't last long. In three straight sets Billie Jean King defeated the boastful Riggs.

It didn't settle much, either.

In the opening chapter of Esther, an unplanned battle of the sexes occurred. With an extravagant display of power and wealth, King Xerxes hosted two banquets intended to underscore his might and supremacy. The unquestioned ruler of a sprawling empire, Xerxes, drunk with wine and his own importance, sent a command that his wife appear before his guests to display her beauty. She refused. The unprecedented response of this spirited woman created a political crisis within the palace and eventually within the nation.

In ancient Persia the "battle of the sexes" didn't settle much either. It did, however, provide the circumstances for God's eventual salvation of his people.

PRINCIPLES

- Wealth inflates a person's pride, resulting in selfishness, anger, greed, and many other sins.
- Drunkenness leads to debauchery.
- Leadership requires wisdom and prudence.
- Decisions made in anger are usually foolish.

APPLICATIONS

- Don't make wealth your aim in life.
- Be content with what you have and "pursue righteousness, godliness, faith, love, endurance and gentleness" (1 Tim. 6:11).
- When facing decisions, seek godly counsel and take time to weigh the alternatives and potential consequences.
- Remember that everything you have comes from God. Cultivate a thankful spirit in order to combat the natural pull of selfishness.

IV. LIFE APPLICATION

Proud as a Peacock

All of us know the meaning of the phrase "proud as a peacock." The peacock embodies excess. Anyone who has ever seen one can envision its small, crowned head or the dazzling blue of its long, shimmering neck. But most memorable are its flamboyant plumes of gold, green, and blue. The male peacock, to draw attention, unfurls his feathers in an expansive fan, rattles his quills, and screams raucously. Quite typically, the female ignores the entire performance.

For six months Xerxes strutted his wealth and power before everyone who was anyone in his kingdom. He spoke and it was done; he commanded and it was accomplished. He dazzled the civil servants of Susa with his glitz and carousal, rattling his supremacy and flaunting his riches.

Those who allow pride to dominate them live in a shrunken world of their own will. The actions of others either boost selfish interests or affront them. Everything becomes redirected toward the self and measured against its desires. In that stifling atmosphere envy whispers in the heart, and covetousness steals in, because the small universe of the ego is insufficient for its own satisfaction.

But even those who, like Xerxes, have vast wealth, success, or power never gain enough to quell the demands of pride—so anger shouts in the heart. Such people come to despise those who threaten their superiority or who, by virtue of their conduct, convict them of their wrongness or question their assumptions. Eventually, pride brings a failure of imagination in which the person so afflicted cannot recognize the humanity of others but sees them only as objects for personal pleasure or use.

Such dangers confront not just the prideful people of this world—those who dominate the citadels of cultural or political power—but Christians as well. Without vigilance and a humble submission to Jesus Christ, pride can dazzle the mind and intoxicate the heart.

V. PRAYER

God of all glory and power, protect our hearts from pride. It tempts with reason; it beckons with self-justification. Holy Spirit, keep us sensitive to sin and aware of grace so that we may serve with humility. Amen.

VI. DEEPER DISCOVERIES

Susa (1:2–6)

Susa was first built by the Elamites in the lush and fertile plains of what is now western Iran. It rose to glory and wealth but eventually fell by sword and fire. In 647 B.C., Ashurbanipal of Assyria, known for his cruelty, destroyed the city—burning its buildings, smashing its tombs, and carrying off all the gold and silver he could find.

In time Susa regained strength and prominence as the gateway to the riches of the Iranian mountains. When Darius became king of Persia, he rebuilt Susa, embellishing the city with gold, ivory, and riches from across his empire. His son, Xerxes, completed the beautification of the city and palatial residences. The walled and fortified royal citadel was built on a hill 120 feet above the city to protect the king and exalt his position. Thereafter, Susa became the winter home of the Persian monarchs.

VII. TEACHING OUTLINE

A. INTRODUCTION

1. Lead Story: Curtain, Please

2. Context: Xerxes spent the opening years of his reign quashing rebellions in Egypt and Babylonia. He also began plans for avenging the Persians' defeat at Marathon by the Greeks. *The Histories* by Herodotus presents Xerxes as ambitious, womanizing, and cruel.

3. Transition: Having secured the throne, Xerxes put on lavish feasts and celebrations to mark his supremacy and power. Some believe his excessive displays of wealth and the marshalling of his officials may have been to plan a war strategy for invading Greece.

B. COMMENTARY

1. The Setting (1:1–9)

    a. Feast one (1:1–4)

    b. Feast two (1:5–8)

    c. Feast three (1:9)

2. Domestic Discord and National Crisis (1:10–22)

    a. The king's request (1:10–12)

    b. The king's response (1:13–15)

    c. A plan devised (1:16–20)

    d. An edict declared (1:21–22)

C. CONCLUSION: THE BATTLE OF THE SEXES

VIII. ISSUES FOR DISCUSSION

1. Discuss the biblical view of wealth. Compare and contrast teachings in the Old and New Testaments.

2. Paul states in 1 Timothy 6:6, "Godliness with contentment is great gain." What does this mean, and how does it relate to goals and personal ambitions?

3. What are some ways that pride can surface in the life of a Christian? What are some strategies for combating and conquering pride?

Esther 2

Providence

I. INTRODUCTION
My Way

II. COMMENTARY
A verse-by-verse explanation of the chapter.

III. CONCLUSION
The Big Band

An overview of the principles and applications from the chapter.

IV. LIFE APPLICATION
Cloudy Weather

Melding the chapter to life.

V. PRAYER
Tying the chapter to life with God.

VI. DEEPER DISCOVERIES
Historical, geographical, and grammatical enrichment of the commentary.

VII. TEACHING OUTLINE
Suggested step-by-step group study of the chapter.

VIII. ISSUES FOR DISCUSSION
Zeroing the chapter in on daily life.

---

*C*harm is deceptive, and beauty is fleeting; but a woman

who fears the LORD is to be praised.

Proverbs 31:30

Esther 2

IN A NUTSHELL

*T*hough God is never mentioned in the Book of Esther, the accumulated "consequences" speak of the providential hand of God on his people and at work in the world. Xerxes's deposal of Vashti set in motion a series of events that eventually led to Esther's ascension as queen of Persia.

Providence

I. INTRODUCTION

My Way

*Y*ears ago Frank Sinatra made popular a song titled "My Way." It was something of an ode to twentieth-century man, a declaration of self-sufficiency and autonomy. Part way through the song, after line upon line of self-focused magnanimity, Sinatra croons, "Regrets, I've had a few." An admission of weakness, an entry point for humility? But in fact, it is only a pause, another occasion for self-congratulations as he brushes away the thought with another chorus of "I did it my way."

Xerxes devoted month after month to self-aggrandizement. And if there was a refrain to each new indulgence, it was that he "did it his way." Each gift proffered, every decree issued, was done for the sake and by the whim of the king. And when his boorish demand to exhibit the queen before his drunken guests was rebuffed, he was enraged. Crossing the will of a selfish person always brings wrath.

Even so, Xerxes stuttered a moment. After his anger subsided he pondered, and there entered a transitory glimmer of regret. But his attendants gathered around and, like the chorus in a Greek tragedy, led him in another verse of "My Way." This time the reverberations of his self-indulgence were felt beyond the palace, disrupting the lives of hundreds of women throughout the kingdom.

II. COMMENTARY

Providence

MAIN IDEA: *Defiance may appear bold, and wealth may seem influential, but willing submission to higher principles carries the power of truth and the inevitability of its triumph.*

A An Edict's Repercussions (2:1–4)

SUPPORTING IDEA: *Because of Xerxes's decision to depose Queen Vashti, a new queen was needed. Again the king relied on the proposals and advice of those near him.*

1. Regrets (2:1)

2:1. Chapter 2 opens with a change in the king's disposition: **Later when the anger of King Xerxes had subsided, he remembered Vashti.** Time had lapsed since the issuance of Vashti's deposition. In the interim the king's temper changed. His anger was past. Perhaps he reflected upon Vashti with softer sentiment and felt the pangs of regret as he recalled **what she had done and what he had decreed about her.** Xerxes was confronted with the consequences of his fury.

2. A plan (2:2-4)

2:2-4. Those who advised Xerxes understood the man they served; they knew what pleased the king. So his **personal attendants** offered him a proposal. To cheer him after his hasty decision, they suggested that **a search be made for beautiful young virgins for the king.** These were to be young women of exceptional good looks.

Just as his decree had been proclaimed to the far reaches of his domain, so now the search would encompass the same. This was a kingdom-wide roundup designed for the king's pleasure. **Hegai, the king's eunuch** in charge of the harem, was to oversee **beauty treatments** for the chosen girls. Then the girl who pleased the king would **be queen instead of Vashti.**

B Esther Becomes Queen (2:5-18)

SUPPORTING IDEA: *All the beautiful young women of the kingdom were gathered at Susa. Among them was Esther, an unknown woman from an unimportant people. Yet, through quiet submission she gained the admiration and support of all who knew her, including the king.*

3. Family background (2:5-7)

2:5-6. Xerxes crossed from chapter 1 to chapter 2 an essentially unchanged man, maintaining his self-indulgent and grandiose charm. But chapter 2 introduces the true protagonist: Esther. Essential to her personhood, her behavior, her wisdom and success was her Jewishness.

Before Esther's entry into the story, however, we learn first of Mordecai, her uncle, who lived **in the citadel of Susa.** His residence in the citadel suggests he held an official government job. Mordecai was **a Jew of the tribe of Benjamin** whose ancestors **had been carried into exile from Jerusalem by Nebuchadnezzar king of Babylon** at the same time Jehoiachin king of Judah was taken away.

2:7. This Jewish man **had a cousin named Hadassah,** who was **lovely in form and features.** Like many Jews in captivity, his cousin had both a Jewish and a Gentile name. *Hadassah,* her Jewish name, means "myrtle"; *Esther* was either Babylonian or Persian in origin. Esther **had neither father nor mother,** so Mordecai had raised her **as his own daughter,** quite possibly adopting her.

4. Harem life (2:8–16)

2:8–9. After communicating Xerxes's edict throughout the realm, **many girls were brought to the citadel of Susa and put under the care of Hegai.** In autocratic governments, individual consent or willingness plays no role in the operations of the state. These girls were brought, regardless of how they or their families felt, and placed in the harem under the care of the king's eunuch. **Esther also was taken to the king's palace.** At this point Esther was one of hundreds of women gathered by the king's emissaries.

Hegai was in charge of the harem and was able to make certain decisions. From among all the girls, Esther **pleased him.** Hegai hurried to begin **her beauty treatments.** Each girl went through a twelve-month regimen of beautification before Xerxes considered her (Esth. 2:12). It seems that, in order for Esther to make her appearance as soon as possible, Hegai lost no time in starting the process.

Hegai assigned to Esther **seven maids selected from the king's palace.** Either Esther was given more maids than all the others, or her maids were of superior ability. In addition, he moved Esther **and her maids into the best place in the harem.** As one who understood Xerxes, Hegai detected in Esther a woman who could please the king.

2:10–11. Esther kept her Jewish nationality a secret **because Mordecai had forbidden her to** reveal it. Esther's attitude was in stark contrast to Vashti's willfulness; Mordecai's familial authority distinguished itself from Xerxes's domestic helplessness. One ruled by relationship, the other by decree.

Mordecai probably wanted to protect Esther from possible anti-Jewish sentiments, the type he experienced from Haman. His sense of concern and responsibility for Esther also drove him to walk each day **back and forth near the courtyard of the harem to find out how Esther was.** This does not imply that he saw Esther or spoke with her. But as an official within the walls of the citadel, Mordecai knew where to get the latest gossip or information.

2:12. Each girl had one opportunity to sway the king in her bid to become queen. In order to assure the greatest impression, and in keeping with the extravagant and ostentatious manners of the palace, each girl **had to complete twelve months of beauty treatments.**

2:13–14. When her turn came, each girl was allowed **anything she wanted . . . to take with her from the harem to the king's palace.** Each girl was permitted whatever jewelry and clothing she desired for her one night with the king; after that it was hers to keep.

In the evening each girl, when it was her turn, would go to the king **and in the morning return to another part of the harem to the care of Shaashgaz . . . who was in charge of the concubines.** The description given by the writer depicts a realm governed by a man driven by appetites as he made his way through hundreds of potential brides, evaluating them only by beauty and sexual performance. After her one night with the king, the girl was placed under the care of a different eunuch and became a concubine. There she was destined to live her life, not returning **to the king unless he was pleased with her and summoned her by name.**

2:15. Against this background, Esther's turn came. Unlike those who had gone before, Esther **asked for nothing other than what Hegai . . . suggested.** She maintained a sense of modesty and propriety by refusing to mimic Gentile habits. She continued her submission to those over her, relying on the knowledge and guidance of Hegai. In addition, the author suggests that Esther went to the king in understated simplicity, allowing her natural beauty and gentle manner to commend her.

2:16. The author next placed the events in context. It was the **tenth month** of the **seventh year** of Xerxes's reign. That means Esther's entry into the king's favor occurred between December and January, 479/478 B.C. About four years had passed since Vashti was dethroned; Xerxes spent those years warring unsuccessfully against Greece.

5. Esther is crowned (2:17–18)

2:17. Hegai's intuitions proved right: **the king was attracted to Esther more than to any of the other women.** So he **made her queen instead of Vashti.**

2:18. After Esther's selection, **the king gave a great banquet . . . for all his nobles and officials.** The contrasts are again striking. Contrary to the opening banquets designed to elevate and display the glories of Xerxes, this banquet was given in honor of his queen. Unlike the previous segregated feasts of Xerxes and Vashti, this celebration included Esther, suggesting marital harmony rather than schism.

Ⓒ Conspiracy (2:19–23)

SUPPORTING IDEA: *Despite the hedonistic culture in which they lived, both Esther and Mordecai retained their moral integrity, as well as their sense of duty and loyalty to Xerxes.*

2:19. Some time passed after Esther's coronation, making the opening phrase (**when the virgins were assembled a second time**) problematic. With Esther as queen, there was no reason to gather virgins a second time. It may, however, indicate the continued licentious behavior of Xerxes. Whatever the phrase connotes, the important information is that **Mordecai was sitting at the king's gate.** The "king's gate" was a term referring to the royal court. Mordecai was not lounging at some courtyard gate, but he was busy in an administrative capacity within the palace.

2:20. The writer inserts a parenthesis emphasizing again that **Esther had kept secret her family background and nationality just as Mordecai had told her to do.** This fact becomes increasingly important as events unfold. Xerxes, and everyone around the royal couple, remained unaware of her Jewish background and her relationship to Mordecai. Though queen of Persia, Esther continued to submit to the guidance of her adoptive Jewish father.

2:21–22. As an imperial official, Mordecai had reasonable access to the queen and to other workers and functionaries within the palace complex. Consequently, he caught wind of a plot. **Bigthana and Teresh, two of the king's officers . . . became angry and conspired to assassinate King Xerxes.** Mordecai overheard the plans and told Queen Esther, **who in turn reported it to the king.**

2:23. At this juncture Esther appears to have had no trouble approaching the king, though it was a terrifying ordeal later (Esth. 4:11). The writer of Esther notes that the conspirators were discovered and **hanged on a gallows.** The integrity and veracity of both Mordecai and Esther were established.

All this was recorded in the book of the annals in the presence of the king. Ancient kings kept records of events. Xerxes kept written reports on officers who behaved admirably in his service and rewarded them accordingly. That Mordecai's loyal actions were noted but not rewarded was inconsistent with the king's habits.

> **MAIN IDEA REVIEW:** *Defiance may appear bold, and wealth may seem influential, but willing submission to higher principles carries the power of truth and the inevitability of its triumph.*

III. CONCLUSION

The Big Band

When I was growing up, my family bought tickets to the University of Washington football games. We would pack blankets to sit on, apples to munch on, and binoculars to peer through (we tended to sit in the cheaper end-zone seats). We then headed for Husky Stadium. Every Saturday before the game the big band marched on to the field with great spectacle to play the national anthem.

Yet, despite the band's glitter and volume, few people paid attention. Some would sing along, but most talked to their neighbors or fidgeted with programs. As the final bars of the anthem played and some singer followed the crescendo to its high-pitched conclusion, the crowd erupted in cheers and yelling—but not for the song. They simply wanted the game to begin.

Then one Saturday the band marched on the field as usual. The musicians stood at their positions, instruments in hand. But this time only one trumpeter played. From beginning to end, no other instrument joined in; no drums flourished. This time one horn carried the song through the autumn air. The crowd was hushed, even after the last notes drifted into silence.

Amidst the opulence of the Persian court came a single clear note of distinction. Esther, just one attractive woman among hundreds, was different. While everyone else busied herself with ornamentation and amassed as much finery as possible, Esther maintained simplicity of spirit and looks. Her attention was focused on learning and obeying the instructions of those who cared for her. As a result, her attractiveness came not from cosmetics and jewelry, but from her natural beauty and submissive spirit.

PRINCIPLES

- God uses the ungodly to accomplish his purposes.
- Submission to authority is highly valued by God.
- God is always present and at work, even when circumstances seem discouraging or confusing.
- God's primary concern and hardest work focus on transforming the inner nature of people.
- Our times are in God's hands.

APPLICATIONS

- Focus your energy and attention on your inner nature so that you grow in godliness.
- Place your confidence in God's revelation of his love, grace, mercy, justice, and care.
- Make God's glory your daily goal. Then, no matter what happens, you will be at peace, resting in his sovereignty.
- Everyone is under someone's authority. Learn to submit yourself to those over you.

IV. LIFE APPLICATION

Cloudy Weather

It's a marvel of God's perpetual design and recreation to watch clouds form, dissipate, re-form, and travel across the sky. From below we see high, wispy clouds spread like gossamer threads. We watch clouds grow, churning in the updrafts, creating towers of roiling vapor. Or we notice low clouds, blanketing the heavens like gray felt. The wonder comes from their multiplicity of form and the influence they project on the earth below.

But snatch a cloud and tie it to earth, and we have something very different. Fog. Surrounded by the cloud's damp breath, all definitions evaporate.

No edges define boundaries; no distance allows understanding. We are caught in the gray. Only a little light penetrates, and our vision becomes imperfect and limited. We are allowed only enough perspective to take the next step.

When Esther was chosen for the king's harem, she had no assurance of the future, no premonition of her forthcoming role or risks. She was taken regardless of her opinions, emotions, fears, or desires. No prophet assured her; no voice inspired her. She could not look heavenward and discern a design or peer into the distance and watch the cumulative effects of her circumstances. She was left to take one step at a time based on the understanding and faith she had. Her submission to Mordecai, and then to Hegai, reveals a gentle spirit of respect as well as reliance on those in authority over her.

Like Esther, we don't have the distance or the perspective to comprehend God's particular purposes or design at a given moment. We can remain confident in his will, love, justice, and grace, but the means he uses and the complex interconnectedness of life lie outside the revelation he has given. But we can be assured that he graces us with enough light to take the next step in confidence through his sovereignty and love.

V. PRAYER

Lord, our faith rests in you. Help us to follow the light of your revelation, not the fog of philosophy or the opinions of others. Thank you for loving people enough to give us your very thoughts and words and the disclosure of your being through Jesus Christ. Amen.

VI. DEEPER DISCOVERIES

Xerxes I (2:1–4, 13–18, 21–23)

Much of what we know about King Xerxes comes from the biblical texts, archaeological inscriptions, and from the Greek writer Herodotus.

After the death of his father, Darius, Xerxes was faced with rebellions in both Egypt and Babylon. With speed and overwhelming force, he quelled the unrest and punished the regions by revoking their autonomy and enforcing strict rule. Then, having settled his own provinces, he turned to Greece. Xerxes spent almost four years preparing, planning, and carrying out his invasion. He marshaled over two hundred thousand soldiers and twelve hundred ships, proclaiming, "I shall pass through Europe from end to end and make it all one country."

Although Xerxes was able to march into Athens and burn its buildings, eventually, like his father before him, he was defeated by the Greeks. The king withdrew to Persia and, from the seventh year of his reign until its conclusion, he spent his efforts on securing his territories and building palaces. It was in that seventh year that Esther was chosen queen.

In 465 B.C., in a scheme by the commander of the palace guard and the royal chamberlain, Xerxes was murdered in his bed.

VII. TEACHING OUTLINE

A. INTRODUCTION

1. Lead Story: My Way
2. Context: Xerxes spent the opening years of his reign crushing revolts. Once his dominance was established, he exhibited his wealth in a series of banquets and festivities designed to impress his own people and the provincial officials under his rule. He was in no mood to be rebuffed, and when the queen refused his official bequest, Vashti was dethroned and banished.
3. Transition: Anger usually results in hasty decisions, and Xerxes appeared to regret his impetuous dismissal of Vashti. To cheer the king, his attendants suggested an empire-wide beauty contest to find the next queen.

B. COMMENTARY

1. An Edict's Repercussions (2:1–4)
   a. Regrets (2:1)
   b. A plan (2:2–4)
2. Esther Becomes Queen (2:5–18)
   a. Family background (2:5–7)
   b. Harem life (2:8–16)
   c. Esther is crowned (2:17–18)
3. Conspiracy (2:19–23)

C. CONCLUSION: THE BIG BAND

VIII. ISSUES FOR DISCUSSION

1. What does submission mean, and why is it highly valued in God's eyes?
2. Discuss some modern-day situations that require submission to authority.

3. Though God is not specifically mentioned, can you detect the action of God in the story of Esther? What does this suggest for your own life and the times in which you live?

Esther 3

A Dangerous World

A scoundrel plots evil,

and his speech is like a scorching fire.

Proverbs 16 : 27

Esther 3

IN A NUTSHELL

*E*sther was made queen of Persia; all appeared well. But offstage a plot was developing, one that would annihilate the Jews within the Persian Empire. Driven by pride and anger, Haman the Agagite used his influence and position in the imperial court to secure a genocidal decree.

A Dangerous World

I. INTRODUCTION

Good Ol' Boys

*Y*ou can find them in politics, in business, at the sports club, and sometimes in the local church—they are the "good ol' boys." They form the small inner circle of influence, and they maintain their position of power by group protection. Their ideas aren't questioned; their dealings aren't scrutinized because, well, they're the good ol' boys. They have always been around, and their loyalties are proven.

As one of the select Persian nobles, Haman belonged to a coterie of privilege, and his promotion by Xerxes assured him of his protected position. Feeling secure and untouchable, Haman engaged in a scheme of backroom politics designed to satisfy his own petty purposes, and Xerxes played his predictable part. The king took Haman at his word, never bothering to question him or investigate his claims. After all, Haman was a good ol' boy in Persian society.

II. COMMENTARY

A Dangerous World

> **MAIN IDEA:** *Pride intoxicates the heart and then poisons it. Ignited by insult and driven by anger, Haman plotted the destruction of the Jews throughout the Persian Empire.*

A Haman Revealed (3:1–6)

> **SUPPORTING IDEA:** *Elevated in position, wealth, and prestige above all others except the king, Haman assumed a sense of his own superiority.*

1. Haman honored (3:1–2a)

3:1. The phrase **After these events** marks a jump in time to the next pivotal incident. **King Xerxes honored Haman son of Hammedatha, the Agagite**. While Haman and his father had Persian names, many believe the author used the descriptive term *Agagite* symbolically, connecting Haman with Agag the Amalekite who was an enemy of King Saul and thus the Jewish people (see "Deeper Discoveries"). Xerxes honored Haman by **giving him a seat of honor higher than that of all the other nobles**.

3:2a. Because of his newly acquired position, **all the royal officials at the king's gate knelt down and paid honor to Haman.** Bowing or prostration before royalty was common practice within the Persian court. Often, as a sign of respect or submission, a person entering the presence of the king would bow and kiss his hand. In the case of Haman, the **king had commanded** the gesture as a recognition of his status.

2. Mordecai's refusal (3:2b–4)

3:2b. The author notes the one exception to the rule of obeisance—Mordecai. He **would not kneel down or pay** Haman **honor.** We find no explanation for his behavior, simply a statement of fact. Among all the people, Mordecai was the one holdout.

3:3–4. Because only Mordecai refused Haman this symbol of respect, he became the focus of curiosity and inquiry, even badgering. The other officials who served alongside Mordecai began questioning him, **Why do you disobey the king's command?** These men interpreted Mordecai's behavior not in relation to Haman but to the king who had issued the directive. It was not a question of honoring Haman but of obeying the king. Consequently, **day after day they spoke to him but he refused to comply.** Depending on viewpoint, one might call Mordecai stubborn, resolute, or proud.

When peer pressure failed, the officials **told Haman about it to see whether Mordecai's behavior would be tolerated.** Evidently, Haman hadn't noticed Mordecai's dismissive conduct. But once it was brought to his attention, it became a test case—a public issue from which there was no retreat. Mordecai's refusal apparently stemmed from the fact that **he was a Jew.** In Mordecai's mind he could not humble himself before someone whose people were historically enemies of the Jews.

3. Haman's response (3:5–6)

3:5. We gain insight into Haman's character once he became aware of Mordecai's behavior: **he was enraged.** The intensity of his response reveals a man so consumed by pride that no room remained for any other desire, motive, or emotion.

3:6. Having learned who Mordecai's people were, Haman revealed the scope of his selfishness and magnitude of his contempt, because **he scorned the idea of killing only Mordecai.** Having felt the sting of Mordecai's disrespect, Haman responded in kind but with an evil ferocity that dismissed personal worth in anyone other than himself.

Haman looked for a way to destroy all Mordecai's people, the Jews, throughout the whole kingdom. In his view the destruction of one person was not commensurate with the offense; Mordecai was not equal to Haman in value and stature. Only genocide would satisfy Haman's lust for power.

B Haman's Plot (3:7–15)

SUPPORTING IDEA: *Clever rhetoric combined with ignorance can exploit a situation, allowing prejudice, hate, and evil to appear reasonable, beneficial, and good.*

4. The lot is cast (3:7)

3:7. It was **the twelfth year of King Xerxes**, some five years after Esther's coronation. It was the first month of the year and, according to custom, **they cast the pur (that is, the lot) in the presence of Haman**. The casting of lots was a new year's ritual conducted by the Persian astrologers to determine the future. Casting the lots in the presence of Haman suggests that, on this occasion, the purpose was to **select a day and month** for the annihilation of the Jews. **The lot fell on the twelfth month, the month of Adar.** Haman had one year to set his plan in motion.

5. Haman before the king (3:8–9)

3:8–9. As chief among the royal nobles, Haman was probably allowed greater access to Xerxes. He used half-truths, lies, generalizations, and faulty reasoning to map out his plans and construct his conclusions for the king. He told Xerxes, **There is a certain people . . . among the peoples in all the provinces of your kingdom whose customs are different from those of all other people.**

This was true, to a point. It was a matter of pride and policy among the Persians that they had a diverse cultural mix in their kingdom. Xerxes's predecessors had encouraged the revival of different traditions, religions, and practices, including that of the Jews. Even so, Haman argued that ethnic and cultural differences constituted a conspiratorial threat.

Haman foresaw the mutiny of an entire population: they do **not obey the king's laws.** It was an accusation for which he had no evidence. Undeterred by truth or facts, Haman advised that it was **not in the king's best interest to tolerate them.** Haman feigned deference to the king in order to advance his own designs: **If it pleases the king, let a decree be issued to destroy them.**

To seal the deal, Haman offered a bribe. He would put **ten thousand talents of silver into the royal treasury for the men who carry out this business.** And so Haman followed the second rule of modern political thought: any economic advantage advances the nation. Ten thousand talents equaled about 375 tons—an enormous amount of silver. One can only imagine how Haman planned to raise these funds.

6. Xerxes's response (3:10–11)

3:10–11. Without so much as a blink or a question, **the king took his signet ring from his finger and gave it to Haman.** Xerxes gave Haman full authority for the extermination of a people, about whose identity he had not bothered to inquire. The king tended to defer to those around him.

Keep the money . . . and do with the people as you please, the king replied. While the evil propelling Haman becomes more obvious and intense as the story unfolds, Xerxes lived out an evil equally as treacherous. He represents the criminality of indifference.

7. The edict (3:12–15)

3:12. The story moves quickly to **the thirteenth day of the first month**. In both Babylonian and Persian cultures, the number thirteen was considered unlucky. The decree of doom for the Jews was issued on this portentous date; it was also, ironically, the day before Passover, the historical celebration of God's deliverance and salvation.

Royal secretaries or scribes were summoned, and **they wrote out in the script of each province and in the language of each people all Haman's orders**. Reflective of the orders sent throughout the kingdom in Esther 1:22, the edict against the Jews was carried out with the same cold bureaucratic formality. To Haman and the king it was all business. The orders were directed **to the king's satraps, the governors of the various provinces and the nobles of the various peoples**. Satraps governed the larger regions of the kingdom; within these regions, and answerable to the satraps, were governors over smaller provinces and cities; the nobles were ethnic and tribal leaders of particular people groups.

Xerxes probably had no direct involvement with the process since he had handed his signet ring to Haman. Even so, the edict received the weight of authority and certainty because it was **written in the name of King Xerxes himself and sealed with his own ring**. The act was deliberate, formal, and calculated. Haman was evil's agent, but Xerxes was the power behind him.

3:13. Every province within the kingdom received **the order to destroy, kill and annihilate all the Jews**. These three words emphasize totality and inevitability. It is amazing that the fate of a people could be decided by a stroke of a pen. People before and since Haman have proceeded with the same arrogance and evil to destroy human life indiscriminately.

The slaughter of the Jews was to occur **on a single day, the thirteenth day of the twelfth month**. For an entire year the Jews would live under the weight of their approaching death. In addition, the distant date allowed for an escalation of anti-Jewish sentiment among the general population. It would also allow for a growing greed as people eyed their Jewish neighbors and their possessions because the edict allowed them **to plunder their goods**.

3:14. The author of Esther emphasizes the inescapable future the Jews faced because the genocidal program was **issued as law in every province and made known to the people of every nationality**. There was no place where the Jews could run, no nation to whom they could appeal. The net of destruction was spread as far as the mind could conceive.

3:15. While the couriers sped with the edict along the royal roads to the corners of the kingdom, **the edict was issued in the citadel of Susa**. The law was posted in all the palatial buildings, and the government workers were informed of the law. Among them was Mordecai.

The dirty work done, **the king and Haman sat down to drink**. Once again this ruler of the world submerged himself in drunken pleasure. With him was Haman, already drunk on his apparent success. Meanwhile, **the city of Susa was bewildered**. For Haman and Xerxes the matter was over and done, but for the general population the matter lay inexorably before them.

> **MAIN IDEA REVIEW:** *Pride intoxicates the heart and then poisons it. Ignited by insult and driven by anger, Haman plotted the destruction of the Jews throughout the Persian Empire.*

III. CONCLUSION

The Intervening Year

On the king's authority, the clock began ticking down toward the destruction of the Jews. Though some theologians see in the story of Esther only an engaging fiction or a literary narrative dotted with hyperbole, the account mirrors our own times with stunning accuracy.

On November 9 and 10, 1938, an apparently spontaneous eruption of violence occurred against the Jews throughout Germany and Austria. The riots became known as *Kristallnacht* ("Crystal Night") because of the shattered windows of Jewish shops, stores, and homes. But the hostilities meted out during those nights were part of a meticulous program that eventually led to the extermination of millions of European Jews. Before the gas chambers could be fed, the Nazis had to marginalize and reduce the Jews' position within society. When the people rampaged through the streets on November 9, their cruelty sprang from a carefully devised strategy in league with the fallen nature of humankind.

Even more recently, in the Balkans War of 1992–1995, a propaganda campaign was launched to justify the deportation, torture, and mass murder of non-Serbians. Known as "ethnic cleansing," the bloody brutality experienced in Bosnia and Herzegovina again proved the propensity of the human heart toward hate and prejudice.

All these, and the "small" injustices we witness daily, spring from a kind of paranoia that results from magnified differences and inherent self-interest—a paranoia that usually serves the selfish ambitions of some group or individual. And, despite what we may believe, they boil just beneath the surface of society.

The days and months following Xerxes's decree were not idle. The instructions reached officials at every level so they would "be ready for that day" (Esth. 3:14). The intervening year required an agenda of prejudice and hate, fear and suspicion toward the Jews. A carefully planned mind-set was needed to justify and implement the violence.

PRINCIPLES

- The world can be a dangerous place for the people of God.
- Pride and anger usually go together.
- The laws of man are changeable and uncertain.
- The laws of God are stable and eternal.
- Prejudice converts differences into moral failure.
- Selfishness negates the humanity in others.

APPLICATIONS

- Don't depend on the stock market, social laws, or peoples' opinions; they are unstable and uncertain. Instead, find your security in the love, sovereignty, and presence of God.
- Practice showing respect to everyone you meet.
- Live with kindness, listen with compassion, remember God's mercy toward you; and you will guard your heart against pride.
- Avoid getting involved in the schemes of angry people. Nothing good comes from such plans.

IV. LIFE APPLICATION

The Final Solution

A few years ago, in an article published in *U.S. News & World Report,* three writers addressed the modern phenomenon known as "road rage." The article offered various explanations for fury behind the wheel—the highway system's insufficiency in handling the volume of traffic, the increased numbers of drivers and vehicles, the current automotive design and the popularity of the SUV. Then, after columns of expert opinion, statistics, and information shuffling, the authors concluded, "But the real key to reducing road rage probably lies deep within each of us."

Rage, whatever its expression, issues from a proud heart. And pride, though rarely so overt, steels the heart in its ambition to be God. Yet the territory of one's own soul is too small for pride's ambitions, and personal power is too weak to fulfill the lust for glory. So the proud seek to control. It is the consummate self-will, demanding its way no matter the cost. It may even lead to destruction of others.

But while pride brings destruction, humility brings life. The humble person has found his or her proper place in the created order. The truly humble individual engages life with a vision beyond the self and beyond this world. Richard Foster captured it well when he wrote, "The God-possessed soul knows only one purpose, one goal, one desire. God is not some figure in our field of vision, sometimes blurred, sometimes focused; he IS our vision" (Foster, p. 103). The humble person has dismissed the desire to rule and has embraced the God who does.

V. PRAYER

Lord, help the weakness of our hearts. By your Spirit illuminate our understanding and strengthen our will to follow after Jesus, who was "gentle and humble in heart," so we may find rest for our souls and freedom from our fears. Amen.

VI. DEEPER DISCOVERIES

Haman the Agagite (3:1)

Throughout the Book of Esther, references to Haman typically describe him as "the Agagite," or they use the pejorative, "enemy of the Jews." To understand the power of these terms, it helps to look back into Israel's history.

After the Jews left Egypt under Moses' leadership, they journeyed through the hostile and harsh environment of the Sinai Peninsula. At Rephidim, the Amalekites attacked. In an exhaustive battle the Israelites eventually won, but the bitter hatred between the two peoples continued. In Deuteronomy 25:19 the Jews were told that when they finally settled in Canaan, they were to "blot out the memory of Amalek from under heaven."

When Israel did settle the land and Saul was king, God instructed him to take his army and annihilate the Amalekites "for what they did to Israel when they waylaid them as they came up from Egypt" (1 Sam. 15:2). Saul attacked, but he disobeyed by sparing their king, Agag, along with the best sheep and cattle. Angered at Saul's disobedience, the prophet Samuel did as God commanded and executed Agag with a sword.

Haman, identified as "the Agagite," is related to the historical enemies of Israel, the Amalekites, and more specifically, to their ruthless king, Agag. The name given Mordecai, "the son of Kish" (Esth. 2:5), connects him in ancestry with King Saul, who was another offspring of Kish. And so the two ancient enemies met again, and the historical animosities converged, this time in Persia between their descendants, Haman and Mordecai.

VII. TEACHING OUTLINE

A. INTRODUCTION

1. Lead Story: Good Ol' Boys
2. Context: Xerxes returned home from his failed conquest of Greece to concentrate on domestic affairs. Among them was the selection of a new queen. He also devoted time, energy, and wealth to the construction of lavish buildings in the imperial cities of Susa and Persepolis.
3. Transition: Xerxes honored those who served him well, and for whatever reason, Haman was promoted to the highest position among the Persian nobles. Glutted with pride and blinded by anger, Haman plotted vengeance against the entire Jewish population because of the offense of one man.

B. COMMENTARY

1. Haman Revealed (3:1–6)
   a. Haman honored (3:1–2a)
   b. Mordecai's refusal (3:2b–4)
   c. Haman's response (3:5–6)
2. Haman's Plot (3:7–15)
   a. The lot is cast (3:7)
   b. Haman before the king (3:8–9)
   c. Xcerxes's response (3:10–11)
   d. The edict (3:12–15)

C. CONCLUSION: THE INTERVENING YEAR

VIII. ISSUES FOR DISCUSSION

1. Discuss some ways our culture encourages or excuses selfishness. List some practical steps you can take to exhibit Christlikeness.
2. Are there groups in our society that are looked on with prejudice or suspicion? How could you and your church combat these attitudes?
3. How can a person develop true humility? What are some practical evidences of humility within a person's life?

Esther 4

For Such a Time as This

---

*R*escue those being led away to death;

hold back those staggering toward slaughter.

P r o v e r b s   2 4 : 1 1

Esther 4

I N   A   N U T S H E L L

*T*he date was set and irrevocable; the Jews were destined for destruction. But the promises of God to his people could not be swept away so easily by the plots of men. In the palace of the king was a woman who could make a difference.

For Such a Time as This

I. INTRODUCTION

Before the Storm

*W*e have all watched reports on television depicting the aftermath of disaster. Whether it's a tornado ripping through the Midwest leaving splintered wreckage or an eruption of violence in the Middle East scattering rubble and twisted metal, the significance of these catastrophes distills in the anguished faces that gaze back at us.

Once Xerxes circulated the new edict appointing a day of annihilation, the Jews living throughout Persia were heard wailing. Yet in their villages no wreckage littered the ground; no rubble marred the landscape. Only a rider had passed through. But in his path he left the familiar faces of tragedy. Before the storm, while the clouds were still gathering, the Jews felt the agony and distress of impending disaster.

II. COMMENTARY

For Such a Time as This

> **MAIN IDEA:** *The Bible consistently teaches a theology of personal responsibility in harmony with divine dependence. We are accountable for our choices and actions as we rely on God to act in accordance with his nature and sovereignty.*

🅰 A Time of Mourning (4:1–3)

> **SUPPORTING IDEA:** *In the face of injustice, people generally respond with protest or sorrow. Protest rises from trampled decency; sorrow from a sense of abandonment.*

4:1–2. Chapter 4 serves as a counterpoint to chapter 3, contrasting Mordecai with Haman. Because of Mordecai's job, perhaps as a royal accountant, and his connections within the citadel, he **learned of all that had been done**. Beyond the official notice Mordecai was privy to more detailed information (Esth. 4:7), and it deepened his indignation. In response, **he tore his clothes, put on sackcloth and ashes, and went out into the city**. The tearing of one's clothes was a sign of deep distress. The use of sackcloth, a type of coarse material, and ashes, usually sprinkled on the head, also acknowledged a troubling crisis.

Mordecai took his offense into the city, **wailing loudly and bitterly.** In other words, he made his lament public. But he was careful to follow Persian protocol and, because of his mourning attire, **went only as far as the king's gate.** The cardinal rule of Persian etiquette was apparently never to upset the king (see Neh. 2:1–2). So symbols of grief were kept beyond the gate, outside the palace walls. But even though the king was kept insulated from unpleasant sights and sounds, Mordecai knew others would notice and hear his cries of grief.

4:3. Mordecai's response was mirrored **in every province to which the edict and order of the king came.** The convergence of critical elements for the Jews' salvation occurs in this chapter: the people sought God's help and deliverance through **fasting,** and through petition—**weeping and wailing.**

B Dialogue (4:4–17)

> **SUPPORTING IDEA:** *The intense demonstrations of Mordecai's grief created the opportunity for communication with Esther. Though they never spoke face-to-face, the discussions between them became the pivot point for all that followed.*

1. Esther takes notice (4:4)

4:4. Mordecai's behavior drew attention. **Esther's maids and eunuchs** reported to her what they had seen. This leads us to believe they knew something of the relationship between Esther and Mordecai (though they probably did not know she was Jewish). Based on Esther's response, they probably told her what they observed—Mordecai's laments and his rough garments.

Her reaction was **great distress,** and **she sent clothes for him to put on instead of sackcloth.** Esther had no knowledge of the decreed annihilation; her emotional response stemmed from understanding the symbols of disaster. Not knowing the source of Mordecai's anguish only added to her own. With proper attire he could enter the palace and explain what troubled him. It was with this hope that Esther offered clothing. But Mordecai **would not accept them.**

2. Esther investigates (4:5–6)

4:5–6. The communication between Esther and Mordecai becomes increasingly intimate. After Mordecai refused to put aside his mourning in order to discuss the situation, she ordered **Hathach, one of the king's eunuchs . . . to find out what was troubling Mordecai and why.**

3. Mordecai's instructions (4:7–9)

4:7. Mordecai told Hathach everything since he wanted Esther to grasp the gravity of the decree and Haman's vicious intent. Since Mordecai knew the **exact amount** of Haman's bribe, he either had connections in the palace, or his official function allowed access to detailed information.

4:8–9. Mordecai **also gave** Hathach **a copy of the text of the edict . . . which had been published in Susa.** Everything he had explained to the eunuch was verified in the official document that could be found all over Susa. Mordecai sent a copy into the palace for him **to show to Esther and explain it to her.** Mordecai intended for Hathach to give Esther the edict to read while he explained the background information told him by Mordecai.

Hathach was also to urge Esther **to go into the king's presence to . . . plead with him for her people.** As her guardian Mordecai was telling the queen what she must do next. Just as he had instructed her to remain quiet about her ethnicity (Esth. 2:10), now he commanded her to identify with "her people," the Jews.

4. Esther's reminder (4:10–11)

4:10–11. It was Esther's turn. Hathach was given a message to take back to Mordecai: **any man or woman who approaches the king in the inner court without being summoned the king has but one law . . . death.** Those were the plain facts. The only exception to the death sentence was **for the king to extend the gold scepter** and so spare the life of the one who came unbidden.

It probably was not fear that motivated Esther, but confusion about how her death could accomplish mercy for her people. To go uninvited before Xerxes seemed pointless, especially since **thirty days** had passed since she **was called to go to the king.** Esther revealed to Mordecai what he could not have known. A month had passed since the king had asked for her and, in the parlance of the court, it could signal his displeasure.

5. Mordecai's reply (4:12–14)

4:12–14. After hearing through Hathach what Esther had to say, Mordecai sent back an answer: **Do not think that because you are in the king's house you alone of all the Jews will escape.** Mordecai wanted Esther to realize that the palace offered no protection, no special privilege. As a Jew, approaching the king was no more dangerous than not doing so because her doom was assured by the edict that Haman had issued.

Mordecai emphasized that deliverance for the Jews could not come from anywhere else. It was with this understanding that he went on to tell her, **you and your father's family will perish.** If Esther failed to act, there was no other hope. Despite her royal position, she and Mordecai would both die in the ensuing slaughter.

But Mordecai did not leave his argument on the purely human level. He translated it into divine providence when he suggested, **And who knows but that you have come to royal position for such a time as this?** Mordecai was expressing confidence that Esther's position was, in fact, designed and purposed by God.

6. Esther's decision (4:15–17)

4:15–17. Esther sent her decision back to Mordecai. She commanded, **Go, gather together all the Jews who are in Susa, and fast for me**. She called for a fast of petition and intercession. This was a religious act, one in which the Jews formed a solidarity with Esther and stood in dependence on God for his favor. The fast was particularly strict. They were not to **eat or drink for three days, night or day**. In such a dire circumstance, extreme measures were needed. Esther vowed to follow the same regimen.

After the three days, Esther promised, **I will go to the king, even though it is against the law. And if I perish, I perish**. Esther understood the situation. Danger hemmed her in on every side. The only choice that offered hope was to seek God's grace and confront the king.

> **MAIN IDEA REVIEW:** The Bible consistently teaches a theology of personal responsibility in harmony with divine dependence. We are accountable for our choices and actions as we rely on God to act in accordance with his nature and sovereignty.

III. CONCLUSION

Context

In the early 1950s, Samuel Beckett's play *Waiting for Godot* opened in Paris. On a predominately bare stage, Beckett's two leading characters do nothing but engage in prattle, trying to pass the time as they wait for Godot, a person without substance, definition, or meaning—a person neither has met and never will. These two homeless men depend on each other to validate their existence. They are homeless not only in Paris but in the world.

It is, perhaps, the quintessential portrayal of existential philosophy—each character void of any essence or character, each needing to create his own existence and meaning from the raw materials of his experience. They do nothing; they mean nothing. In the end one character goes deaf, the other mute.

This is a philosophy that finds practical application in the lives of millions of people each day.

In contrast, Esther and Mordecai played out their conversation in a rich framework of community as well as divine interplay. Before Esther or Mordecai said anything, God and the Jewish people formed a context for their actions, words, and eventual resolve. The mournful crying, the sackcloth and symbols of grief, the admitting of helplessness expressed through fasting—all declared from each human heart a faith in their own inherent value, and a daring to believe in divine purpose.

After their dialogue, Esther's determination gained power through the fasting and petitions of the Jewish community before God. Life had meaning not because it was self-created but because the world and everything in it were God-created. They lived before a God who saw their plight and heard their prayers.

PRINCIPLES

- Physical acts (kneeling, singing, fasting, etc.) reinforce the beliefs and commitments of faith.
- Each person has a unique place in God's design for this world.
- Courage comes from commitment.
- Synergy occurs between individual Christians and the community of faith when they work toward common goals, accomplishing more than the sum of their parts.
- Even in the most hopeless situations, faith persists.
- Christians should act in dependence on God.

APPLICATIONS

- Express your true heart emotions, desires, and concerns to God.
- Stand in solidarity with the persecuted church; pray and work on behalf of those who suffer for their faith.
- Find ways in your community to help establish God's justice and goodness.
- Create strong relationships in your local church. God does not intend for us to work out the life of faith alone.

IV. LIFE APPLICATION

Never Silent

I believe in the sun even when it is not shining.
I believe in love when feeling it not.
I believe in God even when He is silent.

So faith was written on the side of a cellar in Cologne, Germany, where a Jew crouched, hiding from the Nazis.

What drives such trust? What anchors such conviction? Perhaps it comes from a refusal to believe that the cruel evidence of darkness, hate, and evil is not, in fact, the final explanation. Perhaps, like hope, it comes from a conscious decision to choose—a deliberate rejection of brutal assumptions.

But the power to reject the conspiracy of violence and lies—and the strength to persist in the midst of despair—comes from embracing God. Faith invites God into the midst of suffering. With the halting breath of prayer faith must speak, and its very utterance attests God's presence.

The great question posed to Esther by Mordecai was, "If you remain silent . . . then what?" Both knew the answer—hope would vanish, and violence would prevail. Esther's decision to speak to the king was a triumph not of argument or persuasion but of faith. She identified with those marked for destruction, and she invited God into their midst.

V. PRAYER

How easy, O Lord, to talk about faith, especially in our comfort. How petty seem our troubles, how foolish our doubts. Forgive us. Come close; walk beside us. Help us affirm your love and goodness, your faithfulness to all who know you. Amen.

VI. DEEPER DISCOVERIES

A. Fasting (4:3,16)

Fasting was always a spiritual act for the Jews. It served as a demonstration of deep distress and mourning over sin, or an expression of utter dependence on God for deliverance from an enemy. Fasting was a facet of prayer, an urgent plea to God for mercy. The fast that Esther requested of the Jewish community, and in which she and her maids participated, was an absolute fast in keeping with the dire situation that the nation faced.

B. Identification (4:13)

In Mordecai's final words to Esther, he stated a principle found throughout Scripture: identification with God and his people brings persecution. "Do not think that because you are in the king's house you alone of all the Jews will escape" (Esth. 4:13). For Esther it was an inescapable ethnicity, but for those who follow after Christ, the same holds true.

Once we decide to step from the shelter of silence, we should not expect to escape trouble and opposition. Christ guaranteed it: "In this world you will have trouble" (John 16:33). And just as Esther's hope rested in God's mercy, ours does as well: "But take heart! I have overcome the world" (John 16:33). In the mercy of the cross and our identification with Christ in his suffering and resurrection, we find the power to confront the assault of evil.

VII. TEACHING OUTLINE

A. INTRODUCTION

1. Lead Story: Before the Storm
2. Context: In a display of apathy and self-interest, Xerxes allowed Haman to set in motion the machinations needed to destroy the Jews. Once the edict was sent throughout the kingdom, the two men sat down to drink, toasting their egos.
3. Transition: While the king feasted, the Jews fasted, providing the context for Mordecai's grief and adding impetus to his charge that Easter go before Xerxes on behalf of her people.

B. COMMENTARY

1. A Time of Mourning (4:1–3)
2. Dialogue (4:4–17)
   a. Esther takes notice (4:4)
   b. Esther investigates (4:5–6)
   c. Mordecai's instructions (4:7–9)
   d. Esther's reminder (4:10–11)
   e. Mordecai's reply (4:12–14)
   f. Esther's decision (4:15–17)

C. CONCLUSION: CONTEXT

VIII. ISSUES FOR DISCUSSION

1. How do you explain the prevalence of violence and hardship in the world?
2. Discuss what the Christian community's response to suffering should be.
3. Name some obstacles to living by faith. How does a Christian overcome these impediments?
4. Where has God placed you "for such a time as this"?

Esther 5

Walking the Tightrope

I. INTRODUCTION
Protocol

II. COMMENTARY
A verse-by-verse explanation of the chapter.

III. CONCLUSION
A Pound of Flesh

An overview of the principles and applications from the chapter.

IV. LIFE APPLICATION
Mother, May I?

Melding the chapter to life.

V. PRAYER
Tying the chapter to life with God.

VI. DEEPER DISCOVERIES
Historical, geographical, and grammatical enrichment of the commentary.

VII. TEACHING OUTLINE
Suggested step-by-step group study of the chapter.

VIII. ISSUES FOR DISCUSSION
Zeroing the chapter in on daily life.

*P*ride goes before destruction,

a haughty spirit before a fall.

P r o v e r b s   1 6 : 1 8

Esther 5

I N   A   N U T S H E L L

*E*sther began the process of securing the king's pleasure and ex-
posing Haman's evil intent. She invited both men to a banquet. Meanwhile, Haman's rage intensified because Mordecai did not show him
respect or honor.

Walking the Tightrope

I. INTRODUCTION

Protocol

*E*very government and organization has protocols, the rules for correct behavior at official occasions. The U.S. State Department has an office of protocol, a chief of protocol, as well as various protocol officers scattered around the globe, all with the mission of educating government representatives on how to behave properly. There are rules for seemingly every social contingency.

For instance:

> The official place for the ambassador in the car is the backseat, curbside. At ceremonies that take place on ships, the ambassador is the first to step on deck and the first to step off, and at airport ceremonies, he/she is the last to board and the first to disembark.
>
> Reserve the far right-hand seat of a couch, as you sit, for the guest of honor.
>
> Be aware that there are cultural differences about what constitutes casual conversation. . . . Discussing children or food is rude in some cultures.
>
> In some countries, an invitation for 8:00 p.m. means you should arrive at precisely 8:00 p.m. In some other countries, it means you should arrive no earlier than 9:30 p.m.

And this warning: "Even something as simple as bringing a gift to the host can be tricky. . . . In Italy, mums are funeral flowers; think twice about bringing them to a dinner party" (*Protocol for the Modern Diplomat*).

Much of the drama and tension from Esther's decision to go before Xerxes centered on a point of protocol: no one was allowed to come to the king without being summoned; those who dared risked death. Yet, to intervene for the Jews, Esther needed to bend the rules. But once she was received by the king, her every move and word were structured by Persian court etiquette. In every way Esther was a practitioner of government protocol.

II. COMMENTARY

Walking the Tightrope

> **MAIN IDEA:** *Patience and justice characterize wisdom. Selfish interests and immediate gratification consume the foolish.*

A Esther's Wisdom (5:1–8)

> **SUPPORTING IDEA:** *Esther exhibited intelligence and an extraordinary perception of her situation and the people with whom she was dealing.*

1. Esther before Xerxes (5:1–5a)

5:1–2. On the third day Esther put on her royal robes. In accordance with her own command, Esther and her maids had been observing a strict fast, but on the third day she ended it in order to appear before the king. In every way Esther followed court etiquette. She dressed appropriately because no one with symbols of mourning could enter the palace complex. The environment of the king was carefully controlled; sadness and distress were not allowed. She also understood the man with whom she dealt; she knew that he was attracted to beauty.

Esther **stood in the inner court of the palace, in front of the king's hall.** The arrangement of the palace rooms and buildings has faded with antiquity, but apparently she stood in an interior court that was visible from the king's throne room. Since Xerxes was sitting on the throne, it seems that he was occupied in official business, or perhaps he was between sessions with his officials and nobles.

When he saw Queen Esther standing in the court, he was pleased with her. The same expression used here was used in Esther 2:9 when Esther impressed the king's eunuch Hegai. It carries the sense of earning favor or winning approval. Most likely, when the king looked up from his throne, he was struck by Esther's beauty. Xerxes was a man driven by pleasure, appetites, and self-indulgence. It was enough that Esther's beauty was stunning; he **held out to her the gold scepter that was in his hand.**

She had passed through the first danger. As we learned in Esther 4:11, the gold scepter represented life. As expected in Persian protocol, **Esther approached and touched the tip of the scepter**—a sign of respect and honor.

5:3–4. Xerxes asked, **What is it, Queen Esther? What is your request?** The king knew this was not a social call; Esther risked her life in coming before him unbidden. Xerxes also realized that a weighty matter was on her mind, an issue requiring his intervention. Then, with the offhanded extravagance we have come to expect from the king, he offered her **up to half the**

kingdom. Everything in Xerxes's speech to this point was given in the parlance of the court. The bestowal of half his kingdom was not to be taken seriously. It simply indicated the favor with which she was received at that point.

Following court etiquette, Esther replied, **Let the king, together with Haman, come today to a banquet I have prepared for him**. Banquets were the socially acceptable platform for discussing negotiations or serious issues. Esther was behaving properly. The inclusion of Haman allowed for her eventual public revelation of his wickedness.

5:5a. Bring Haman at once, the king ordered. Everything about the will of the king was done quickly not because it was urgent but simply because his word was imperial edict. In the king's own words, the urgency was also **so that we may do what Esther asks**. Here the narrator included some irony because Esther's true desire was not the banquet but Haman's exposure.

2. The first banquet (5:5b–8)

5:5b–6. The king and Haman attended Esther's banquet. As they were drinking wine, the king asked, **Now what is your petition? It will be given you**. In Near Eastern culture no serious discussions were conducted while eating. Once the meal was finished and they entered the more relaxed atmosphere of drinking wine, then important issues were allowed. Xerxes opened the negotiations by repeating his formulaic speech.

5:7–8. Many scholars wonder why Esther pursued such an apparently evasive strategy in responding to the king when it seems he was ready to grant whatever she asked. But Xerxes's repetitive question was not an agreement but a request of his own . . . that she disclose her petition. Frederic W. Bush sees in Esther's response a stratagem that captured the king's curiosity and secured her success. He translates Esther's opening remark as an enticing question, "My wish and my request?" (Bush, p. 407). She followed this with a formality drawn from court propriety, her language rich in respect and social grace: **If the king regards me with favor**.

This time, however, her request was not just to attend another banquet. She rephrased the invitation in order to secure her success: **If it pleases the king to grant my petition and fulfill my request, let the king and Haman come tomorrow to the banquet I will prepare for them**.

By deciding to attend the second banquet, the king publicly agreed *in advance* to honor whatever the queen asked. In this way Esther circumvented Xerxes from seeking advice from his counselors or nobles about her petition. If Xerxes and Haman would come to the banquet then, confident her request would be granted, she promised to **answer the king's question**. And so, as D. J. Clines notes, Esther made it appear that she would be doing the king a favor, rather than the other way around.

𝕭 Haman's Psychology (5:9–14)

SUPPORTING IDEA: *Consumed with pride, Haman became further enraged by Mordecai's behavior. Consequently, he listened to the advice of fools who encouraged him in violence and reckless folly.*

3. Haman encounters Mordecai (5:9–10a)

5:9–10a. Haman left the first banquet and headed home **happy and in high spirits**. A private banquet with the king and queen was heady stuff; Haman was exultant over his continued success and privilege—an elite among the elite.

Once again, however, Haman's well-ordered world was challenged. Encountering **Mordecai at the king's gate**, Haman **observed that he neither rose nor showed fear in his presence**. The three-day fast had ended, and Mordecai had resumed his usual attire. But in his struggle between distress and hope, Mordecai emerged a bit more confident, even defiant. Not only did he refuse Haman obeisance, he withheld any show of respect. Worse, Mordecai denied Haman what he most desired—fear. Even with the edict of death hanging over him, Mordecai showed no signs of dread toward the man who had bartered the slaughter of the Jews. Haman **was filled with rage against Mordecai**.

4. A counsel of fools (5:10b–14)

5:10b–13. Once home Haman gathered together **his friends and Zeresh, his wife**. It was another party of sorts, and Haman provided the main entertainment. He **boasted to them about his vast wealth, his many sons, and all the ways the king had honored him**. He was, by his own estimation, at the top of the Persian world economically, socially, and politically. His wealth was immense; fathering ten sons proved his personal manliness; he had advanced beyond all the other nobles.

But there was more. The capstone of his greatness was that he was the **only person Queen Esther invited to accompany the king to the banquet she gave** . . . and he was invited again tomorrow. In Haman's mind he was an intimate of the royal couple; he was invincible. But he would not be satisfied as long as he saw **Mordecai sitting at the king's gate**. His pride had pushed him beyond anger. No longer was the problem Mordecai's lack of respect; his existence was the issue.

5:14. Like the king's advisors, no one among Haman's privileged pals dared contradict him. His wife encouraged his hatred while the others joined in agreement: **Have a gallows built, seventy-five feet high, and ask the king . . . to have Mordecai hanged on it**.

His wife and friends understood that, to satisfy Haman, the king must decree Mordecai's death and so clear him of personal vengeance. But he must be displayed in public humiliation for all Susa to see. The "gallows" was, for the Persians, a sharpened pole upon which dead bodies were impaled and displayed.

Haman was **delighted** with this suggestion, **and he had the gallows built.**

> **MAIN IDEA REVIEW:** *Patience and justice characterize wisdom. Selfish interests and immediate gratification consume the foolish.*

III. CONCLUSION

A Pound of Flesh

In Shakespeare's classic play, *The Merchant of Venice,* the two protagonists, Antonio the Venetian merchant and Shylock the Jewish moneylender, become linked by way of a loan. Antonio borrows money using his merchant ships as collateral; Shylock awards the loan on the condition that any default will allow him to collect one pound of Antonio's flesh. A bit macabre but Shylock has a loathing for Antonio that longs to find violent expression. For his part, Antonio seems the charitable yet naïve businessman though we learn he has humiliated Shylock in the past.

There are subplots to the play, but the driving action comes from the economic bond between Antonio and Shylock. Of course, one by one Antonio's ships sink in storms and disasters, leaving him unable to fulfill his debt obligation. Delighted, Shylock determines to collect. Although he is offered bribes of gold, he refuses them in anticipation of collecting a pound of Antonio's flesh.

Haman operated by the same mentality. He would have his "pound of flesh," his revenge against Mordecai, the Jew who refused to tremble in his presence. If Mordecai would not bow, then Haman would better the offense. If Mordecai snubbed him, Haman would publicly humiliate him for all Susa to behold. He would follow his dark heart to wherever it might lead.

Haman was consumed by the object of his hate; he was controlled by the person whom he despised.

PRINCIPLES

- While we depend on God, we are responsible to make plans and take action.
- Grace and humility should precede any request.
- An angry and proud person is easily offended.

- The appetite of hate is never satisfied.
- The advice of fools leads to folly and ruin.
- Pride blinds a person to truth and reality.

APPLICATIONS

- Make requests of God and tell him your concerns, then leave them with him; trust his love and wisdom.
- When people ask your advice, direct them toward love, kindness, and forgiveness.
- Never encourage another person in his anger or discontent.

IV. LIFE APPLICATION

Mother, May I?

As children, most of us probably played some form of the game Mother, May I? One child, dubbed "mother," stood alone at the end of the playground or field; she held the power to grant or deny the requests made by all the other kids. The object was for everyone to advance across the playing field until one could, by tapping the current "mother," replace him or her as the reigning authority.

Even as children we understood the inherent nature of a request—it could be denied, modified, or granted. You might ask for two steps, and it would be approved. You could petition for three steps and be told to take one step backward. You might be told a flat no to whatever you asked. The decision was out of your control. But nobody found this unfair because we understood that the "mother" held the power to grant or deny requests.

When Esther began enacting her plan to help rescue the Jews, twice she presented requests to the king, and each time she understood that Xerxes held the power of consent or refusal. A request, in contrast to a demand, acknowledges that the other person has the right of decision. More importantly, however, before approaching the Persian king, Esther made a request of God. Through fasting and prayer she agreed that prerequisite to all else, God decided requests. No human authority could advance against God's will or pleasure; no king could overturn the decision of heaven.

When Jesus described the heart of kingdom living he said, "Ask and it will be given to you; seek and you will find; knock and the door will be opened to you" (Matt. 7:7). Jesus tells us that what opens the door of God's blessing is the request. But those who expectantly ask do so because they have chosen to live by kingdom values. Disciples learn to attach affections to eternal treasures—those things that belong to God's activity in the world.

We will only dare make requests to God if we share his values and trust his nature. From first to last, Christian obedience centers on the request.

V. PRAYER

God, we will ask of you only if we have confidence in you. We will trust you only if we believe in your goodness and wisdom. This one thing we ask right now is, Lord, help us in our weakness. Amen.

VI. DEEPER DISCOVERIES

Eating at court (5:5–8)

Throughout the story of Esther, much of the actual action occurs while eating, drinking, or banqueting. While the impression might be that Xerxes was available to his officials and dined with guests, the actuality was that he lived a secluded life. Few people ever saw him, and even fewer ate with him. He maintained his bodyguards, but everyone was either summoned or excluded—hence Esther's genuine fear of appearing before him without being requested.

According to Herakleides: "Of the King's guests some dine outside in full view of the public, others indoors with the King. But even the latter do not dine with the King. . . . The King can see them through the curtain in the doorway, but they cannot see him. . . . The King generally breakfasts and dines alone, though on occasion his wife and some of his sons dine with him" (Yamauchi, p. 229).

Knowing the king's reclusive and protected existence, one can also understand why Haman thought himself of such high privilege to be asked to dine alone with the king and queen.

VII. TEACHING OUTLINE

A. INTRODUCTION
1. Lead Story: Protocol
2. Context: For three days the Jews of Susa observed a strict fast, refraining from all food and drink in order to ask God's deliverance and protection for Esther. But she was not idle; during those three days she devised a plan and made preparations for two separate feasts.
3. Transition: Esther completed her fast, then prepared herself to meet the king. She knew this could mean her death. Even so, she acted on the belief that God would intervene in the heart of Xerxes.

B. COMMENTARY

1. Esther's Wisdom (5:1–8)
   a. Esther before Xerxes (5:1–5a)
   b. The first banquet (5:5b–8)
2. Haman's Psychology (5:9–14)
   a. Haman encounters Mordecai (5:9–10a)
   b. A counsel of fools (5:10b–14)

C. CONCLUSION: A POUND OF FLESH

VIII. ISSUES FOR DISCUSSION

1. Discuss how to balance the Bible's instructions to wait and depend on God, and its teachings to plan and take personal responsibility.
2. What is the source of anger? How can a person control anger?
3. It's easy to get caught up in gripe sessions and negative thinking. What are some ways to defuse negative attitudes or redirect people who are complaining?
4. List some ways you can guard your heart against pride.

Esther 6

Remembrance and Honor

| Q u o t e |

*E*vil men will bow down in the presence of the good, and

the wicked at the gates of the righteous.

P r o v e r b s   1 4 : 1 9

Esther 6

I N   A   N U T S H E L L

*T*he tempo of events quickens. To the casual observer, each new twist and turn of plot seems amazing coincidence, but they reveal the providential interaction of God for those who put their trust in him. Haman's world begins to unravel.

Remembrance and Honor

I. INTRODUCTION

According to Nature

*N*ovelist and theologian Dorothy Sayers wrote perceptively about God's sovereignty and man's free will. Her insights, from which I borrow below, apply to the converging events in Esther.

Storytellers understand that characters and events within a narrative must not only drive the plot, but they must do so according to their nature. There should be no artificiality. A timid person does not suddenly display valor and boldness unless the seeds of these traits were evidenced earlier. A character should not be rescued from death by some heretofore unmentioned and unknown uncle three times removed. Such devices ruin the veracity of the author, the story, and the characters involved; integrity results from all parts adhering to their natures.

Some protest that the story of Esther, especially at this juncture, has too many "coincidences"; they argue that the plausibility of the king not being able to sleep that particular night, his decision to listen to the chronicles, the happenstance of Mordecai's loyalty being read, his service having gone unrewarded after so long, and Haman happening into the court when he did—all result in a forced plot lacking literary and historical credibility.

I think not.

In every instance, each person acted according to his nature as revealed in earlier situations. In keeping with a good story and actual life, these people were consistent with their inner character and previous behaviors.

We know Xerxes as a selfish, hedonistic monarch consumed with his own exploits and sense of grandeur. He seems never to have acted without seeking advice. He had a reputation for rewarding loyal service, lavishing gifts on those who pleased him.

Haman forms a dark portrait of overweening pride, personal ambition, and lust for power; he was consumed and energized by an eager hatred.

Throughout, these men behaved with continuity and faithfulness to their inner makeup and habits. The recorded events were not implausible; God's sovereign design brought them to a purposeful unity. God's objectives are well conceived, so pulling together the proper players to achieve his purposes rarely requires dramatic intervention; like an author, he simply needs to allow each character to perform according to his nature.

II. COMMENTARY

Remembrance and Honor

> **MAIN IDEA:** *People act out their lives according to a small repertoire of habits, values, and ambitions; God arranges and brings together those elements that propel his purposes and achieve his intentions.*

A A Restless Night (6:1–9)

> **SUPPORTING IDEA:** *In Susa's citadel, two men could not sleep. One plotted murder; the other proposed honor.*

1. Insomnia (6:1–3)

6:1–2. That night the king could not sleep. The king's sleeplessness begins a series of events that, in the mind of the author of Esther and his Jewish readers, verifies the sovereign rule of God.

In order to sooth his restlessness, Xerxes **ordered the book of the chronicles . . . to be brought in and read to him**. The chronicles were a chronological account of what had occurred during the king's reign—from a royal point of view. These were official, historical reports, and Xerxes wanted to listen to the **record of his reign**. The king had these records read by a servant. As he droned on, **it was found recorded there that Mordecai had exposed Bigthana and Teresh**.

6:3. At that point in the reading, Xerxes interrupted and asked his attendants, **What honor and recognition has Mordecai received for this?** He learned that nothing had been done to honor Mordecai.

2. Advice (6:4–9)

6:4–5. Xerxes's question was still hanging in the air when he heard someone in the outer court. So he asked his attendants, **Who is in the court?** We are told that **Haman had just entered the outer court of the palace to speak to the king about hanging Mordecai.** Haman, like everyone else, could not enter the king's presence without being summoned. In his eagerness to gain an early audience with the king and set his murderous plan into action, Haman had arrived early at the palace. The king asked that Haman be brought before him.

6:6. Xerxes wanted some advice. Haman's fortuitous arrival provided the king a trusted advisor. So when Haman came into the king's presence with the full intention of requesting Mordecai's death, the king asked him, **What should be done for the man the king delights to honor?**

In an ironic twist, Xerxes did not mention whom he wished to honor. He withheld the person's name, just as Haman had withheld the identity of those he planned to annihilate. The two men mirrored each other's attitudes, methods, and temperament throughout the story. The irony deepens because Haman thought to himself, **Who is there that the king would rather honor than me?**

6:7. So Haman answered the king, **For the man the king delights to honor** . . . He was so absorbed in his own fantasies of glory that he dropped courtly etiquette in order to outline what he thought would be his great triumph.

6:8. Let **them bring a royal robe the king has worn**, Haman recommended. Evidently the robes worn by a king were considered a great gift and honor, some believing that royalty or power were conferred in its wearing. Further, he wanted **a horse that the king has ridden, one with a royal crest placed on its head**. Among the Persians, horses were often decorated with turbans or other ornamentation. Haman could not imagine anything greater than to touch royalty.

6:9. But Haman desired more. He wanted to flaunt his greatness by having one of the king's most noble princes oversee the occasion. Then he envisioned being led **through the city streets** as the noble proclaimed, **This is what is done for the man the king delights to honor!** He wanted as many people as possible to know that he was a favorite of the king.

B Mordecai Honored (6:10–14)

SUPPORTING IDEA: *The Lord vindicates the righteous and upsets the plans of the wicked.*

3. Mordecai's public recognition (6:10–11)

6:10–11. But Haman had constructed his own humiliation. The king was delighted with everything he suggested: **Go at once. . . . Get the robe and the horse and do just as you have suggested for Mordecai the Jew.** Haman had developed a deep ethnic hatred toward the Jews; now he must honor the one Jew whom he most despised.

Since Mordecai had kept his ethnicity secret until after the assassination plot, Xerxes had probably learned of his ancestry through the palace servants. The king still was unaware that the Jews were marked for destruction; Haman never revealed whom he wanted annihilated, and the decree was written and distributed under Haman's watchfulness. Although everyone else seemed to know about the Jews' impending doom, the king did not; his secluded lifestyle made this possible.

Before Haman left, the king added, **Do not neglect anything you have recommended.** These final words were the most biting irony in Haman's ears. Every detail of Mordecai's recognition, even his own role, all came from his own mouth; Haman personally designed the whole extravagant show. He was forced to carry out the ceremonial, proclaiming through the streets as he led Mordecai on the horse, **This is what is done for the man the king delights to honor!**

4. Reactions (6:12–14)

6:12–14. It appears that Mordecai took the parade in stride, not being impressed, shaken, or affected in any way. He simply **returned to the king's gate**; life went back to normal. For Mordecai, nothing had changed. The Jews still lived under the threat of extermination.

But Haman reacted violently to all that had happened. He **rushed home, with his head covered in grief.** Shocked and humiliated, he assumed the posture of a person mourning a death. As he did before, Haman **told Zeresh his wife and all his friends everything that had happened to him.** Now, however, everything changed. Those who previously encouraged him in his reckless pursuit of killing Mordecai now predicted Haman's ruin.

Then **the king's eunuchs arrived and hurried Haman away to the banquet Esther had prepared.** Haman felt devastated by his humiliation, but the edict condemning the Jews still held, and Esther's plan still needed to follow its course. Before Haman had time to recover, he was whisked away to the banquet, his friends' prediction about his ruin still ringing in his ears.

MAIN IDEA REVIEW: *People act out their lives according to a small repertoire of habits, values, and ambitions; God arranges and brings together those elements that propel his purposes and achieve his intentions.*

III. CONCLUSION

Fifteen Minutes of Fame

Television's so-called "reality" shows have created a new genre of crudity and exhibitionism that reflect little of life's reality. But they do attest to a growing sense of insignificance in many people's lives and that "quiet desperation" which Thoreau deemed the condition of so many.

At an audition for one of the shows, Adrienne Katzman of Washington, D.C., stated, "I think fame will give meaning to my life. I mean, who am I right now—a face in a million. If I become famous, then I really will feel like I am someone, and I will have a sense of accomplishment in my life. I will be known" (Associated Press, The Web, July 20, 2003).

There exists within people a drive to "be known"—a cry for significance. And today that desire screams into a godless void, causing people to resort to lewd, violent, or ridiculous behavior to quiet the yearning. More and more people grasp for those "fifteen minutes of fame" predicted by pop-artist Andy

Warhol. But even the absurd becomes predictable, and the "famous" fade from sight or merge into a new background of banality.

Haman, too, was animated by the need for notoriety. Though we aren't told how he rose to prominence, we know that his social, economic, and political accomplishments were significant. Even so, his desire for personal glory was unabated. It explains, in part, why he imagined himself the object of Xerxes's plan to confer honor, and why he gloated in the exclusivity of dining with the king and queen. He stood above not only the common crowd, but the noble elites as well. He was "somebody."

But like the celebrity "wannabes" who exchange principle and dignity for a moment's recognition, Haman wagered his soul for the next accolade. In the end he discovered that "whoever wants to save his life will lose it" (Matt. 16:25).

PRINCIPLES

- People make plans, but the purposes of God prevail.
- God's sovereign rule and man's free will work in harmony to achieve God's glory.
- Pride perverts the imagination.
- Those who plan evil often succumb to their own plots; the violent are pursued by violence.
- The selfish despise the success of others; the humble are happy when others do well.

APPLICATIONS

- Do not pursue fame or recognition. If you do, you will think of others as competitors for the honor you desire.
- Commit yourself to doing good deeds; in time you will be rewarded. God never forgets.
- Trust in God's sovereign control over people and nations.

IV. LIFE APPLICATION

For What It's Worth

Haman's drooling fixation with status seems a bit absurd, even comical. When his imagination soared, the best he could come up with was a vicarious triumph in the king's clothes. But he exhibited a deep-seated human longing. He is as contemporary as our neighbor . . . or ourselves.

While browsing the Internet, I found that in the year 2000, a Honus Wagner sports card (how many know who he was?) sold for $1,265,000. A 1921 Paul Strand photograph titled "Rebecca" auctioned off for $335,750. Someone bought a framed painting by Rothko depicting white, red, and black bars titled "No. 9" for more than $14,000,000. And, in the quintessential bid at fantasy, a buyer paid $3,225 for a Star Trek tunic made for, though never worn by, William Shatner.

Within the heart of each of us pounds a longing to touch upon the famous, to dally with the powerful, and to rub shoulders with someone greater than ourselves. And lest we scoff too quickly, watch how we clutch for the hand of a passing President, drop the name of a celebrity we've glimpsed, and battle the mob to get that athlete's autograph—even though none of them will ever remember us from out of the crowd.

We need not settle for second-hand honor. Believers in Jesus Christ truly know the King of all kings, the artist of the universe, the source of all knowledge and wisdom. He invites us into the intimacy of family; he entrusts his work into our care; he clothes us with his own nature. Yet we prefer mob-sanctioned heroes and crowd-defined greatness.

Haman was enamored with Xerxes, as we should be with God. But while his relationship with the king fed his pride and reduced his personality to a mere caricature of a man, intimacy with God deepens humility and enlarges us as individuals to develop beyond our earthbound capabilities. When we become satisfied in Christ, we assume our proper place in the drama of God's unfolding kingdom and his eternal glory for which we were made.

V. PRAYER

Lord, help us not to sleepwalk through life, consuming the standards of society, bartering in worthless ambitions. Day by day may we choose to know you in increasing closeness and obedience; satisfy our souls. Amen.

VI. DEEPER DISCOVERIES

Royal honor (6:7–10)

Haman's imagined honor by the king may appear a bit odd by modern standards, but judging from Xerxes's reaction, it seems to have been received as a sensible suggestion. Plutarch writes of similar modes of recognition. Demaratus, an exiled Spartan king, was commanded to choose a gift. Plutarch wrote, "He asked to be permitted to ride in state through Sardis, wearing his tiara upright just like the Persian Kings." The Greek writer also related an instance when the Persian king, Artaxerxes, gave a robe to a man but commanded him never to wear it. The belongings of the king, such as a robe or horse, were thought to convey power to their owner.

VII. TEACHING OUTLINE

A. INTRODUCTION

1. Lead Story: According to Nature
2. Context: On the advice of his wife and friends, Haman ordered the construction of an enormous stake, or "gallows," on which to execute Mordecai and display him for all Susa to see. His excitement over this violence compelled him to enter the royal palace at the first hints of dawn, confident in securing Xerxes's approval.
3. Transition: Haman's restlessness was mirrored in the king's chamber as Xerxes spent a wakeful night. Unable to sleep, he commanded his attendants to read. Lacking a good novel, they read the histories of his reign, including Mordecai's exposure of an assassination plot.

B. COMMENTARY

1. A Restless Night (6:1–9)
   a. Insomnia (6:1–3)
   b. Advice (6:4–9)
2. Mordecai Honored (6:10–14)
   a. Mordecai's public recognition (6:10–11)
   b. Reactions (6:12–14)

C. CONCLUSION: FIFTEEN MINUTES OF FAME

VIII. ISSUES FOR DISCUSSION

1. Discuss why admiration by others is so appealing to most of us. What can you do to free yourself from this desire?
2. List the status symbols in our society. Do you find yourself wanting to acquire some of them? Are they harmless? What attitude should a Christian have toward these signs of prestige?
3. What does it mean to find your contentment in God? Contentment often sounds like settling for second best; brainstorm ways in which contentment represents a drive toward excellence.

Esther 7

Divine Justice

*M*any seek an audience with a ruler, but it is from the

LORD that man gets justice.

P r o v e r b s   2 9 : 2 6

Esther 7

IN A NUTSHELL

*H*oping to gain some consolation from his private dinner with the king and queen, Haman's expectations turned to terror when Esther revealed him as the man responsible for plotting against her life and all the Jewish people.

Divine Justice

I. INTRODUCTION

Playing the Market

I once watched a news clip showing the trade floor of the New York Stock Exchange in full action. I was stunned as men in various colored jackets yelled and shouted, signaled, scribbled, and yelled some more. Then the bell rang, the day ended, and the floor was littered with a kind of trade-and-industry confetti. I was awed that out of such apparent bedlam rose the fortunes of our national economy.

Wall Street analysts, brokers, and investors study the market carefully. They rely on the formulas of finance, the historical performance of particular stocks, the monitoring of key economic indicators, and the analysis of profits and losses. Even so, dealing in investments can be chancy. There are no guarantees in the volatile world of speculation; you can never predict the forces that might converge to send the stock market index soaring or crashing.

We have followed Esther in her calculated effort to liberate the Jews and her family from the genocidal edict devised by Haman. She has shown acumen in dealing with Xerxes and Haman, as well as a high level of insight. She has reduced her risks by studying every contingency. Her comprehension and exploitation of court protocol and rhetoric have gained her favor and audience with the king.

Yet Esther had no assurance of Xerxes's reaction once she accused Haman. The king was a volatile man prone to moodiness, and Haman held a favored position. She could take no consolation from his expansive mood; everything could still spiral out of control.

II. COMMENTARY

Divine Justice

> **MAIN IDEA:** *Violence begets violence, and evil intentions turn back on themselves, resulting in ruin or destruction.*

Accusation (7:1–6)

> **SUPPORTING IDEA:** *Esther's well-calculated plan comes to a climax with the revelation of Haman's evil and violence.*

7:1–2. After the eunuchs hustled Haman away from his home, **the king and Haman went to dine with Queen Esther.** The banquet followed the same routine as the previous one, and Haman probably regained his calm. Morde-cai may have had public recognition for a day, but now he was back at the gate; Haman, on the other hand, was dining with the royal couple . . . again.

The three relaxed around the wine course of the banquet. Just as he had done the day before, the king asked **Esther, What is your petition? It will be given you. What is your request? Even up to half the kingdom, it will be granted.** Xerxes's inquiry was again framed in the formal language of court etiquette.

7:3. Esther came right to the point: **If I have found favor with you, O king, and if it pleases your majesty, grant me my life—this is my petition. And spare my people—this is my request.** Esther used the king's own phras-ing but with a twist. Whereas the king's repetitive phrasing signified a single appeal, Esther used them to present two pleas. Yet her two requests are insep-arably linked because she dared to identify herself with the Jews. In that moment of solidarity with her people, she placed herself at great risk, since she did not know what the king would do.

7:4. The two parts of her request united in one depiction of injustice: **For I and my people have been sold for destruction and slaughter and annihila-tion.** Esther was never specified in the edict, since neither the king nor Haman knew she was Jewish, but Esther's identification with the Jews was complete and irrevocable. In explaining the calamity, Esther used the exact language of the edict (Esth. 3:13). However, because the king was also impli-cated in the unjust transaction and decree, she carefully worded her explana-tion in the passive voice, avoiding direct reference to the king.

She further minimized the financial aspect by conceding, **If we had merely been sold as male and female slaves, I would have kept quiet.** She also sought to reduce possible tensions, embarrassment, or irritation within the king by acknowledging that **no such distress would justify disturbing the king.**

7:5. With a sense of outrage, King Xerxes asked, **Who is he? Where is the man who has dared to do such a thing?** Xerxes apparently had no recol-lection of anything Esther described. As easily as he had consigned a people to destruction, he just as easily forgot about the whole thing. But Haman was keenly aware of all that was happening.

7:6. Esther quickly answered, **The adversary and enemy is this vile Haman.** Her plan unfolded as she had hoped and prayed. As for Haman, he became **terrified before the king and queen.**

𝕭 The Verdict (7:7–10)

> **SUPPORTING IDEA:** *After a life devoted to selfish interests and the accumulation of wealth and prestige, Haman's ruin was swift and complete.*

7:7. Xerxes had a history of boiling rage. Esther's revelation of Haman's plot threw him into another fury, and he got up from the table **in a rage**. This time there were no counselors to consult. In fact, his most trusted adviser turned out to be the source of his anger. Xerxes had to make a decision on his own and, perhaps confused and uncertain, the king **left his wine and went out into the palace garden**. He probably left either to settle down or to consider his options.

Haman, however, had a clear picture of his predicament, **realizing that the king had already decided his fate**. Ironically, his journey from arrogant hatred to callous violence began when a Jew would not bow down to him; now, with his own life on the line, he groveled before a Jew.

7:8. **Just as the king returned from the palace garden, Haman was falling on the couch where Esther was reclining.** Esther seems to have remained reclined at the table, as was the custom in Persian dining. Haman threw himself before the queen, hoping to find mercy. In his panic, he broke all rules of decorum, since no men, other than assigned eunuchs and the king, were allowed within seven paces of harem women. Xerxes exclaimed, **Will he even molest the queen while she is with me in the house?** He accused Haman of sexually attacking the queen.

7:9. The king's attendants realized how quickly fortunes had turned, so they offered some advice to assist the king and support his mood. **Harbona,** one of the king's eunuchs, said, **A gallows seventy-five feet high stands by Haman's house. He had it made for Mordecai, who spoke up to help the king.** It seems the servants knew more than those at the top. Harbona provided Xerxes yet another provocation for assigning Haman to death. Haman had intended to kill someone who had saved the king's life.

7:10. With this information, Xerxes needed no more evidence. He ordered, **Hang him on it!** With a word, Haman was condemned. **So they hanged Haman on the gallows he had prepared for Mordecai.** It was the final irony.

With Haman's death, **the king's fury subsided**. But the edict Haman had put into effect still stood. Xerxes's anger had focused on the affront to his queen, not on the larger concerns of an entire people condemned to death.

With the villain gone, the king appeared unaware of the greater implications of his duty or the unresolved issues he faced.

> **MAIN IDEA REVIEW:** *Violence begets violence, and evil intentions turn back on themselves, resulting in ruin or destruction.*

III. CONCLUSION

Myopia

Haman was dead, and Xerxes was mollified. The shocking exposé of Haman's dealings and plots were viewed through the half-light of Xerxes's ego. Even the threat to Esther was redefined as an attack on imperial honor, and Haman's prostrations in search of mercy were recast as violence against the king. All the events were reinterpreted as direct assaults on Xerxes. He had no vision for the effect on others and the greater catastrophe that still hung over the Jews.

Once again we see pride and the damage it wreaks—for those consumed by it and those who feel its cold indifference. Once pride gains control, the light of understanding and imagination diminishes. It becomes difficult to envisage another viewpoint, to comprehend someone else's feelings or concerns. Pride eclipses everything outside its solitary concern. Our impatience, our disinterest, our irritation, and a host of other unbecoming habits can be traced back to a devilish pride that haunts the human condition.

Both Haman and Xerxes epitomized the self-focused life—nearsighted and hopelessly narrow.

Jesus warned, "Whoever wants to save his life will lose it, but whoever loses his life for me will find it. What good will it be for a man if he gains the whole world, yet forfeits his soul?" (Matt. 16:25–26). It's easy to nod agreement to these familiar words but quite another task to live by their mandate. Xerxes and Haman, unrestrained and commanding the political and military power of the known world, exhibit uninhibited pride and self-indulgence. But we each map out the borders of our own kingdoms and tenaciously defend them. Christ calls us to relinquish these petty fiefdoms and expand our vision to encompass the kingdom of God.

PRINCIPLES

- God responds to the prayers of the righteous.
- Evil eventually comes back upon itself.
- Violence creates more violence.
- Timely spoken truth has great power.
- Pride destroys the prideful as well as others.

APPLICATIONS

- When you experience injustice or unfair treatment, never resort to revenge or "getting even."

- In circumstances where deception or wrong behavior must be exposed, do so in humility. Don't elaborate or exaggerate.

- Be patient. God's timing is perfect.

- Remember that your responsibility is to serve God and others. He will defend you.

IV. LIFE APPLICATION

Spring Planting

My mother grew up on a small farm in South Dakota where the measureless prairie began just outside the back door. She could drive by a field, see the first green shoots breaking the soil, and tell you what that farmer planted. She could eye a crop and determine how long it was until harvest.

She could do this because she was familiar with the cycles of planting and gathering, and with the predictable properties of various crops. She knew that a kernel of corn produces broad leaves and a sturdy stalk; that the tear-shaped seeds of oats form airy clusters of grain, whereas small barley seeds produce compact heads with sharp-edged husks.

It is the nature of a seed to propagate; that is its purpose. Without the proper conditions and attention, it remains only a probability. But no matter how long it has lain dormant, it will sprout and grow under the right conditions.

Pride, hate, love, gentleness, brutality, forgiveness, bitterness, and a truckload of other characteristics and attitudes are invested with this same innate power to reproduce. Haman, Xerxes, Esther, and Mordecai exhibited traits in harmony with what they nourished and fed in their lives. If we examine our own lives and habits, our demeanor and responses, we will understand where we have tended our souls, and where we have allowed ungodly and destructive thoughts to take hold and grow into a way of life.

V. PRAYER

Lord, help us to nurture a godly spirit and to starve and uproot the selfish and destructive attitudes that war against our souls. Amen.

VI. DEEPER DISCOVERIES

Justice

Esther 7 raises some questions about the nature of justice. On one level, justice involves the application of established law. In societies based on law, it is presumed that lawbreakers will receive the punishment that the offense deserves. In such a way justice is satisfied.

Justice also operates outside codified law. In fact, any legal system is based on the shared moral assumptions that supersede written laws. When these moral convictions are upheld, they provide the measuring stick by which all laws and behaviors are deemed right or wrong, good or bad, beneficial or destructive; when they are discarded, ignored, or overruled, the basis for justice and a fair ordering of society diminishes.

The most just system of law and behavior is sustained by adherence to the character and revelation of God. Because God is good, everything reflective of his character and original intent is good as well. Conversely, everything opposed to his nature and purpose is not good. When ungodly intentions or thoughts become attached to a person's will, the result is evil. The scale of such evil depends on the range of one's will to act. But whatever the extent, the personal will acting outside God's will always results in a miscarriage of justice.

VII. TEACHING OUTLINE

A. INTRODUCTION

1. Lead Story: Playing the Market
2. Context: Esther's plan was still unfolding—but in ways she could not imagine. In concert with the queen's strategy and all the principal players, God brought together events and personalities to enact justice and provide salvation.
3. Transition: Haman had just come from a humiliating reversal of events. Rather than supervising Mordecai's execution, he was forced to parade him through the streets of Susa in honor. At home his wife and friends predicted his personal ruin and further fed his anxiety. Haman, distraught, was rushed off to dine again with Xerxes and Esther.

B. COMMENTARY

1. Accusation (7:1–6)
2. The Verdict (7:7–10)

C. CONCLUSION: MYOPIA

VIII. ISSUES FOR DISCUSSION

1. Can a person be lawful and yet unjust? Give examples to support your position.
2. Amos 5:24 states, "Let justice roll on like a river, righteousness like a never-ending stream!" What is the connection between justice and righteousness?
3. If violence begets violence and anger inspires more anger, how should a person respond to these emotions and actions in others? In society?

Esther 8

The Tables Turned

When a wicked man dies, his hope perishes; all he expected from his power comes to nothing.

Proverbs 11 : 7

Esther 8

IN A NUTSHELL

Haman was dead, but his edict against the Jews still stood. In a great reversal, a new decree was issued on behalf of the Jews.

The Tables Turned

I. INTRODUCTION

Snakes and Such

*M*atthew 10 relates how Jesus sent his disciples throughout Israel to preach about the kingdom of heaven. But he knew he was sending them into a hostile environment. Before they departed, he gave them instructions about their mission and how to respond to opposition. He told them, "I am sending you out like sheep among wolves. Therefore be as shrewd as snakes and as innocent as doves" (Matt. 10:16).

Vulnerability can be frightening. It carries with it the knowledge that you are open to harm and unable to defend against it. In some respect you stand powerless before the threat. That was why Jesus advised his followers to be "wise as serpents" (KJV). Snakes do not expend unnecessary energy, nor do they waste their time chasing their prey. They patiently wait for the most opportune time—then strike. Jesus commended a purposeful and intelligent approach to danger and opposition; he recommended sound judgment and unhurried resolve.

But this calculated cunning should not react in a predatory manner. While one's intelligence must be sharp and timely, one's moral composition must remain innocent. Shrewdness should not be practiced at the price of honesty. Like the harmless dove, motives must be inoffensive and intentions should be honorable.

Though Haman was dead, Esther was still exposed to the dangers of his decree and the king's whim. The Jewish people still lived under the sentence of death. She persisted in asking for a reprieve for the Jews. Esther struck again while the moment was favorable. Even so, she had no hidden agenda; she focused on one objective—to save the Jews from slaughter.

II. COMMENTARY

The Tables Turned

> **MAIN IDEA:** *There is no certainty in human governments. Our confidence must rest in God and in his Christ, whose constancy and care remain unshakable.*

🄰 In the Palace (8:1–8)

> **SUPPORTING IDEA:** *Haman was dead, but the major problem remained—the edict allowing the slaughter of the Jews. Esther continued to plead for her people.*

1. The fortunes of Esther and Mordecai (8:1–2)

8:1–2. King Xerxes failed to grasp the larger issue that Haman's decree presented. Instead he acted in an almost bewildered, perfunctory manner once his sense of outrage was pacified: **That same day King Xerxes gave Queen Esther the estate of Haman, the enemy of the Jews**. Rather than addressing the edict, Xerxes turned to bestowing honors. In the case of traitors, the Persians often appropriated their property—not just the real estate but also the entire household, including the family.

In addition, **Mordecai came into the presence of the king**; he was elevated in status similar to that held by Haman. To conclude the royal tribute, Xerxes **took off his signet ring . . . and presented it to Mordecai**. This was the imperial ring once worn by Haman; this ring had sealed the edict sentencing the Jews to annihilation. Now it was given to Haman's nemesis, and he was empowered by its authority. In addition, **Esther appointed him over Haman's estate**. In this final act, Mordecai became the owner of all to which Haman had aspired.

2. Esther pleads (8:3–6)

8:3–4. At this point Esther allowed her emotions to show by falling at the king's feet and weeping. This signifies a growing intimacy, or at least a lessening of formality, between the king and queen. Esther **begged him to put an end to the evil plan of Haman the Agagite**. Xerxes encouraged Esther to express her concerns.

8:5–6. Esther prefaced her plea with deference to his royal opinion: **If it pleases the king . . .** and he **thinks it the right thing to do**. However, she also appealed to the heart of Xerxes—**and if he is pleased with me**—a direct reference to her beauty. At last she let her request fall: **Let an order be written overruling the dispatches**. She wanted another law overruling the first law. She cleverly called them "dispatches" rather than a decree or edict, and diplomatically pinned their authorship and transmission on Haman. She further indicted Haman and cleared the king by reminding Xerxes that it was Haman who **devised and wrote** the "dispatches."

Esther concluded, **How can I bear to see disaster fall on my people?** She understood that Xerxes had no particular fondness for the Jews; he was neutral in the matter. But she depended on the king's affection for his queen and his desire to please her.

3. Xerxes shrugs (8:7–8)

8:7. In Xerxes's mind he had compensated as much as possible for Haman's indiscretions and vile behavior. He turned to Esther and Mordecai and explained, **Because Haman attacked the Jews, I have given his estate to Esther, and they have hanged him on the gallows.** It is unclear how giving Esther an estate, or even executing Haman, would alleviate the Jews from their impending doom.

8:8. Just as Xerxes had handed over the Jews to Haman and his murderous plot, he now placed their future in the hands of Mordecai. The king absolved himself in the bid to help the Jews as he had in his collusion to kill them. He told Mordecai to **write another decree in the king's name**, this time in behalf of the Jews. He instructed Mordecai to **seal it with the king's signet ring—for no document written in the king's name and sealed with his ring can be revoked**. Both Haman's decree and the new one by Mordecai would bear the king's seal, making both irrevocable. Whatever Mordecai wanted to do was fine with him.

🅑 A New Edict (8:9–14)

> **SUPPORTING IDEA:** *It was left to Mordecai to reverse Haman's edict by the creation of a new decree.*

8:9. **The royal secretaries** were enlisted to transcribe the edict **on the twenty-third day of the third month, the month of Sivan.** The author fixed the date probably because of its significance to the Jewish community. The new edict granting deliverance from death was written seventy days after that composed by Haman. The seventy days mirrors the seventy years of the captivity; the diaspora Jews would have recognized its symbolic relevance. **The Jews** were listed first among those receiving the royal edict, followed by **the satraps, governors and nobles of the 127 provinces stretching from India to Cush**.

As with Haman's decree, **these orders were written in the script of each province and the language of each people.** But the Jews gained a new place of distinction, or at least equality. The new decree went **also to the Jews in their own script and language.** Their inclusion underscored the new respect given the Jews.

8:10. As Haman had done before him, **Mordecai wrote in the name of King Xerxes,** and **sealed the dispatches with the king's signet ring.** The new decree bore the irrevocable authority of the king. While before it was briefly noted that Haman's dispatches went out by couriers (Esth. 3:15), Mordecai's documents were sent by **mounted couriers, who rode fast horses especially bred for the king.** Everything about the new decree was weighted with imperial power.

8:11. The new edict **granted the Jews in every city the right to assemble and protect themselves.** Under Haman's order the Jews were powerless since it came by royal command. But Mordecai's edict empowered the Jews to take up arms. Significantly, however, they were not allowed to **destroy, kill and annihilate** without limits. The Jews could defend against attack, but they were not free to participate in an orgy of violence; they were not to initiate the hostilities. But they were allowed **to plunder the property of their enemies.**

8:12. Like Haman's decree, Mordecai's new edict was effective in **all the provinces of King Xerxes** and would take place on **the thirteenth day of the twelfth month, the month of Adar**—still nine months away.

8:13. The decree was sent throughout the kingdom not so the general populace and governmental officials could be ready but so **the Jews would be ready on that day to avenge themselves on their enemies.** The proclamation allowing the Jews to defend themselves was made general knowledge. When Adar 13 arrived, there would be no surprises. In the intervening months, the people of the empire would have time to consider what they would do that fateful day.

8:14. In the same manner that Esther 3 concluded, **the couriers** went out to distribute the new edict. This time, however, it was noted that they rode **the royal horses,** and that they **raced out,** both references to imperial authority. As with Haman's decree, Mordecai's **was also issued in the citadel of Susa.** The people of the kingdom as well as those in the governmental fortress were informed of the new law. Whereas Haman's decree caused confusion among the populace, Mordecai's created a different response.

Ⓒ Ascendancy of the Jews (8:15–17)

> **SUPPORTING IDEA:** *Throughout the narrative, Mordecai reflected the situation of the Jewish population. His rise to prominence was paralleled by increased influence and power among the diaspora Jews.*

8:15–16. The concluding verses of this chapter summarize the dramatic reversals that occurred after Haman's death. Some time had passed since Xerxes spoke to Mordecai about writing a new edict. The author's inclusion that **Mordecai left the king's presence wearing royal garments of blue and white** describes not a specific event but changed circumstances. His blue and white clothing indicated his new position within the royal hierarchy; these were regal colors. Mordecai was among the elite, those allowed personal audience with the king. Additionally, he wore a **large crown of gold and a purple robe of fine linen**. These signified Mordecai's rise in position.

Immediately **the city of Susa held a joyous celebration**. This was in contrast to the confusion that gripped the city after Haman's edict was posted. The spontaneous eruption of joy suggests relief over the averted disaster for the Jews, as well as delight in Mordecai's promotion. Although the general population apparently joined in this happy mood, it was especially **the Jews** who celebrated. The mourning, fasting, weeping, and wailing of Esther 3 were replaced by **happiness and joy, gladness and honor**.

8:17. This time, as the king's rider passed through the villages, joy was left in his wake: **in every province and in every city . . . there was joy and gladness among the Jews**.

In addition, many people of other nationalities became Jews **because fear of the Jews had seized them**. Mordecai's decree seems to have convinced a number of people that supernatural power sided with the Jews. The fear that gripped these people was spiritual or religious.

In the final irony Haman's design to eradicate the Jews ended by actually increasing their numbers.

MAIN IDEA REVIEW: *There is no certainty in human governments. Our confidence must rest in God and in his Christ, whose constancy and care remain unshakable.*

III. CONCLUSION

Vortex

I remember as a kid playing outside after a hard rain. The storm's runoff fed into a gutter on the edge of the road, creating a small stream. I put rocks and sticks along the water's course, trying to obstruct the flow. More often than not, it carried my debris down the street and into the drain. But if the rain was particularly heavy, it was greater fun to position myself by the drain where a small whirlpool formed. Whatever I placed near the swirling edges was quickly snatched, spun briefly, and then sucked out of sight.

Evil has inherent energy. But it remains weak and confined until attached to the human will. When these two forces join, however, they generate a power beyond themselves; they reach a critical dynamism. When evil finds expression in a person, nothing remains the same. The closer to the center, the more profound the effect as it pulls everything possible into its vortex.

Because of his political position, Haman's hatred reached to the far corners of the Persian Empire. His anger broke the floodgates of his own soul and spilled out on his family, Susa, and eventually the provinces. As a result, the entire kingdom was caught in a dangerous swirl of events that initiated from Haman's heart and will. The more hatred filled his soul, the more violent and twisted his thoughts and actions became.

When Mordecai wrote an edict to counter Haman's, he set the currents swirling in an opposite direction. By establishing the Jews' right to self-defense, he initiated a reversal. The countermand did not guarantee violence; hostilities would erupt only if people followed Haman's decree. The second edict had meaning only if the first edict was enacted.

Today, many people charge that Christianity is divisive, narrow, or exclusionary. But the allegation only has meaning if the currents of society decree truth as a meaningless concept, ethics as inherently relative, and God as a totally human construct. In such a context our insistence that truth is revealed, that morality is founded in absolutes, and that God is deserving of worship will generate some turbulence. Love and mercy must always empower our position, but to compromise on the essentials is untenable. God's power for good can have great influence when it encounters the energy of evil and self-will.

PRINCIPLES

- The most effective life incarnates God's revelation.
- Vengeance belongs to God.
- God delights in justice and in those who act fairly.
- Spiritual renewal often occurs while we are experiencing difficult circumstances.
- God honors those who honor him.
- Both evil and good have strong influence.

APPLICATIONS

- As you help others, learn to identify with them. Be willing to take their concerns and difficulties as your own.
- When you face hardships, pain, or uncertainty, spend time in prayer and Bible study. Ask God's Spirit to instruct and lead you into deeper spiritual understanding.
- When you interact with difficult people or unfair circumstances, resist the temptation to respond in kind. Focus on honoring God and Jesus Christ.
- Determine in all you do to live by the power of God; do not give Satan a foothold.

IV. LIFE APPLICATION

Incarnation

At the second banquet, when Esther finally told Xerxes her request, she framed it in these terms: "Grant me my life . . . spare my people" (Esth. 7:3). Later, after Haman's execution, she again confronted the king with a plea to overturn the first edict. In both instances her daring and reasoning rested on a strong association with her people. She identified with those marked for destruction.

When God entered the world in Jesus Christ, he claimed the name Emmanuel—"God with us." From the moment of conception, God claimed his humanity and was never ashamed of it. His birth delivered to us a God who was present with us not only in spirit, or simply in flesh, but with us to the very inner spaces of our experience.

After his crucifixion, Christ was raised from the dead. He later ascended into heaven. But he left in the world his body, the church, to continue the presence of God—the "God with us"—for all people. We are to bring into flesh and bone the transforming power of Christ in this world. This demands that we go out of our way to find people in need and stand in unity with them. It requires identifying with those marked for destruction; it means owning our humanity while proclaiming the redemption of God.

V. PRAYER

Father, help us be persons of peace, to work for unity, understanding, and compassion. Help us live sacrificially, placing others above our own concerns. But may we never compromise your truth or subvert the power of your Holy Spirit. To you be all praise and glory. Amen.

VI. DEEPER DISCOVERIES

Royal couriers (8:10,14)

The writer of Esther emphasized that Mordecai's edict went throughout the kingdom by couriers who used "fast horses especially bred for the king" (Esth. 8:10). The Persian kings, beginning with Darius, had developed a highly efficient postal system throughout the empire. It was the ancient version of the pony express. Royal horses were bred for speed, much as race-horses are today.

The postal system worked on a relay system. A rider covered a prescribed distance, then handed the message on to the next rider. Herodotus wrote,

"Nothing stops these couriers from covering their allotted stages in the quickest possible time—neither snow, rain, heat, nor darkness." This motto was adopted thousands of years later by the U.S. Postal Service.

VII. TEACHING OUTLINE

A. INTRODUCTION

1. Lead Story: Snakes and Such

2. Context: After a sleepless night, Xerxes relaxed in the congenial company of friends to enjoy a meal, only to have it end in accusations and the eventual execution of his closest adviser. It was an emotional and exhausting day, and it still was not over.

3. Transition: In a rather irritated mood by this point, Xerxes felt he had done his part by executing Haman and giving his worldly goods to Esther. But more needed to be done. The rescue of the Jews had yet to be effected.

B. COMMENTARY

1. In the Palace (8:1–8)

   a. The fortunes of Esther and Mordecai (8:1–2)

   b. Esther pleads (8:3–6)

   c. Xerxes shrugs (8:7–8)

2. A New Edict (8:9–14)

3. Ascendancy of the Jews (8:15–17)

C. CONCLUSION: VORTEX

VIII. ISSUES FOR DISCUSSION

1. What does it mean to identify with others? What are some practical ways this can be done for people you know and for other Christians?

2. Why does our spiritual life tend to deepen during hardships? Share some things you have learned about following Christ during difficult times.

3. List some habits or attitudes that weaken our effectiveness in influencing other people for Christ. What can be done to reverse these and positively affect our world?

Esther 9–10

Purim

| Q u o t e |

*W*hen the storm has swept by, the wicked are gone,

but the righteous stand firm forever.

P r o v e r b s   1 0 : 2 5

Esther 9–10

I N   A   N U T S H E L L

*E*sther concludes by describing the events of Adar 13, the day when both Haman's and Mordecai's edicts were enacted. The historical account serves as the foundation and rationale behind the annual Jewish celebration of Purim.

Purim

I. INTRODUCTION

Laws and Nonsense

In the state of New York, it is illegal to speak to a person while riding in an elevator and you must fold your hands while looking forward. (This piece of legislation has apparently taken hold throughout the country without the necessity of enforcement.) Within four hours of eating garlic, a person may not enter a movie house, theater, or ride a public streetcar in Gary, Indiana.

Law is necessary in any well-ordered society. It is one of the great stabilizing influences among peoples and nations. Our own country governs by laws established under the broader guidance of the Constitution and the Bill of Rights. But if laws are not grounded in general principles, if they just address a current crisis or narrow concern, they become either ludicrous or counterproductive.

Throughout the Book of Esther, King Xerxes confronted each new situation by the issuance of a decree. Whether it was the resolution of marital defiance, the amount of wine to serve, or the wholesale annihilation of a people, principle gave way to imperial whim; values were subordinated to personal feelings and ambitions. This approach to governance allowed two opposing edicts to be issued; this lack of responsible leadership allowed the crisis and bloodshed of Adar 13.

II. COMMENTARY

Purim

MAIN IDEA: *Typically God expresses his judgment and deliverance through the natural dispositions of people and the established structures of society. Our responsibility is to become the kind of people God can use for his glory.*

A Deliverance (9:1–19)

SUPPORTING IDEA: *Anti-Semitism was allowed its day, but the Jews were permitted their own defense. In the ensuing conflict, the Jewish community triumphed.*

1. *The dawn of change (9:1–4)*

9:1. Nine months passed between Mordecai leaving the presence of the king robed in royal finery, and **the thirteenth day of the twelfth month, the**

month of Adar. This was the anticipated and dreaded day when the edict commanded by the king was to be carried out. Two conflicting edicts were commanded for that day, but the historical notes of interest involve only the Jewish perspective.

The author of the Book of Esther provides a general overview of Adar 13, the day the enemies of the Jews had hoped to overpower them. Haman's edict, while directly related to his own personal loathing, depended on hatred toward the Jews by other groups and nationalities. Those harboring anti-Semitic sentiments were eager and ready for that day, anticipating the help of imperial forces (Esth. 3:12). Instead, the tables were turned and the Jews got the upper hand.

9:2–3. Wherever the Jews lived throughout the vast Persian Empire, they rallied together to attack those seeking their destruction. This was not a defensive position in which they waited for their enemies. The Jews acted preemptively, striking those who had determined to destroy their community. In the months following Mordecai's decree, a political shift had apparently occurred throughout the empire, one that recognized the Jews as increasingly powerful: No one could stand against them, because the people . . . were afraid of them.

This changed attitude was reflected in the government officials: all the nobles . . . the satraps, the governors and the king's administrators helped the Jews. These royal bureaucrats had been placed in the precarious position of having two opposing edicts upon which they were to act. Haman's decree promised imperial forces to help slaughter the Jews, but the second decree threw the troop commitment into question. However, Mordecai's quick advance into power within the king's administration resolved the dilemma in favor of the Jews because the provincial officials were seized with fear of Mordecai.

9:4. Respect and dread of Mordecai were well founded, since he was prominent in the palace. This must have created new political jockeying within the system. Mordecai's reputation spread throughout the provinces, and he became more and more powerful. Everyone wanted to align themselves with this rising star.

2. Triumph (9:5–16)

9:5–10. The Jews struck down all their enemies with the sword, killing and destroying them. Although the Jews took offensive action, they did so from a defensive necessity. Entire groups and nationalities within the Persian Empire were committed to their destruction, and their desires had been sanctioned by royal decree. The report that in the citadel of Susa, the Jews killed and destroyed five hundred men shows how deeply the anti-Jewish hatred had penetrated.

The Jews also killed **the ten sons of Haman . . . the enemy of the Jews.** Haman had always been identified as an enemy. Perhaps it stands to reason that his sons would align themselves against these people whom their father hated. Their hatred toward the Jews probably deepened when they lost their home and inheritance to Mordecai. Their deaths also abolished the lineage of Haman. Although the ordinance allowed it, the Jews **did not lay their hands on the plunder.**

9:11–12. On the same day that the violence occurred, the body count from **the citadel of Susa was reported to the king.** In response, Xerxes passed the information on to Queen Esther, telling her of the destruction of **five hundred men and the ten sons of Haman.** He never evinced much concern over the lives of people. The king's next question to Esther, **What have they done in the rest of the king's provinces?** suggests a detached interest. He also asked, **What is your request? It will also be granted.** His statement reflected a willingness to continue the killing.

9:13–14. Esther requested a second day of attack: **Give the Jews in Susa permission to carry out this day's edict tomorrow also.** Esther's request seems to assume a Jewish offensive, not a self-protective stance. But the purpose of the author of the Book of Esther was not to explain strategies or motives. His point in describing the fighting was to explain the celebration of Purim, and to that end the second day of fighting in Susa needed mentioning.

Esther also requested that **Haman's ten sons be hanged on gallows.** The public display of a body needed an imperial edict. Hanging Haman's sons on spikes was a method of public disgrace and sent a strong message of power, especially to any who might question Esther's or the Jews' authority and rising dominance.

So the king commanded that this be done. Just as Esther had asked, so it was accomplished. This may indicate the queen's growing power.

9:15–16. As they had done on the decreed day, the thirteenth, so the Jews did on the fourteenth: **the Jews in Susa came together . . . and they put to death in Susa three hundred men.** Away from the fighting in Susa, the Jews who were in the king's provinces **also assembled to protect themselves.** These violent exchanges were not hate-inspired retaliation but attempted relief. The emphasis throughout is rest—freedom from danger and fear. So the report that **they killed seventy-five thousand** enemies was not to gloat in numbers but to admit to the widespread anti-Jewish sentiment that existed throughout the Persian Empire. The author of Esther reminds his readers that they **did not lay their hands on the plunder.** The objective was relief not gain.

3. Rest (9:17–19)

9:17–18. In the provinces, **on the fourteenth** of Adar, the Jews **rested and made it a day of feasting and joy.** But while their country relatives feasted, the Jews in Susa were fighting. Consequently, the Jews in the capitol rested on the fifteenth and made it a day of feasting and joy.

9:19. The author interjects a parenthesis to explain why **rural Jews** (more correctly, those living outside the capitol) **observe the fourteenth of the month of Adar as a day of joy and feasting, a day for giving presents,** while those living in Susa celebrated on the fifteenth. He provided the historical explanation for a contemporary practice.

Ⓑ The Celebration of Purim (9:20–32)

SUPPORTING IDEA: *The annual celebration of remembrance sprang from the extraordinary events that led to the Jews' deliverance from annihilation and the spontaneous festivities that followed.*

4. Mordecai's letter (9:20–25)

9:20–22. Mordecai recorded these events, and he sent letters to all the Jews throughout the provinces. Mordecai's rise in status carried practical implications. His notoriety as both a Persian high official and loyal Jew strengthened his influence in the Jewish community. The "events" of which he wrote were probably the circumstances that led to the two edicts. The Jews living outside the citadel had no knowledge about the intrigue of Haman and the counteractions taken. They knew only of the edicts' demands and provisions. After the dust settled, Mordecai wrote to give the basic background of what had occurred. His overview is found in Esther 9:24–25.

Mordecai's main purpose in writing to the Jews was **to have them celebrate annually the fourteenth and fifteenth days of the month of Adar as the time when the Jews got relief from their enemies.** Mordecai recognized both days as valid celebrations (the author having provided the two-day clarification in Esther 9:17–19). He instructed the Jews to celebrate the two days each year after the same manner as the original, spontaneous festivities.

The holiday was to become a great remembrance party because **their sorrow was turned into joy and their mourning into a day of celebration.** Earlier there had been "weeping and wailing" (Esth. 4:3), but everything changed. So Mordecai wrote that their celebrations were to reflect the great reversal. Instead of fasting and sorrow, there would be **days of feasting and joy and giving presents of food to one another and gifts to the poor.**

9:23. So the Jews agreed to continue the celebration they had begun, doing what Mordecai had written. The people bound themselves to the annual festivities to continue not only the manner of celebration but the different dates.

9:24–25. To justify the place of this holiday among annual traditions, Mordecai offered a summary of events. The result was not a precise rendering of the facts as we have watched them unfold. Mordecai's overview retained Haman as principal villain: **Agagite, the enemy of** *all* **the Jews** (emphasis added). But while Haman had, indeed, **plotted against the Jews to destroy them and had cast the pur**, he cast lots to decide on the date not their annihilation.

The other primary players—Esther, Mordecai, and Xerxes—assumed quite different roles in the retelling. The complicity of the king in the first edict was totally discarded, while Haman's death and the second decree melded into one command: **when the plot came to the king's attention, he issued written orders that the evil scheme** should come back on Haman's head, **and that he and his sons should be hanged on the gallows**.

In a manner of speaking, this was all true, but the king assumed a more proactive role than previously witnessed. In fact, Haman's sons were hanged only after Esther's request. The retrospect ignored Esther and Mordecai's involvement, recasting Xerxes as champion of the Jews. The reason may be because the situation of those involved was dramatically changed, and the new version of events compelled the king to work as a powerful ally.

5. Purim (9:26–28)

9:26–28. Once again the author of Esther inserted a parenthesis, this time to explain that the **days were called Purim, from the word** *pur.* Mordecai's instructions, combined with the community's experience—from the hatching of Haman's plot to the final deliverance—convinced the Jews to bind themselves to the custom that they and their descendants **should without fail observe these two days every year**. The language gives it the same force as irrevocable Persian law. Purim is still celebrated by the Jewish community today.

6. Queen Esther's letter (9:29–32)

9:29. Esther issued a letter after Mordecai's in which she confirmed all he had written. She brought the full force of her authority as queen of Persia, and as a Jew (**daughter of Abihail**), in making Purim binding.

9:30–31. The letters were sent **to all the Jews in the 127 provinces of the kingdom of Xerxes**. This designation of provinces underscores the far reach of the Jewish diaspora. It also suggests the royal nature of the letters. The queen, in establishing the days of Purim, did so gently but firmly, with **goodwill and assurance** to all her people.

9:32. **Esther's decree confirmed these regulations about Purim, and it was written down in the records**. The decree, the letters, and the will of the people converged in this obligatory holiday. It was also written into the official Persian records because the imperial government demonstrated interest in the observance of religious and ethnic holidays.

C Postscript (10:1–3)

SUPPORTING IDEA: *Though the book bears Esther's name, it concludes by praising Mordecai, a man devoted to the welfare of the Jews.*

10:1–2. We have, it appears, an odd insertion: **King Xerxes imposed tribute throughout the empire, to its distant shores.** The purpose, however, was to compliment Mordecai's position in the kingdom. The king could only impose taxes upon those whom he ruled, so it is one way of describing again the vast extent of Xerxes's empire. He controlled the entire realm, even to its distant western shores and islands of the Mediterranean Sea. The king was also complimented by attributing to him **acts of power and might.**

But the real point of these descriptions was **the greatness of Mordecai.** A respectable Jew, Mordecai was favored by Xerxes. The author of the Book of Esther appealed to history to validate his story and his claims—**the book of the annals of the kings of Media and Persia**—the chronicles of the Persian Empire.

10:3. Referred to simply as **Mordecai the Jew**, he was **second in rank to King Xerxes.** Not only valued by the Persians, he was **preeminent among the Jews, and held in high esteem by his many fellow Jews.** Mordecai lived out a rags-to-riches story; he started as an unknown employee of the imperial workforce in Susa, and ended up as a trusted and powerful ruler alongside the king, respected and admired by his countrymen.

Mordecai was venerated **because he worked for the good of his people and spoke up for the welfare of all the Jews.** He was loyal to the Jewish people and, through God's providence, wielded great influence. The Jews had an advocate at the highest reaches of political power.

MAIN IDEA REVIEW: *Typically God expresses his judgment and deliverance through the natural dispositions of people and the established structures of society. Our responsibility is to become the kind of people God can use for his glory.*

III. CONCLUSION

Cooking Lessons

Steve's wife decided to cook his favorite meal—a beef roast. He was puzzled when she took the meat, cut a chunk off each end, and placed it in the roaster. When he asked her about it, she replied, "My mother always did it that way."

One afternoon Steve's mother-in-law was visiting, so he asked her, "Why is it important to cut off the ends of the beef roast before cooking it?"

"Well, it's a family secret," she replied. "The meat always turns out very tender. I learned it from my mother."

The next day Steve called his wife's grandmother. "We're trying to unravel a mystery," he told her. "Why is it you cut the ends off a beef roast before cooking it?"

"Well, it's the only way I can get the thing to fit in my roaster!"

Often what starts as a meaningful and necessary action becomes a pointless custom over time. As the memory fades, only the rituals remain.

In order to assure the tradition of Purim as well as its meaning within the Jewish community, the violent days preceding the feast were recorded, and the edicts from Mordecai and Esther were established. The celebration gained depth when seen in the context of the turbulent events initiated by Haman's edict against the Jews; it gained purpose when viewed as the historical peace from the Jews' enemies. The remembrance of Purim gave hope of God's deliverance to future generations. As a result, this festival is still the most jubilant celebration within the Jewish religious year.

PRINCIPLES

- God often works in ways that are not obvious; in ways that appear natural or ordinary.
- God always preserves his people.
- God rewards faithfulness.
- Evil is always punished.
- Remembrance declares people and events worthy of honor.
- Salvation should be celebrated with joy.

APPLICATIONS

- Focus your energy on being a person whom God can use. Your inner spirit will determine the role you play in God's work in this world.
- When you go to worship services each week, remember to celebrate God's great salvation.
- Always do what is right and good, knowing God's justice will prevail.
- Live your life for the approval of God, serving faithfully in obedience to his commands.

IV. LIFE APPLICATION

Remembrance

A great deal of effort, time, and money goes into remembering. We carry calendars, daily planners, palm organizers, and phones that track appointments. We post "sticky notes" and even jot on our hands. We establish national days, weeks, or months for almost every concern; we designate particular holidays of commemoration. We build monuments. We etch names in stone or on tabletops—all in an effort to remember or to be remembered.

To understand the need for remembrance, you need only recall a time when you were forgotten. Whether it was an appointment that failed to show or a call that never came, a birthday that was overlooked or a meeting that was neglected, forgetting communicates a loss of value. It strikes at the heart of our existence. Someone or something else has taken your place; in the hierarchy of importance, you have not made the list.

Establishing Purim as a festival in perpetuity was an attack against forgetfulness. It was an agreement to value the salvation of that day. The Jews understood that God was their deliverer, and Purim served as a reminder of his preservation and care—year after year. The celebration was a promise to honor not only the memory of that historical event but also the God of that event and the enduring nature of the community of faith.

The Christian community has a celebration of remembrance as well, a time of honoring salvation. Just before his crucifixion, Christ told his followers to eat the bread and drink the wine of Passover as a new memorial. It was to be eaten in memory of him as the one who rescued us from the terrors of eternal punishment; the one who delivered us into abundant life; the one who brought rest for our souls. It was to be a meal of joy, observed until his return.

This observance is a defense against forgetfulness. It is an agreement to value our salvation. It declares that God through Jesus Christ is our deliverer. It celebrates not just a historical event but the living Christ who deserves our worship.

V. PRAYER

God our deliverer, Jesus our salvation, we delight in the new life into which you have brought us. We celebrate the rescue of our souls and the joy of life that you provide. May we never forget your love. Amen.

VI. DEEPER DISCOVERIES

Purim (9:17–32)

For thousands of years the Jews have observed the festival of Purim. Today, Jews set aside the fourteenth or fifteenth of Adar (usually in March), to commemorate the miraculous triumph over their enemies. Though some customs and requirements vary depending on whether a person subscribes to Orthodox, Conservative, or Reform Jewish traditions, Purim has some basic ingredients common to all.

The day before Purim the Jews observe the Esther Fast. It is a minor fast commemorating the three-day fast that Esther requested of the Jews of Susa before she stood before Xerxes.

Purim itself is a time of merriment. The people gather for the reading of the Esther Scroll. A reader chants the entire story. All goes well through the first two chapters. But at chapter 3, wildness breaks out. At each reading of Haman's name, those in the audience boo, hiss, stamp their feet, or twirl a noisemaker. The audience delights in this raucous behavior as they try to blot out the name of Haman.

The traditions of Purim also require the Jews to eat, drink, and be merry. The people dress up in costumes and wear masks. The roots of this tradition are unclear, but it may relate to Esther's keeping her ethnicity a secret. The Jews also give gifts of food, drink, and money to one another and to charity.

VII. TEACHING OUTLINE

A. INTRODUCTION

1. Lead Story: Laws and Nonsense
2. Context: Haman was dead. In the aftermath of his folly, his family lost everything, and Mordecai was elevated into a royal position of power. But the thirteenth of Adar was approaching—the day of appointed violence.
3. Transition: When Adar 13 arrived, the attitude toward the Jews had changed. Enemies still awaited their opportunity, but a new respect had swept the empire; the royal officials in the provinces decided to support the Jews.

B. COMMENTARY

1. Deliverance (9:1–19)
   a. The dawn of change (9:1–4)

C. CONCLUSION: COOKING LESSONS

VIII. ISSUES FOR DISCUSSION

1. What should be expected of a Christian who holds a political office?
2. What happens when we fail to remember? What are some positive results from observing traditional celebrations? What are some potential dangers?
3. In your church or personal experience, is the observance of the Lord's Supper marked by joy? If not, how can joy be introduced while still maintaining reverence? List other ways to celebrate God's salvation.

Glossary

chronicler—A writer, one who records the histories and events of a nation, people, or individual.

confession—To agree or declare as true, especially to agree with God's viewpoint. It is most often used regarding sin but can also denote agreement about God's worthiness, glory, beauty, and perfection. To confess is to align oneself with God's revealed truth.

exile—Forced existence outside one's own country or home. In Israel's history, it referred to times of captivity by a foreign power, as in the Babylonian captivity.

faith—Trust, confidence. *The* faith can refer to the body of accepted orthodoxy as revealed by God and his messengers; the exercise of faith refers to the combined energy of a person's intellect, emotions, and will as he or she surrenders to the truth of God's revelation, choosing to live in accord with God's authority, truth, and purposes.

fasting—Abstinence, usually from food, for a prescribed time in order to pray to, or petition, God.

grace—Goodwill, kindness. Grace is favor that God bestows on all people, regardless of merit. More particularly, he demonstrates eternal goodness to those who trust in his redemptive work.

holy—Separateness, akin to sanctification. Holiness is a state of completeness, untainted and without need or want. It is perfect in every respect, especially in regard to morality.

Levites—Members of the tribe of Levi who assisted the priests in the temple.

Palestine—The Jews' homeland, covering the area between the Jordan River and the Mediterranean Sea.

Pentateuch—The first five books of the Bible known as the books of Moses (Genesis, Exodus, Leviticus, Numbers, and Deuteronomy).

pluralism—The existence and acceptance of different ethnic, religious, political, and cultural groups within one society. Religious pluralism is a philosophical attitude that espouses all beliefs to be equally valid and true.

prayer—Communication between man and God. It is mankind's means of conversing with the divine. Prayer can be offered by an individual or by a group; it can encompass silence, confession, requests, praise, and simple expressions of feeling or thoughts.

priests—Those chosen from the descendents of Aaron for service before God on behalf of the Israelites. Their main service was the offering of sacrifices at the temple.

prophecy—The telling of what cannot be known by natural understanding. At times predictive, though not necessarily so, prophecy is a declaration of God's word and purpose.

redemption—Deliverance, the buying back from harm or slavery. It speaks of God's pursuit of Israel and, later, all people, in rescuing them from sin, death, and futile living.

revelation—To reveal, to uncover what is there, yet hidden, and to make it known. God pulls back the curtain of our ignorance and human limits, allowing something of himself to be comprehended.

Sabbath—The seventh day of the week. Given as a gift from God to humankind, the Sabbath establishes a day of rest and the promise of his provision.

sanctified—Set apart for God's exclusive use.

satrap—The governor of a designated province in ancient Persia.

satrapy—One of many provinces in ancient Persia governed by a satrap, or a ruler assigned by the king.

scribe—A man who was both student and teacher of the law.

sovereignty—The freedom and power to do as one pleases. In regards to God, sovereignty is his absolute power, authority, and capacity to do as he wishes, determined by the perfection of his nature.

worship—To revere, to bow in homage. Worship motivates a person to acknowledge God's worthiness and to surrender to him in adoration.

Bibliography

Adeney, Walter F. *Ezra and Nehemiah*. Minneapolis, Minn.: Klock & Klock Christian Publishers, Inc., 1980.

Associated Press, The Web, "Tech Creates Breed of Attention-Seekers," July 20, 2003.

Baldwin, Joyce G. *Esther*. Tyndale Old Testament Commentaries. Downers Grove: InterVarsity Press, 1984.

Barber, Cyril J. *Nehemiah and the Dynamics of Effective Leadership*. Neptune, N. J.: Loizeaux Brothers, 1991.

Bennett, Arthur. *The Valley of Vision, a Collection of Puritan Prayers and Devotions*. Carlisle, Pa.: The Banner of Truth Trust, 1975.

Boice, James Montgomery. *Nehemiah: Learning to Lead*. Old Tappan, N. J.: Fleming H. Revell Company, 1990.

Brown, Dale M., ed., *The Holy Land*. Alexandria: Time-Life Books, 1992.

_____, ed., *Persians: Masters of Empire*. Alexandria: Time-Life Books, 1995.

Brown, Raymond. *The Message of Nehemiah: God's Servant in a Time of Change*. J. A. Motyer, ed. Downers Grove, Ill.: InterVarsity Press, 1998.

Bruce, F. F. *Israel and the Nations*. Downers Grove: InterVarsity Press, 1997.

Buckley, Jerome Hamilton, ed. *Poetry of the Victorian Period*. Glenview, Ill.: Scott, Foresman and Company, 1965.

Budge, E. A. Wallis. *Babylonian Life and History*. New York: Dorset Press, 1992.

Bush, Frederic W. *Ruth/Esther*. Word Biblical Commentary. Dallas: Word Books, 1996.

Butterfield, Herbert. *Christianity and History*. New York: Charles Scribners' Sons, 1950.

Chase, Alston. *Playing God in Yellowstone*. New York: The Atlantic Monthly Press, 1986.

Clayton, Charles, and Dan McCartney. *Let the Reader Understand*. Wheaton: Bridge Point Books, 1994.

Clines, D. J. *Ezra, Nehemiah, Esther*. The New Century Bible Commentary. Grand Rapids: Eerdmans Publishing, 1984.

Fairbairn, Patrick, ed. *Fairbairn's Imperial Standard Bible Encyclopedia*. Grand Rapids: Zondervan, 1975.

Foreign Service Institute. "Protocol for the Modern Diplomat." Washington, D.C.: U.S. Department of State, 1998.

Foster, Richard. *Freedom of Simplicity.* New York: Harper & Row Publishers, Inc., 1981.

Frye, Richard N. *The Heritage of Persia.* Cleveland: The World Publishing Co., 1963.

Gaebelein, Frank E., ed. *I Kings-Job.* The Expositor's Bible Commentary. Vol. 4. Grand Rapids, Mich.: Zondervan Publishing House, 1988.

Harmon, Nolan B., ed. *I Kings-Job.* The Interpreter's Bible. Vol. III. New York: Abingdon Press, 1954.

Hayden, Martin. *The Book of Bridges.* New York: Galahad Books, 1976.

Herodotus. *The Histories,* translated by Robin Waterfield. New York: Oxford University Press, 1998.

Hicks, Jim, ed. *The Persians.* New York: Time-Life Books, 1975.

Jamieson, Robert. *Joshua-Esther.* Critical and Experimental Commentary. Vol. II. Grand Rapids, Mich.: Eerdmans, 1967.

Kuiper, B. K. *The Church in History.* Grand Rapids: Eerdmans Publishing, 1998.

Laney, J. Carl. *Ezra-Nehemiah.* Chicago: Moody Press, 1982.

Luck, G. Coleman. *Ezra and Nehemiah.* Chicago: Moody Press, 1961.

McQuilkin, J. Robertson. *Understanding and Applying the Bible.* Chicago: Moody Press, 1983.

Nouwen, Henri J. M. *Lifesigns: Intimacy, Fecundity, and Ecstasy in Christian Perspective.* New York: Doubleday, 1986.

Peterson, Eugene H. *Run with the Horses.* Downers Grove, Ill.: InterVarsity Press, 1983.

Piper, John. *Brothers, We Are Not Professionals.* Nashville: Broadman & Holman Publishers, 2002.

Remnick, David. *Lenin's Tomb: The Last Days of the Soviet Empire.* New York: Vintage Books, 1994.

Riley, Gregory J. *The River of God.* New York: HarperCollins Publishers, Inc., 2001.

Roux, George. *Ancient Iraq.* Cleveland: The World Publishing Co., 1964.

Sayers, Dorothy. *The Mind of the Maker.* San Francisco: Harper Collins Publishers, 1987.

Schlesinger, Arthur M., Jr., *The Disuniting of America: Reflections on a Multicultural Society.* New York: W. W. Norton & Co., 1992.

Tenny, Merrill C., ed. *The Zondervan Pictorial Encyclopedia of the Bible.* Grand Rapids: Zondervan Publishing, 1975.

Tozer, A. W. *The Knowledge of the Holy.* San Francisco: Harper Collins Publishers, Inc., 1961.

Wilber, Donald N. *Persepolis, the Archaeology of Parsa, Seat of the Persian Kings.* New York: Thomas Y. Crowell Co., 1969.

Willard, Dallas. *The Divine Conspiracy.* San Francisco: Harper Collins Publishers, 1998.

Williamson, H. G. M. *Ezra, Nehemiah.* Word Biblical Commentary. Waco: Word Books, 1985.

Wilson, William. *Wilson's Old Testament Word Studies.* Peabody: Hendrickson Publishers.

Yamauchi, Edwin M. *Persia and the Bible.* Grand Rapids: Baker Book House, Co., 1996.

Zacharias, Ravi. *Cries of the Heart.* Nashville: Word Publishing, 1998.